DECOLONIZING
DIALECTICS

RADICAL AMÉRICAS

*A series edited by Bruno Bosteels
and George Ciccariello-Maher*

DECOLONIZING
DIALECTICS

GEORGE CICCARIELLO-MAHER

Duke University Press   Durham and London   2017

© 2017 Duke University Press

Designed by Heather Hensley
Typeset in Chaparral Pro by Westchester Publishing Services

Library of Congress Cataloging-in-Publication Data
Names: Ciccariello-Maher, George, author.
Title: Decolonizing dialectics / George Ciccariello-Maher.
Other titles: Radical Américas.
Description: Durham : Duke University Press, 2016. |
Series: Radical Américas | Includes bibliographical references
and index.
Identifiers: LCCN 2016028024 (print)
LCCN 2016029328 (ebook)
ISBN 9780822362234 (hardcover : alk. paper)
ISBN 9780822362432 (pbk. : alk. paper)
ISBN 9780822373704 (e-book)
Subjects: LCSH: Dialectic. | Postcolonialism. | Critical theory.
Classification: LCC B809.7 .C54 2016 (print) | LCC B809.7 (ebook) |
DDC 190—dc23
LC record available at https://lccn.loc.gov/2016028024

Cover art: H. L. Stephens, *Blow for Blow* (detail), ca. 1863;
reproduction number LC-USZC4-2523. Courtesy of the Library
of Congress.

G. W. F.
W. E. B.
C. L. R.
F. O. F.
H. C. F.

CONTENTS

ACKNOWLEDGMENTS

This book was conceived in Berkeley, written largely in Caracas, and completed in Philadelphia—it bears the marks of each within it. Forever ago, it was not a book at all, but a dissertation, and before that a list of theoretical provocateurs. For helping guide and shape its metamorphosis, my greatest debt goes to my dissertation committee: Wendy Brown, Mark Bevir, Pheng Cheah, Kiren Chaudhry, and Nelson Maldonado-Torres. Wendy guided and pressed me to overcome my own limitations and blind spots, to think harder and to think better, and to prize commitment, all with a firm generosity that I can only hope to emulate. I arrived a pretender without much in the way of social graces, and she was kind even when I put my foot in my mouth. No single individual has seen more of what follows than she has, and even what she has not seen bears her indelible mark. Few of us are so lucky.

When I asked Wendy whether my dissertation project was a good idea, she didn't hesitate for a second—was I really going to do anything else? No, I wasn't. When I decided to move to Caracas for no apparent reason, and then to write a different book—*We Created Chávez*—when I should have been writing my dissertation, no one objected to such apparent lunacy. Kiren even memorably suggested that it would be the perfect place to get into just enough trouble; she was more than right, and I am more than grateful. Mark instilled in me a no-nonsense historical sensibility that has been consistently valuable. Pheng's commentary always combined a lucid rigor with an only occasionally daunting bluntness.

Nelson Maldonado-Torres welcomed me warmly into the fold of ethnic studies: by introducing me to Fanon and Dussel, inviting my participation in the Caribbean Philosophical Association and last-minute trips to Zapatista territory in the Selva Lacandona, he helped to set me down the path I now tread. He brought me into a supportive community including Jorge Gonzalez, Ramón Grosfoguel, Roberto D. Hernández, Richard Pithouse, Aníbal Quijano, Neil Roberts, Daphne Taylor-García, and many others, not to mention the inimitable Jane Anna Gordon and Lewis Gordon, and the entire board of the Caribbean Philosophical Association—which remains one of the most welcoming and supportive intellectual communities in existence. Nelson further encouraged me to translate Latin American theory, a sometimes-thankless task but one without which this book would never have been what it is. Enrique Dussel has been a disarmingly kind collaborator and supportive interlocutor along the way.

Wendy's dissertation group provided essential feedback in the early stages of this project, and was the perfect ratio of comradely and challenging: Diana Anders, Libby Anker, Ivan Ascher, Ali Bond, Mona Bower, Matt Baxter, Yasmeen Daifallah, Jennifer Denbow, Tim Fisken, Jack Jackson, Asaf Kedar, Sarah Kendall, Annika Thiem, Zhivka Valiavicharska, Yves Winter, and others I have inevitably forgotten. Senior cadres—particularly Jimmy Casas Klausen, Robyn Marasco, and Sharon Stanley—led us by example, as they continue to lead.

While at Berkeley, I taught some of these thinkers alongside Jeffrey Paris in the Prison University Project at San Quentin State Prison. To our students, whose insatiable taste for the concrete did not undermine the pleasure they took in abstraction: seeing some of you escape the gulag is more than I could possibly ask for.

As I was finishing my time at Berkeley, the upsurge came—and it is this same upsurge that we are still living today. The murder of Oscar Grant on New Year's Day 2009 was one of many, but one that thankfully came to matter more than most. From the flames of Oakland came the occupations at Berkeley, from which Occupy was born as a strange progeny. I treasure my friends and comrades from that period, in particular Nima Bassiri, Jasper Bernes, Joshua Clover, Robeson Taj Frazier, Satyel Larson, and Annie McClanahan, not to mention the original troublemakers at *Reclamations* journal: Chris Chen and Zhivka Valiavicharska. My appreciation as well to the University of California Police Department for its sheer incompetence, for never discovering my identity despite the fact that I worked right next door every day.

This book is inextricable from the context of Venezuela, where I moved in 2006 to begin teaching and learning, learning by teaching, struggling and being struggled with by student-militants at the Venezuelan School of Planning. In many senses, *Decolonizing Dialectics* is a theoretical companion piece to *We Created Chávez*, since I read and thought with these thinkers amid the combative heat of the Venezuelan crucible. It should be said, however, that from Venezuela I have taken far more than I have given, from those revolutionary movements that have provided me not only inspiration but also the concrete foundation required for any thought to become real. Today, Venezuelans continue to teach what it means to not back down, turning defeat into new victories, one step back into two steps forward.

My colleagues at Drexel have been sympathetic and supportive, and the university has been both understanding and patient, despite the hate mail it has brought. Julie Mostov in particular has been unfailingly kind. At the University of Pennsylvania, Tulia Falleti, Jeff Green, Andy Lamas, Anne Norton, Rogers Smith, and Bot Vitalis have been encouraging, as have many UPenn graduate students, Osman Balkan in particular. I am more than grateful for the recent support that many have shown for this project: particularly Amy Allen, Linda Martín Alcoff, and Charles Mills, not to mention my theory comrades of various shades of red: Paul Apostolidis, Anita Chari, Glen Coulthard, Andrew Dilts, Jeanne Morefield, Robert Nichols, Corey Robin, Jakeet Singh, and Antonio Vázquez-Arroyo.

The arguments that make up this book have been tested and enunciated, in written form but just as often in the streets. In their clearer expressions, they have been presented at APSA, WPSA, APA, APT, and the CPA; Rethinking Marxism; the Sciences Po; the University of Pennsylvania Political Theory Workshop; Ed Emery's autonomist conference at Cambridge some years back; the Georgetown University Institute for Global History; the International Association for Philosophy and Literature; and the International Congress of Americanists. Early versions of some arguments have appeared in *The Commoner*, *Contemporary Political Theory*, *Human Architecture*, *Listening*, and *Theory & Event*. The last of these warrants special comment, since past and current editors of *Theory & Event*—Jodi Dean, Davide Panagia, and James Martel, in particular—welcomed me immediately and warmly as a combative fellow traveler.

Courtney Berger at Duke University Press has been unnecessarily supportive of this project from the outset. I thank her for reminding me, gently but firmly, that Duke is where this book belongs—as usual, she was right. Moreover, both she and Gisela Fosado embraced my early suggestion for a book series geared toward our new hemispheric reality, and the series that this volume inaugurates—Radical Américas—is the result. My appreciation to comrade Bruno Bosteels for being willing to co-navigate these waters with me in the hopes of turning the tide. The entire Duke team has been a pleasure to work with, joke with, and tweet with throughout the years—Laura Sell in particular; I look forward to more of the same. Anonymous reviews from two different presses improved the manuscript enormously, and Andrew Dilts and Jason E. Smith both read closely and gave thoughtful feedback. Participants in the Tri-College Political Theory Workshop—Susan Liebell, Joel Schlosser, Molly Farneth, Craig Borowiak, Jill Stauffer, Osman Balkan, Gabe Salgado, Zach Smith, Tom Donahue, and Paulina Ochoa Espejo—provided invaluable comments and advice on the penultimate draft of the introduction.

As a dissertation, this project was not about dialectics in name, but soon enough—in good dialectical fashion—its content outstripped its form through the tight spiral of theory-practice-theory. In the 1970s, the Sojourner Truth Organization (STO) began to train its militants in dialectics, through an intensive curriculum entitled, with a hubris that only Lenin could have inspired, *How to Think*. As a member of Bring the Ruckus—an organizational heir to STO—we continued to study and teach dialectics according to their model, based on readings from Hegel, Marx, Engels, Lenin, Luxemburg, C. L. R. James, and W. E. B. Du Bois, alongside those readings that grounded our political tradition in the centrality of white supremacy in the United States. In Bring the Ruckus, we practiced a self-consciously combative dialectics that we often described as drawing hard lines. The painful discovery that not everyone draws those lines in the same place doomed us, but not without strengthening the resolve of those who still walk the crookedly dialectical path. To comrades past and present, this book is an imperfect attempt to put what we have been doing into words.

One comrade, Taryn Jordan, knows better than any other the pain of combat, but also that rage—while explosive—is the best fuel. Thanks to my Philly comrades for their patience above all else, and for never backing down. In 2015 Philadelphia—as in 2009 Oakland—a small group of those that Huey Newton would call "the implacables" helped to tip the balance and press an entire city in new and unforeseen directions. Joel Olson, political theorist and founding member of Bring the Ruckus, left us nearly five years ago. A walking, talking double helix of militant theory and practice, Joel was completing a book on fanaticism when he died. At our best, all we can hope is to be half as fanatical as he was. I count among my most treasured friends and comrades those who continue to build upon his legacy, including Alberto Toscano, Jord/ana Rosenberg, and the decolonial fanatics coalescing around *Abolition* journal, for which Eli Meyerhoff's efforts have been heroic and indispensable.

I learned combat young and of all those who have had my back in a fight, my parents were the first and the most important. My best memories are of them fighting for their children and themselves; my worst memories are of the pain that left them no choice but to do so. They showed by example why it's important to struggle, and I'm sure they have occasionally regretted just how well the lesson stuck. My gratitude to the Ciccariello family for lending me their name—I'll give it back, I promise. My deepest thanks and mustache emojis to Andrew Dilts and John Drabinski—confidants and sounding boards—and what the hell, to Sheela Cheong and Rich Porter too, whoever you are. Sina Kramer has been generous and patient in pressing me to think Hegel better, and Marisa Parham coached me best when I needed it. As always, Alicia, Jeff, and Lyla Bell are a refuge.

Finally there is Oakley Francisco, who if he wants—and I suspect he will—may one day suffer the painful dialectics of parenthood. There is nothing worse than struggling against pristine young beings, setting before them the barriers they must overcome if they are ever to learn for themselves. In every overcoming we take one step closer to self-consciousness, and nothing is more selfish than robbing them of that opportunity. My deepest gratitude to Abbey Irene for her patience with him and with me, crying, laughing, or more often laugh-crying, while we shake our heads to the same question as always: "what even *is* this child?"

Frantz Fanon once blamed the lateness of a book on his boiling blood. But having found in him a kindred spirit like no other, I don't believe that—in his brief life—his blood ever truly stopped boiling. Wary of zealotry, Fanon was in fact the best kind of zealot. In any case, I have no such excuse. This book could have been written before, and the temperature has not dropped but only risen. I can only hope that in this world, which every day proves itself unworthy of existence, this book may be useful, if only for the sharpening of weapons.

RUPTURES

OURS IS A NEWLY DIALECTICAL AGE, the much-touted teleological resolution of the "end of history" having collapsed like the myth that it always was into fragmentation, division, and dynamic oppositions, new struggles erupting over old questions. For too long, however, *dialectics* has not served to denote such moments of combative division that give its name, but instead the opposite: a harmonious closure often announced but rarely experienced. For this, Hegel bears as much responsibility as anyone: driven by a profound anxiety toward rupture and "intense longing" for unity, Hegel's dialectical vision would enable conservative resolutions even as it opened radical possibilities.[1]

It is perhaps little surprise, then, that the most famous recent attempt to recruit Hegel for the task of declaring history over—Francis Fukuyama's *The End of History*—took much the same form as Hegel's own preemptive dialectical closure nearly two centuries prior, albeit in a more transparently conservative way. Blind to the internal tensions of globalizing capital, Fukuyama even more than Hegel fell back on a faith in the impossible: the resolution of the utterly contradictory, the reconciliation of humanity with its opposite, through the same vehicle: civil society.[2] Today, more than two decades after the banner of civil society was hoisted to topple the Soviet Union and usher in a temporarily unipolar neoliberal world, that banner now dangles in tatters, its internal tensions bared and its complicities with power ever more apparent—the vehicle of choice for removing intransigent regimes from Yugoslavia to Haiti, Ukraine, and Venezuela.[3]

By contrast, new struggles are emerging, new ruptures throwing forth new and renewed identities that deepen contradictions and press toward different possible futures. I do not refer to what for years was offered to disprove liberal optimism—namely, the resurgence of political Islam—although this too is a clear enough indication that history has yet to reach its terminus. I refer instead primarily to those struggles that have surged forth in opposition to the neoliberal onslaught and which pose the possibility of a postneoliberal world: the Latin American "pink tide" (especially in its darker red variants), a veritable global wave of riots and rebellions returning like the repressed to the heart of the Old World (Paris, London), and more recently the broad upsurge comprising the Arab Spring, the Spanish *indignados*, and the Occupy Movement. New identities, new struggles, and new forms of sociability, the novelty of each never expressed in absolute terms, but instead as an occasionally painful process of strategic and tactical refinement whose defeats and reversals are as pronounced as its victories and advances.

Not surprisingly, this newly combative moment has been accompanied by and intertwined as both cause and effect with a rebirth of dialectical thought. Whether in recent attempts to rethink the Hegelian legacy, to renovate the Marxist and communist tradition, or to mobilize against the current political and economic crises racking the globe, the question of dialectics—the dynamic movement of conflictive oppositions—is once again firmly on the table.[4] In this process, the dialectical questions par excellence—what to preserve and what to discard, how to move forward without reproducing the errors of the past—are re-posed with heightened urgency. But in the context of struggles that are powerfully global, at the intersection of the inverse but complicit dynamics of outsourcing and exodus-migration, white supremacist containment and suburban rebellion, we cannot escape the historically fraught relationship between dialectics and decolonization, one long characterized by mutual suspicion.

On the one hand, while Hegel and especially Karl Marx have long served as go-to sources for struggles emerging from the global periphery, these same authors have been viewed with skepticism due to their shared Eurocentrism and the linear, progressive, determinist, and teleological elements of their approaches. As a result, most postcolonial theory has "eluded engagement with . . . the reworking of dialectical thinking."[5] Viewed from the opposite direction, however, this postcolonial suspicion is not without reason, since despite the undeniable resources that Hegel and Marx furnished for later decolonial thought, many contemporary neodialec-

ticians have done little to alleviate the concerns of their would-be decolonial allies. Reacting to poststructuralist and postcolonial critiques of
the universal, thinkers from Slavoj Žižek to Alain Badiou have effectively
bent the stick in the opposite direction, occasionally to a troubling degree.
Where Badiou has assailed an "ethics of difference" that is complicit with
capitalist multiculturalism, his alternative is the unalloyed universalism
of a "generic humanity" that is fundamentally *"indifferent to differences."*[6]
Žižek, with a characteristic zeal for the provocative, has gone even further
in urging the Left to openly embrace Eurocentrism.[7] But as a boomerang
effect of the poststructural politics of difference, much is missed in this
precipitous return swing toward the universal.

Troubling Unity

Despite the palpable divisions increasingly embraced in theory and incar-
nated in practice, political logics of the present remain curiously trained
on unity. In a maneuver that Michel Foucault describes as *recentering* and
even *recolonization*, unitary logics stalk political oppositions, seeking to
deactivate unruly movements in the name of power and sovereignty. Political leaders from Right to Left, Republicans and Democrats alike, maneuver and jockey less over substantive differences than over who can claim
the mantle of speaking for everyone and whose unity is therefore preferable. Thus we unify against our enemies under Barack Obama as we did
under George W. Bush, with the sole proviso that Afghanistan is a "good
war" while Iraq was a "bad war," a merely qualitative metric for determining
who "our" absolute enemy is.

So too in domestic affairs, where the question is not "what price unity?"
but instead, "who is the *us* that is unified?" Obama's famous 2008 "race
speech" was accordingly titled "A More Perfect Union," but four years later
his cynical pretensions shone through when he admitted that "the nature of
this office is also to tell a story that gives them a sense of unity and purpose
and optimism." Here Hegelian themes are clearly on display: totality (we are
unified), teleology (we have a purpose), and the promise of progress (we
are optimistic). The inescapability of this logic of unity was clear as day just
two months later when Mitt Romney violated this cardinal rule in a leaked
video, scornfully dismissing the laziness of the 47 percent. Having acciden-
tally proven his unsuitability for "the nature of this office," Romney paid the
price for speaking the inverted truth of a class warfare he rejected in public.

The differences between the two candidates would prove more rhetorical than substantive as a result: Obama's watered-down immigration

reform is a drop in the bucket compared with record deportations; in terms of human rights abuses abroad, one unnamed government official spoke of "no change at all . . . an almost seamless transition from Bush to Obama";[8] Obama's much-touted Affordable Care Act has left the private insurance sector firmly in the driver's seat; and the long-promised integration of Black Americans into this unified nation has been little more than window dressing. Rather than the crowning resolution of struggles past, Obama's election has instead represented, as Glen Ford presciently predicted, "the antithesis of Black Power"—a dialectical identity if ever there was one—its deactivation and incorporation into the status quo ante.[9]

If we had any reason to doubt this diagnosis in an age of mass incarceration and resurgent white fascism, then the names turned hashtags Oscar Grant, Trayvon Martin, Renisha McBride, Tamir Rice, CeCe McDonald, Sandra Bland, and Mike Brown—among thousands of others—serve as a painful reminder. The nation remains fundamentally unchanged, albeit adorned with fewer Confederate flags. But even the most cynical campaign rhetoric and even the emptiest promises can produce social blowback: if theorists of revolutionary change have long emphasized how rising and frustrated expectations can spark social upheaval, we find this confirmed in the militant resistance that broke out at the dawn of the age of Obama and has only escalated in the falling dusk of his promised hope and change, in those local names turned national symbols: Ferguson and Baltimore. And lest we dismiss the unitary rhetoric of sovereignty as *simply* a ruse, reducing it to the disingenuousness of political power, such logics permeate far more deeply, cutting into and across oppositional movements and discourses themselves, disarming movements from within and preparing them for reincorporation into the governing apparatus.

Here, the Occupy Movement provides a dire warning. While Occupy gained initial traction as a clarion call for social equality by re-posing class conflict in the now-famous ratio of the wealthiest 1 percent against the remaining 99 percent, swirling immediately in and around the occupied camps was the sharp interrogation of this ratio, not from advocates of unity, but from those posing division in different terms. Those criticizing the slogan of the 99 percent from a class perspective rightly worried that this ratio displaced hostility from capitalist exploiters to the recently popularized category of the "super-rich," usually associated with high finance. Inversely, others argued that there was little practical use for a category in which one could still earn over $300,000 annually and technically be a member of the "99 percent": in this view, demonizing the super-rich simply acquitted the just plain rich of their exploitative role. Others shunned a strictly economic approach entirely, insisting that the fault lines racking U.S. society have more to do with anti-Black racism, colonization (whose relation to calls to "occupy" is tense at best), or gender. Ultimately, the most militant of occupations—in Oakland, California—divided into two wings known as "Occupy Oakland" and "Decolonize Oakland," although the question of whether this particular division of one into two was a dialectical one, remains open.[10]

Those who defended the idea of the 99 percent, and especially those who enforced it in practice in the Occupy encampments, testified to both the lure of unity and its dangers. For many, the strength of the slogan of the 99 percent was its *inclusivity*, the laudable aspiration to gather rather than disperse our forces. But by asymptotically approaching the inclusion of everyone, we run the risk of sliding into far more treacherous territory, moving from rupture, division, and opposition toward the aspirational recasting of a near-total unity. If anything, *this* is the most ideological gesture of all, one that seeks to reconcile rupture with its opposite, taking refuge in the comforting idea that we are all in this together rather than engaging in risky solidarity *against*. While dangerous in its own right, this slide toward unitary logic also enacted-while-concealing concrete *exclusions* as well: critics were tarred as "divisive," as a mortal threat to the unity of the 99 percent, and this label was reserved especially for those who sought to establish people of color or women's caucuses within the camps.

In banishing difference, this homogeneous universalism jealously reproduced the unity it had once claimed to oppose, and demands for internal unity proved complicit with the even more dangerous openness that some camps demonstrated toward the power structure itself: welcoming local mayors and police into the warm embrace of the 99 percent all the while silencing internal dissidents. In many places, Occupy thereby became a safe space for those already safe, refusing to even exclude white supremacists, anti-immigrant activists, and Ron Paul supporters, while embattled radicals drifted away. It was only a matter of time before Occupy candidates began to make electoral bids, and large sectors of the movement were reincorporated into the same power structure it had sought to oppose. As I write this, moreover, it is clear that such threats were not limited to Occupy: observe the ease with which political opportunists and foundation funders are currently working to recolonize the oppositional energy of the Black Lives Matter movement by exploiting the political naiveté of some of its leaders—we can only hope that the explosiveness of Ferguson and Baltimore will not be bought off so cheaply.

Beyond revealing the seductions of unity, such dynamics point toward the contested nature of the identities in question and tenacious debates about the relationship between race, class, nation, and gender.[11] How to negotiate these dynamics, these microdialectics that cut into and across oppositional movements themselves, while always keeping a wary eye toward that dangerous lure that Cristina Beltrán calls "the trouble with unity"?[12] Whether in the theoretical chasm between Žižek's universalism and postcolonial theory or the on-the-ground clash between "Decolonize" and "Occupy," I argue that much is neglected in between. It is this vast and generative space—one constituted by the unavoidable judgment of where and when to draw hard lines, divide unities, and press oppositions—that I hope to probe in this book, with the following questions in mind.

First, against those postcolonial thinkers who discard dialectics out of hand, is it possible to subject the dialectical tradition to its own decolonizing *Aufhebung*, transcending its limitations by preserving what is useful and shedding what is not? Second, and inversely, is there a dialectical understanding capable of accommodating the continuing project of decolonization, and the questions of race and nation that this process inevitably confronts, or is the historical baggage of dialectical thought simply too heavy to be worth the trouble? My response to both lies in the affirmative: just as any attempt to systematically grasp the conflicts and identities that structure our world requires that we rupture the boundaries of European thought, we cannot grasp the parameters of decolonization as a profound and ongoing process without recourse to some modified understanding of that dynamic and combative motion that many give the name "dialectics."

Decolonizing Dialectics

In this book, I approach the task of decolonizing dialectics by excavating a largely subterranean current of thought, what I call a *counterdiscourse*, that I argue constitutes a radicalization of the dialectical tradition while also opening outward toward its decolonization. This is a dialectical counterdiscourse that, by foregrounding rupture and shunning the lure of unity, makes its home in the center of the dialectic and revels in the spirit of combat, the indeterminacies of political identities slamming against one another, transforming themselves and their worlds unpredictably in the process. This is a dialectical counterdiscourse that, by grasping the momentary hardening of group identities, grants weight to a separatist *moment* in dialectics—at the expense of premature reconciliation—but does so without succumbing to a hermetically essentialist separatism, be it of class, race, nation, or otherwise. Identities are forged in struggle, and there too are they reforged. This is a dialectical counterdiscourse that, as a result, tosses off many of the shackles of a conservative dialectical tradition that traffics under the phrase, only dubiously attributable to Hegel: "the real is rational."[13] In confronting the antidialectical immobility of false universals that portray the present as complete, the thinkers considered here resist all teleology, determinism, linearity, refuse all comforting promises of inherent progress, and defer all premature declarations that history has indeed reached its conclusion. Their horizon remains a horizon.[14]

I begin with the turn-of-the-century French syndicalist Georges Sorel to distill the basic contours of a radicalized dialectic of European class struggle. Confronting the false promise of social unity that had deactivated the class struggle, Sorel concluded that working-class conditions (class-in-itself) were no guarantee of an oppositional working-class identity (class-for-itself) and that the latter must be actively constructed and subjectively projected in an openly combative struggle. In part through Sorel's peculiar attentiveness to the importance of ideology—and thereby the centrality of class identity—he is able to glimpse at a surprisingly early moment the contours of a broad Marxist dialectics of history stripped of all determinism and teleology, in which the identitarian intervention of the working class serves as the fundamental but not invincible motor force. Despite, or better put, *as a result of* his intransigent class-centrism—one that foregrounds ideology, identity, and active intervention—Sorel's immanent critique of European Marxism provides *not* the origin of decolonized dialectics, but a radically combative baseline that is open to subsequent decolonization

I then turn to the Martinican-born and French-trained psychiatrist turned Algerian revolutionary Frantz Fanon, who serves as a bridge between Europe and the colonies and thereby from a European to a more openly decolonial dialectics. Not unaware of Sorel's work, Fanon nevertheless took an ostensibly different approach, engaging race (rather than class) in the European context and doing so through a critical engagement with the Hegelian master-slave dialectic (rather than the Marxist dialectic of class struggle). Surface differences conceal substantive similarities, however: where Sorel saw a dialectic frozen by the ideology of unity, Fanon saw one short-circuited by white supremacy, in which the basis for reciprocity—which Hegel took for granted—did not yet exist. Like Sorel, he advocated subjective, identitarian struggle to jumpstart dialectical motion, but by injecting subontological racial difference into Hegel's formulation, he also crucially "decolonized" the master-slave dialectic itself. After shifting to the revolutionary Algerian context, Fanon confronted a similar context, albeit one characterized not by frozen unity, but by the congealed opposition that he famously diagnosed as Manichaean. In response, he would project this radicalized dialectic onto the global scale, posing a broad opposition between the decolonial nation as a complex, shifting, and dialectical entity and those (neo)colonial forces intent on freezing its motion both from within and from without.

Finally, I turn to the exiled Argentine philosopher of liberation Enrique Dussel Ambrosini, who poses what would appear to be a direct challenge to both the coherence of this counterdiscourse and to the possibility of a decolonized dialectics more generally. Influenced by Emmanuel Levinas's ethics of alterity, Dussel is sharply critical of dialectics and instead embraces what he calls an *analectics* rooted in the embrace of the Other as exteriority. However, as I show, Dussel's break with dialectics is far from complete, and rather than refuting a decolonized dialectics, his insistence on incorporating the category of exteriority into a dialectics of national and popular identity provides an essential ingredient for my own project that—through a sort of productive parallax—is visible in Fanon's work as well.

It is this dynamic fusion of internal oppositions and decolonial appeal to excluded exteriorities that, I then argue, we see playing out in the combative dialectics and multiple subdialectics swirling around and coalescing in Venezuela's "Bolivarian Revolution." In the last chapter, I test the traction of this decolonized dialectical approach through a reading of the dynamic movement of "the people" (*el pueblo*) in a moment still shaped by the combative specter of the late president Hugo Chávez. While some Eurocentric critics dismiss popular identity as inherently unitary and homogenizing, I show how its contextual function in Venezuela—and much of Latin America—tends instead to be combative and divisive. The dynamic movement of the Venezuelan people in recent years has done more than simply draw together different sectors in struggle; it has marked for many the overcoming of ontological exclusions discernible only through a decolonized dialectical lens, their entrance into being itself.

A word on terminology and categories: the thinkers that I draw together here write in markedly different registers. Thus Sorel, a more unabashedly political and practical thinker, speaks scornfully of unity and "social harmony." Fanon, who oscillates between political and ontological registers, takes aim instead at false universals, whether at the foundation of Hegel's own system or in the politics of formal emancipation. In Dussel, finally, the philosophical register takes center stage with his frontal critique of "totality," which he nevertheless translates into the categories of colonization and exclusion. To smooth such terminological disjunctions, I use the language of the authors themselves, while anchoring the discussion conceptually to Martin Jay's typology of the category of totality: specifically, the distinction between descriptive and normative totalities, as well as the more powerful conceptions of expressive totality (history as the unified expression of a single principle) and longitudinal totality (a temporal unity in which that singular history moves progressively forward).[15]

Why Dialectics?

Each of the thinkers considered here is a sharp critic of the dialectical tradition in its different manifestations. Sorel goes so far as to denounce dialectics as illusory, Fanon aims his sharpest theoretical barbs at Hegel's dialectic of recognition, and Dussel turns to exteriority against what he reads—transposing concepts with geopolitics—as a sort of dialectical imperialism. Each rejects elements so common to dialectical thinking as to be considered by some its essential ingredients: teleology, determinism, progress, class-centrism, and two-sidedness, among others. If dialectics—or better, "*the* dialectic"—is necessarily totalizing, deterministic, or teleological, one could argue that the thinkers in question here move, each in their own way, and perhaps without knowing it, irreversibly beyond anything that could be called properly dialectical. More precisely, one might argue that what passes for dialectics in this book, especially a decolonized dialectics that foregrounds the category of subontological difference and exteriority, has crossed the crucial Hegelian threshold that divides *difference* (an internal relationship) from *diversity* (the indifferent difference of a purely external relation).[16] Without the ties that bind opposing elements by necessity to one another—without, in other words, the unified ground of totality to grant meaning to oppositions—nothing remains but unrelated multiplicity.

Why then attempt to unite such a motley band of theoretical heretics under the banner of dialectics in the first place? Is it not fairer and safer to circumvent thorny philological and Marxological debates by simply opting out? While tempting in its simplicity, I believe that to evade dialectics entirely would be a cop-out, for at least three reasons: two theoretical reasons that point, from inverse directions and at opposite extremes, toward the danger of bad dialectics on the one hand and bad multiplicity on the other. These two theoretical reasons then ground the potentially too-obvious practical argument for a dialectical approach that nevertheless, in its simplicity, conceals its own theoretical rationale: that the thinkers in question considered themselves to be doing the same.

First, to surrender the name *dialectics* would be to hand dialectical thinking over to its more conservative proponents, as a phenomenon oriented toward internal closure or centered too stringently on the internal nature of oppositions. If we hold too tightly to what binds the two sides to one another in a predetermined logic, we foreclose on a radicalized dialectics by succumbing to what Fredric Jameson describes as "the possibility that difference might vanish altogether in some premature identity."[17] This threat should not be a surprise, since the question of unity constitutes a fundamental tension and perennial temptation for even the inaugurators of the tradition. Whether it be Hegel's own anxieties toward dialectical rupture and desire to theorize systematic reunification, or Marx's posing of a less systematic but still reconciled logic and end of history, master dialecticians past were not immune to those elements so scrutinized in the past century: teleology, determinism, linearity, progressivism, and the lure of totality.

This is not and cannot be a book about Hegel or Marx however—about those who draw them together or oppose them—for space limitations, for the interminable debates this would provoke, and above all because we must set such questions aside if we are ever going to get where we are going. What can and must be said is that the powerful ambivalence both Hegel and Marx display toward unity bespeaks radical kernels of possibility at the very least, kernels that the thinkers discussed in this book seize upon, transform, and exploit in more unabashedly combative directions.[18] This is not to suggest that there have been no previous efforts to decolonize the dialectical tradition, and much less to strip that tradition of its more conservative residues.[19] Suffice it to say, however, many attempts to liberate the dialectical tradition from such fetters have ended up inadvertently reproducing elements of the same, with even the best examples showing just how far epistemic decolonization still has to go.[20]

My approach, and that of the thinkers—not to mention the political processes and movements discussed here—will be more directly trained on the dual task of radically rethinking dialectics in a manner faithful to the combative dialectical spirit *and* decolonizing dialectical thought in the process, insisting all the way that this ostensibly dual task is in fact but a single one. If radicalizing dialectics to the very point of incommensurability runs the risk of moving beyond dialectics entirely, it has the virtue of bringing into the dialectical purview oppositions that are too often obscured. If radicalizing dialectics means attempting to strip away all teleology, decolonizing dialectics underscores how the telos of Hegelian and Marxian conceptions of history emerges from a particular location (Europe), and assumes forms of dialectical resolution specific to it (*Sittlichkeit* through civil society for Hegel, the resolution of the industrial proletariat-bourgeoisie class opposition for Marx).

If a radicalized dialectics resists the idea that the dialectic moves inexorably and deterministically according to its own internal oppositions, a decolonized dialectics recognizes both the historical source of that motion *outside* Europe in the colonies as well as the brutal reality that for colonial subjects, history often seems to move backward rather than forward, if it moves at all. If a radicalized dialectics questions the fixed linearity of dialectical movement and recognizes the subjective capacity to set relations into motion and change course, a decolonized dialectics sets out from the historical experience of those who have been instructed to either catch up with Europe by completing the necessary "stages" or to await "objective conditions" that are possible only under a full-fledged capitalism.

Although it is possible to radicalize dialectics without decolonizing, as Sorel does, I argue that it is not possible to decolonize without radicalizing. Any process of decolonization that shies away from incessant dialectical tensions, the contingency of struggle, and the indeterminacy of the future risks reiterating the history of actually existing decolonization that Fanon unceremoniously dismissed as the "dead end" and "sterile formalism" of bourgeois nationalist rule.[21] To the extent that we refuse this straitjacketed view of a dialectical difference that refuses or subsumes diversity—foregrounding instead division, rupture, and dynamic opposition—we will always be confronted with a subversive and unpredictable remainder that, as we move toward decolonization, gains a distinct valence in what Fanon calls "nonbeing" and Dussel calls "exteriority," that which lies beyond the realm of division and which by appearing makes a more profound rupture manifest. And to the extent that the turn toward this remainder pulls us from internal to external difference, our dialectics will lose all the comforts of predictable motion or inevitable progress.

Second, if we do not put up a fight for the name *dialectics*, we risk abandoning the field of dynamic oppositions—especially those macro-oppositions that cut across society and globe—to the many theories of multiplicity so prevalent today, theories that would see us willfully neglect or deny the broad swing of motion such oppositions often entail. In what follows, I resist this danger not only by reclaiming dialectics, but also—simultaneously and from the opposite direction—by reclaiming Foucault's conception of counterdiscourse as itself dialectical, thereby robbing uncritical theories of multiplicity of a caricatured Foucault reducible to the micropolitical. It was against such bad multiplicities—and that of Gottfried Wilhelm Leibniz in particular—that Hegel sought to fold diversity immediately into dialectical opposition, and while mindful of this concern, I hope to instead slow this folding, to sit with and inhabit the category of diversity and the external relation it poses as a key to decolonizing Hegel himself.

Third: it is between these two reasons—bad dialectics on the one hand and bad multiplicity on the other—that we can then walk the practical line set out by the thinkers considered here, not to mention an entire trajectory of decolonial organic intellectuals. In other words, this is a dialectical project in part because the thinkers involved took the dialectical tradition—however critically understood—as a central point of reference. These are thinkers who saw Hegel, Marx, or both as powerful and necessary interlocutors, and in this they were not alone: for more than a century, for better or for worse, the dialectical tradition has served as a go-to weapon in the struggle for not only class liberation but also—all ambiguities and tensions aside—for racial and national liberation.

These ambiguities and tensions are not to be set aside entirely, however, but are instead a central part of the story. An entire litany of radical and decolonial thinkers—George Padmore, Richard Wright, and Aimé Césaire, to name only a few—were even members of official communist parties before breaking with those parties precisely amid sharp debates over race and colonialism.[22] These are thinkers who found in Hegel and Marx values of autonomous selfhood and liberation, tools to diagnose and critique global capitalism, methods that began—as they knew they should—not from negotiation but from struggle, and weapons to sharpen against the "slavery and social death" left in the wake of colonization.[23]

But these are also thinkers who often found Hegel and Marx unable, and their political heirs unwilling, to grapple seriously with the legacy of *actual* slavery. Once we add those such as Frederick Douglass, who as I will argue in the conclusion puts forth a decolonized dialectics without having read either, it becomes clear that to argue, as Timothy Brennan does, that "the parentage of the postcolonial is, ultimately, a communist one," is misleading at best, and furthermore evades entirely the central tension posed here.[24] Rather than skirt the questions that this tension raises on both sides—and losing in the process either the importance of communism for decolonization or its failings, *why* so many were members but also *why* they left—my goal here is to confront the tension head on as one to be grappled with.

Which is another way of saying that we must walk in theory the same fine line that decolonial militants have often walked in practice: neither rejecting nor uncritically embracing the dialectical tradition, but instead attempting to rescue a theory of dynamic oppositions from being recolonized by logics of unity or dispersed into meaningless multiplicity. These are thinkers who, while stubborn in their insistence on the rupture of the existing order, are simultaneously and for the same reason deeply hostile to the recuperation of dialectics into unitary logics. As a result, the radicalized dialectical approach they produce, with its combative oppositions and refusal to see divisions subsumed into the whole, is arguably *more* faithful to the dialectical spirit than even some who gave the approach its name. Viewed this way, the thinkers considered here, as a result of their liminal position that straddles the very border of dialectical thought, might just be the best defenders of any dialectics worth its salt.

Here again, Jameson is productive for his nuanced mapping of the terrain to be traversed between the uncritical unity of conservative dialectics and the uncritical multiplicity of deconstructive temptations, between which lay the terrain of a radicalized dialectics:

> the dialectic moves jerkily from moment to moment like a slide show, where deconstruction dizzily fast-forwards . . . both work to bring up into the light the structural incoherences of the "idea" or conceptual "positions" or interpretations which are their object of critique. But where the dialectic pauses, waiting for the new "dialectical" solution to freeze over in its turn and become an idea or an ideology to which the dialectic can again be "applied" . . . deconstruction races forward . . . devour[ing] its own tail, and thus itself in the process. One of the outcomes thus devoured and unraveled is of course the dialectic itself, which paused too long, and became an ideology in its own right, yet another object of deconstruction.[25]

It is in this generative space between the stalled hesitancy of a dialectic that waits too long and the ravenous appetite of a deconstruction that, in the absence of sustenance, is content to feed on itself, that my project also moves.

In lieu of offering a preemptive definition of dialectics that might violate the spirit of the term, I begin provisionally from Jameson's own methodological insistence that "any opposition can be the starting point for a dialectic in its own right," allowing a proliferation of local dialectics and dynamic oppositions, and I follow him in generally shunning the definite article denoting "the" dialectic.[26] However, my approach is different in two ways: first, I trail slightly closer to deconstruction in the degree to which contingency, indeterminacy, and an open hostility to totality imbue the multiple and local dialectics of the thinkers considered here. Furthermore, I move toward a dialectics understood above all as a *practice*, or what C. L. R. James aspired to do in his *Notes on Dialectics*: "not explanations of the dialectic but directly the dialectic itself."[27] The thinkers considered here are more organic intellectuals than world-historical philosophers looking down with a bird's-eye-view from above, thinkers who do theory on the basis of actors pressing the dialectic forward themselves through collective solidarities and combat. If this sounds like a strange way to speak of dialectics, this is precisely because the closer we trail toward a conservative dialectics, the less often we hear of one *acting* dialectically or *engaging* in dialectical struggle. In this caricatured view—certainly more Hegel than Marx, and a conservative Hegel at that—the dialectic (and here it is almost always *the*) is something that happens to us and acts upon us, in which we are enmeshed whether we know it or not, unconsciously doing the grand work of history.[28]

The thinkers considered here are *doing* something different, and to approach dialectics as practice helps to partially allay the dangerous flights that have characterized some previous attempts to think dialectics beyond its conservative forms: to take refuge in paradox or incommensurability in which there is no motion but the (not inconsequential) whirring of the philosopher's mental gears. Actual struggles, ongoing and permanent, can thereby recede into the background, or worse still, be unilaterally dismissed by master dialecticians. If dialectical thought is instead localized and embedded in concrete material practice, however, to be a dialectician gains a wholly new meaning: that of pressing subjectively forward in collective combat, embodying Lenin's "leaps, leaps, leaps!" without any certainty whatsoever that a better world will be the inevitable result.[29]

Why Counterdiscourse?

As should be clear by now, we cannot decolonize dialectics solely by prying open the cracks of immanent critique—although this is crucial, and the thinkers that make up this volume embody such cracks each in their own way. Rather, radicalizing dialectical oppositions to the very breaking point at which internal verge on external differences, and opening such oppositions toward the substantive exteriority of a decolonial critique, requires that we step to the very limits of dialectics—or even beyond—before casting our gaze back. If this involves stepping beyond the *geographical* boundaries of traditional dialectics, so too with *methodological* boundaries, and it is here that Foucault offers some useful tools. I turn and return to Foucault more than simply to reclaim his theories for a radicalized dialectics, but also because he provides concrete cues for both the method and content of this project. However, as will become clear, Foucault—like the thinkers that constitute this book—is more liminal to than outside of the scope of the dialectical, and while he would locate the incommensurable oppositions he identifies as being beyond dialectics, I see these as instead marking and opening its outer limits.

This claim might seem a scandalous affront to Foucault, the avowed antidialectician, not to mention those who understand Foucault's genealogical method as a purely critical project. But while tracing the surface and measuring the mass of Foucault's oeuvre certainly reveals more critique than positive construct, lying beneath and slightly to the side of Foucault's critical genealogies are subjugated counterdiscourses, counterhistories, and countermemories to be excavated and set into motion.[30] To bind counterdiscourse to genealogy—the form of discourse to the mode of its recovery—is moreover but a single gesture, as the two are utterly inseparable from one another and from the subject matter of this study. Critique, for Foucault, aims "to dig" subjugated knowledges "out of the sand," but it is the very existence of these knowledges—grounded in "struggles and the raw memory of fights"—that makes critique both possible and effective.[31] This is more than mere excavation, and the fight is not limited to memory: the goal is instead one of "reactivating" combative memories toward "contemporary tactics," "to set them free . . . *to enable them to oppose and struggle*."[32] The result of this reactivation of oppositional counterdiscourses and their setting into combative motion is, I argue, dialectical in both form and content. Genealogy, through the counterdiscourse it frees, presses toward dialectical motion.[33]

With regard to content, counterdiscourses stand against the unitary pretensions of what Foucault calls "science" (traditional dialectics included). Genealogies are thus "antisciences" because they incite an "insurrection of knowledges" against the "centralizing power-effects" of scientific discourse, which legitimizes some knowledges and disqualifies others, establishing the ground of what does and does not count.[34] The problem with Marxism, for Foucault—and indeed with dialectics tout court—is not that it *lacks* scientific rigor, but that it *aspires* to be a science in the first place (this is a sentiment that Sorel shared). Hence genealogy as *method* is doubled in terms of the very *content* that renders it effective: what is recovered is not just *any* historical discourse that has been occluded from sight, but rather those discourses that pose a challenge to prevailing logics and practices of unity.[35] Nowhere is this coincidence of method and content clearer than in Foucault's excavation of what is arguably *the* paradigmatic counterdiscourse: what he calls, revealingly and provocatively, the "race war."

Toward the end of the sixteenth century, according to Foucault, European states consolidated their monopoly on violence and "war was expelled to the limits of the State," to the border, exiled from society to interstate relations.[36] But a counterdiscourse to this milestone in sovereign unity emerged almost immediately, according to which "a battlefront runs through the whole of society, continuously and permanently, and it is this battlefront that puts us all on one side or the other."[37] Such a "binary" view has clear epistemological implications: if society is divided, then no subject can be "universal, totalizing, or neutral," and all knowledge is "perspectival . . . interested in the totality only to the extent that it can see it *in one-sided terms*, distort it and see it from its own point of view." "The truth is, in other words," he writes, "a truth that can be deployed only from its combat position." The idea of the "race war" as absolute incommensurability stands against not only ruling discourse but all unitary discourse, "tears society apart and speaks of legitimate rights solely in order to declare war on laws."[38]

But the immediate danger that confronts all radically oppositional discourses is that they "will be recoded, recolonized by the unitary discourses."[39] The counterdiscourse of the race war was no exception, and as a result, Foucault shows how this formerly "decentered" counterdiscourse was eventually "recentered" to "become the discourse of power itself."[40] While one path this recentering took was the biological reification of race in Nazism, less noted but equally insidious for Foucault was the *dialectical* recentering of the "race war": "the dialectic codifies struggle, war, and confrontations into a logic, or so-called logic, of contradiction . . . ensures the historical constitution of a universal subject, a reconciled truth, and a right in which all particularities have their ordained place. The Hegelian dialectic and *all those that come after it* must . . . be understood as philosophy and right's *colonization* . . . of a historico-political discourse that was both a statement of fact, a proclamation, and a practice of social warfare."[41]

In his attempt to reject *all* dialectics, however, Foucault provides potent guidance for how best to rescue and reclaim a radicalized dialectical vision. If the fundamental danger is that combative discourses will almost inevitably suffer reincorporation, recolonization, and recentering into governing doctrines of unity, it is precisely this danger that we must resist. To do so also obviously means to overcome Foucault's own unambiguous hostility to dialectics and the mistakenly sweeping generalization, "all those that come after it must . . ." Such reverse totalization—a perennial difficulty of poststructuralist approaches that slide too easily from critique to the insistence that nothing exists beyond the object of that critique—seems to openly contradict Foucault's own methodological sensibilities. But it also comes on the heels of a long list of qualifiers—totalization, rationality, irreversibility, universal subject, reconciled truth—to be added to a conspicuously singular term, *the* dialectic. What if there were to exist many dialectics that do not carry these pernicious attributes of *the* dialectic and that instead prioritize oppositional combat over unity?

Despite being frequently associated with the micropolitical, itself a much abused term, Foucault's own critiques of logics of unity go hand in hand with an arguably dialectical account of the strategic (macro)unification of the tactical (micro)moments of power. As he puts it, "No 'local center,' no 'pattern of transformation' could function if . . . it did not eventually enter into an over-all strategy," and as a result, power relations "form a general line of force that traverses the local oppositions and links them together."[42] While certainly incompatible with what Foucault most loathes about dialectics, such a view *is* nevertheless compatible with the radicalized and decolonized dialectics that emerge from the thinkers considered in this book, for whom the subjective moment of combative, one-sided rupture (Foucault's "social warfare") is jealously maintained at the expense of any final resolution, any determinist progression, in short, any foreseeable horizon for reconciled unity. Again, it is *only* with the help of Foucault and others who similarly walk the fine line between dialectics and its opposites—and here I count Sorel, Fanon, and Dussel—that we can approach the task of truly radicalizing and decolonizing dialectical thought.[43]

In a crucially different time and place, Foucault would grant dialectics the same indeterminate duality he ascribes to other discourses, the ability to serve different and even opposing purposes. This time the dialectics were Marxian and the place was Tunisia, where "everyone was drawn into Marxism with radical violence and intensity and with a staggeringly powerful thrust." "For those young people," he continues, "Marxism did not represent merely a way of analyzing reality; it was also a kind of moral force . . . And that led me to believe that without a doubt the role of political ideology, or of a political perception of the world, was indispensable to the goal of setting off the struggle."[44] Violence, ideology, myth, and subjectively "setting off the struggle"—all explicitly echo elements of the radicalized dialectical counterdiscourse that I sketch in this book. Far from the French Communist Party, whose influence had overdetermined Foucault's entire understanding of dialectics, the "scientific character" of Marxism— its claim to a unified truth—receded into the background as "an entirely secondary question."[45] In other words, the primary practical function of Tunisian Marxism was the opposite of what had so alienated Foucault from its European counterparts.[46]

It was no coincidence that this transformation occurred in the Tunisian context, beyond the "motionless movement" of Europe, where for Fanon "dialectics has gradually turned into a logic of equilibrium."[47] And nor is it any mistake that Foucault named his paradigmatically oppositional discourse the "race war" and described its eventual recentering as a process of "recolonization." Even if this equation of recolonization with recentering gains a concrete literalness in the hands of decolonial thinkers, Foucault is already pointing us in the right direction. Decolonization for Fanon as for Dussel entails and indeed requires a fundamental break with the paradigm of totality, a deferral of dialectical closure, and the rejection of a more straightforwardly colonial variant of Foucault's "science," one that disqualifies not only knowledges (epistemological disqualification) but those very beings deemed innately incapable of producing such knowledges (ontological disqualification).

Black *Anti*-Jacobins?

A final note before I begin. Latent in all that has been said above is an ambitious comparative project, one that is both broader and narrower than what currently goes by the name "comparative political theory." If we strip away the thinkers, contexts, and methods, we are left with four identities that are too often considered to be utterly irreconcilable: class, race, nation, and people. But this irreconcilability is grounded in naturalized unities, some of which are thankfully receding into the past: structural notions of class, biological conceptions of race, the nation as a priori, or the people as a modern expression of undivided sovereignty. Built into the structure of this book, then, is an insistence on the equivalence and coevalness of different forms of political identity, and a rejection of the all-too-frequent contempt for so-called identity politics. The idea that class is "real" whereas race is simply a backward idea to be abandoned, or that nations are "imagined communities" and nothing more, is bound up with the idea of reason in history that is so central to the same conservative dialectics we hope to bury.[48] Just as class identity is fully capable of losing its political meaning if severed from class condition, so too does race exist in a dialectic of *identifying* and *being identified* that is itself a form of class-ification.[49]

This is not to suggest that no communities are imagined, but instead that *all* communities are, that imagination is a part of all political identities—class very much included—and this imagination is never divorced from material practices. It is to release those political identities from the straitjacket of teleological determinism, to allow and indeed demand that they stand forth and function, assuming their proper position at the heart of any dialectics worthy of the name. Inversely, if conservative dialectics is complicit with a hierarchy of identities, to radicalize and decolonize dialectics in a way that foregrounds the active subjectivity of their constituents is to open up a space to consider their functions comparatively, a space for the contingency of multiple overlapping and clashing identities that is better suited to what Aníbal Quijano calls the "historical-structural heterogeneity" of ostensibly postcolonial societies.[50]

If there is a model for the sort of comparative political theorizing I hope to undertake here, for the joint analysis of race, class, nation, and people—not to mention a radicalized dialectic of decolonization in which contingency and unpredictability stand firmly in the foreground—it is C. L. R. James's *The Black Jacobins*. While James's concrete task was to recover the memory of the most systematically expunged and "disavowed" event in "modern" history, the Haitian Revolution, the implications of his work far exceed this already monumental task.[51] The radical kernel of *The Black Jacobins* lies in the fact that it was not merely a history of the world's first successful slave revolution, but also of that decisive event with which it did not run parallel—a metaphor loaded with misleading equidistance—but was instead fully intertwined and, finally, entangled: the French Revolution. One revolution systematically erased, the other upheld on a pedestal as *the* "bourgeois" revolution—tipping point in a world-historic dialectical progression—the colonial veil separating the two cannot survive the piercing blow of James's analysis, and with it goes much else.

James's insistence on the coevalness of these intertwined revolutionary processes sets into motion an uncontrollable avalanche whose theoretical devastation arguably exceeds the author's own intentions, leading to the collapse of strict class oppositions, and with them the notion of historical stages and inevitable progress. If the pedestal cracks under James's blunt insistence that so prefeudal a phenomenon as slavery constituted "the economic basis of the [bourgeois] French Revolution," feet of clay collapse as the narrative unfolds.[52] Rebellions on the old continent fueled freedom dreams on the new, and the unprecedented—and unthinkable—resistance of heretofore nonhumans propelled French revolutionaries to ever more radical lengths. Were it not for Thermidor, Toussaint would never have been thrust toward independence; were it not for France's utter reliance on the colonial economy, Bonaparte would never have given the final and decisive push.

More subversively still, James—a Marxist—transposes the political identities Marxists had reserved for Europe onto the colonial world and vice versa: the French masses were analogous to the Black slaves, the French aristocracy to colonial planters, and the French bourgeoisie to the privileged mulattoes of San Domingo. In sum: "Had the monarchists been white, the bourgeoisie brown, and the masses of France black, the French Revolution would have gone down in history as a race war."[53] That James uses the same term that Foucault would deploy to describe the binary division of European societies is as productive in its suggestive similarity as in the gap it reflects. The slaves were the *same* as the proletariat, these "half-savage slaves of San Domingo were showing themselves subject to the *same historical laws* as the advanced workers of revolutionary Paris."[54] But this sameness unleashed a radical difference according to which Black slaves even prefigured the European proletariat itself: "working and living together in gangs of hundreds on the huge sugar-factories . . . they were closer to a modern proletariat *than any group of workers in existence at the time*."[55]

To subject slaves to these "same historical laws," however, was to open a Pandora's box that explodes their status as laws: without sharp class oppositions—as Sorel also insisted—there can be no historical determinism, and it was instead the revolutionary self-activity of the masses in Paris and Port-au-Prince that drove the revolutions forward, and fear of the same that would prompt their retreat.[56] Class is race, and European civilization is little more than barbaric brutality.[57] Amid the swirling contingency of transatlantic combat, no single dialectic can claim either centrality or inevitability. The pretense of automatic forward motion—itself tightly bound up with Eurocentric history—disintegrates into James's famously tragic view of history: "Sad though it may be, that is the way that humanity progresses. The anniversary orators and the historians supply the prose-poetry and the flowers."[58] But tragedy is only tragic if we know what is coming, and the collapse of dialectical determinism is in itself a liberation in the knowledge that, in Fanon's words, "the war goes on . . ."[59]

I hope, however immodestly, to walk in the footsteps of this radically comparative theoretical project, drawing together multiple dialectics whose central identities—class, race, nation, and people—are neither distinguished categorically from nor reduced to one another. But to embrace *Black Jacobins* as a methodological model for thinking a decolonized dialectics raises a peculiar question: How to square the bold assertion contained in James's title with the radicalized dialectical counterdiscourse running through Sorel, Fanon, and Dussel that, I argue, can be understood on some level as "anti-Jacobin"? We are getting ahead of ourselves, however. In the wildly swirling dialectical eddies of this "tragic" history; the dynamic interaction between masses and leadership; and the fraught role of Black identity, tradition, and positivity, James's initially celebratory view of Jacobinism gives way to something far more ambivalent and indeterminate that is characteristic of a decolonized dialectics.

Where Sorel presses the dialectic of the European class struggle to its very breaking point, insisting that between worker and capitalist the only relation is one of war, Fanon and Dussel will theorize more fully the edges of the dialectic where its internal oppositions give way to not meaningless difference, but new grounds for decolonization. And if Fanon insisted that "decolonization is truly the creation of new people" through a process in which "the colonized 'thing' becomes a person through the very process of self-liberation," then Venezuela today stands as confirmation of both the radical potential of this dialectics and its lack of guarantees.[60]

Hannah Arendt, in her critical zeal, tacitly attests to C. L. R. James's ambitiously expansive homology between metropole and colony, arguing that both the slaves and the unfortunate *malheureux* of the French Revolution "carried with them necessity, to which they had been subject as long as memory reaches, together with the violence that had always been used to overcome necessity. Both together, necessity and violence, made them appear irresistible—*la puissance de la terre*."[61] But to this *puissance* celebrated by Saint-Just, I hope to reply with a different constellation, one that spans *not* the distance separating the Bastille and Saint-Domingue— as in the Jamesian version—but rather between the puissance of the twentieth-century French working class and the process, still unfinished, of revolutionary decolonization. But to do so requires that we instead shift toward that subterranean source of decolonial dialectical motion that lay not above *la terre* but below it, in those condemned nonbeings known as the *damnés*.

CHAPTER 1

JUMPSTARTING THE CLASS STRUGGLE

"The art of reconciling opposites by means of nonsense."[1] It was with this characteristically heretical zeal that Georges Sorel denounced the dialectic in *Reflections on Violence*, earning him the accusation of "abuse" by a more recent defender of the dialectical method.[2] When this strange French autodidact, trained as a civil engineer in the provinces but recently transplanted to the capital, stepped into the fray of Marxist debates at the end of the nineteenth century, he proved eminently capable of dishing out abuse to enemies, Right or Left. If my goal is to salvage dialectics, why begin with a thinker so abusive of the approach? Because it is not dialectics per se that Sorel despises, but rather an abusive practice in its own right, in which the dialectic—here uniformly singular—is deployed as a method for *"resolving all contradiction."*[3] What Sorel calls the "dialectical illusion" is in fact an antidialectical masquerade, which emphasizes not rupture and conflict, but their resolution through moderation—a sort of Aristotelian golden mean.[4] Rather than an abuser of the dialectic, might Sorel, like Foucault, therefore be counted among the best defenders of dialectics in the plural? In what follows, I wager that it is precisely from the jaws of such a ferocious critique of "nonsense" masquerading as dialectics that a radicalized dialectics might be snatched and put to use.

The ferocity of Sorel's critique was an eccentric product of an equally eccentric moment, the overlooked historical interlude after Marx but before Lenin, after the rise of socialism as an electoral force but before the cornerstones had been laid for what would come to be called Western Marxism—central among these what Sorel devotee Antonio Gramsci would name hegemony. Only decades after Marx's death, Marxism was an expanding and ambitious political force. This was not yet a time of Winter Palaces, however, but instead of party building and elections, in which the legacy of Marx was very much up for debate. Was Marxism a doctrine of unrestrained class struggle or reasoned debate? Was it—in Rosa Luxemburg's famous opposition—about reform, or was it about revolution?[5] Was it a moral or an economic force? And was its communist consummation an inescapable destiny or a product of willful intervention?

Surveying this political context, Sorel saw more unity than struggle, more stasis than dialectical motion. He found a dialectic blocked not only by material developments, but crucially by an ideology of social harmony to which his contemporary socialists were not immune, and in which many were even willing participants. Thus when dialectics was trotted out as a prop toward compromise, Sorel seethed. But sharp words for *the* dialectic notwithstanding, I argue that he did not abandon the task of rethinking dialectics, even if he rarely granted the word a positive valence. Against both dogmatic revolutionary mantras and the reformist politics of social reconciliation with which they were complicit, Sorel radically reformulated a Marxian dialectics of class struggle that would remain faithful to Marx's spirit rather than his word—foregrounding the moment of subjective intervention, in which the working class presses its shoulder to the stalled wheel of history, re-creating itself as a class in the process.

It was through oppositional combat and deepening enmity toward the bourgeoisie, Sorel argued, that class identity could be reestablished and consolidated, ultimately pressing into motion a conspicuously open-ended dialectic. In the process of centering conflict and willful intervention, Sorel abandoned the determinism, teleology, and "necessary order" that made an illusion of dialectical movement.[6] Against all such illusions, Sorel instead forged a dialectics that, while still grounded in European class oppositions, was nevertheless freed of many internal fetters and available for subsequent decolonization. But if Sorel's radicalized dialectic was the heterodox product of a heterodox moment—forged in the crucible of Parisian Marxist debates at the turn of the century—it had its roots in pre-Marxist reveries penned far off in the provinces.

Myths of Totality

Like Frantz Fanon and Enrique Dussel after him, Sorel was an unwilling conscript into the cause of revolutionary dialectics. In fact, his earliest works were not dialectical at all, and much less were they characterized by the unmitigated rupture and conflict he would later embrace. Instead, like the angel of history described by Walter Benjamin—another heterodox Marxist who later drew upon this maligned source—at first, Sorel faced stubbornly backward, glorifying a mythically harmonious ancient past as the "wreckage upon wreckage" of the present began to pile around his feet. Like the angel, Sorel would have preferred to "make whole what has been smashed," but he first had to embrace the wreckage itself—which took an active form in the concrete struggles of the French proletariat—eventually turning to face the future by embracing the present.[7] Like Fanon and Dussel after him, the very process whereby Sorel abandoned his own nostalgic illusions of harmony would shape his dialectics to come.

This mythical, harmonious past was pre-Socratic Athens, the heavily idealized backdrop for Sorel's *The Trial of Socrates* (*Le Procès de Socrate*), published in 1889. This polemical account of the downfall of Athenian virtue at the hands of philosophy casts Socrates himself not as victim but as culpable. Socrates's guilt was symptomatic of broader class transformations, however, and Sorel's indictment was therefore "a sociological study of Socratism . . . as itself a social phenomenon."[8] In Sorel's idiosyncratic view, pre-Socratic Athens was a unified and harmonious society rooted in a sort of equality among warriors—"All are equal: this is the ideal of Attic democracy."[9] The cement binding this social totality together was none other than Homeric poetry, the unrecognized original source for Sorel's theory of the myth. Sorel found a direct correlation between the egalitarian content of the poetry and its mythopoetic form: poetry imparted a simple virtue that required no specialized schools, only the traditional family structure. Heroism and love alike were available to all, and both—grounded as they were in enthusiasm—resisted intellectualization: one can neither fight nor love in a wholly rational way.[10]

Socratic philosophy, in Sorel's peculiar reading, interrupts the egalitarian simplicity that Homeric myth taught and the family nourished, introducing into both love and war the pernicious principle of hierarchical expertise. In terms of love, Sorel accused Socrates of denigrating everyday, material love in favor of an abstract and cerebral love available only to the properly trained, thereby weakening the family as the primary vehicle for transmitting Athenian equality to the next generations.[11] In the martial sphere, too, he saw Socrates as a corrupting influence who injected expertise into warfare where heroic virtue once predominated. If this military science contained in nuce the Socratic attack on Athenian virtue, Sorel's critique thereof contains an embryonic form of his mature dialectics.[12]

Where Socrates sought "the perfection of military science," Sorel saw this as a contradiction in terms. To introduce science into war is to disrupt the psychological operations of courage, which require the sort of willful blindness that Homeric myth cultivated on the battlefield. Heroism is not calculable, and in fact, calculation short-circuits and destroys it. After all, who risks their life in battle if they are but a single and irrelevant datum in the hands of calculating experts? With heroism, equality too is lost, since "the old basis of Athenian democratic virtue in which mass action could be combined with excellence and in which heroism could emerge from anywhere in the ranks is now called into question."[13]

If Sorel's critique of scientific expertise and attentiveness to its hierarchy-effects is arguably proto-Foucauldian, so too with his emphasis on the relationship between knowledge formations and social power more broadly.[14] His indictment of Socrates reflected an anxiety about the role of savants in what was already and increasingly a society divided by social class. "There were no more soldiers or sailors," Sorel lamented, "but only skeptical and witty shopkeepers."[15] Knowledge and power emerged as mutually reinforcing phenomena, and the "old soldiers of the Marathon" were no match for the new urban classes for which Socrates stood as both cause and effect.[16] "When a society is divided into distinct classes in terms of knowledge, the question of oligarchy is soon posed," and this was an "oligarchy of the small shopkeepers and artisans of Athens—proud and cunning, liars and braggarts."[17]

Wearing his contemporary concerns plainly on his sleeve, Sorel called this dangerously ambitious rationalism that replaces equality with the hierarchical rule of experts *Jacobinism*. In his view, Socratics and their political protégés, like the intellectual elites of the French Revolution, "were submerged in the theory of the *absolute*; they did not recognize the importance of historical law, this made them revolutionaries."[18] And for the moment, Sorel was an unalloyed opponent of revolutions. Jacobins past and present considered themselves to be "perfectly logical. They alone possessed the revolutionary Idea." And since "right [*droit*] does not reside in numbers," they felt emboldened to wipe the slate of society clean no matter how much "the masses cling to their traditions."[19]

The Jacobin for Sorel is thus the revolutionary imbued with the absolute, the philosophical idealist with nothing but contempt for the majority and their traditions and whose privileged access to truth justifies any and all means toward its enactment. In this sense, while Socrates was not a revolutionary himself, he may as well have been. "When the Good has been formulated and defined . . . there is no lack of fervent spirits ready to draw all of the consequences from a doctrine," and to do so "by *sword and fire*" if necessary.[20] If the tyrant Critias was arguably "the first Robespierre," for Sorel, Socrates was his Rousseau.[21] It is this portrait of the Jacobin—as the violent, minoritarian absolutist—that provides the oft-overlooked red thread uniting this earliest of Sorel's books with his later work.

Sorel's anti-Jacobin orientation would come to provide the egalitarian *content* for the mythopoetic *form* that was the basis for Sorel's dialectic of class combat. Thus not only does attention to *The Trial of Socrates* help us avoid the lazy if almost universal tendency to attribute Sorel's concept of myth to the later influence of Henri Bergson, but it also helps us avoid even more dangerous errors in interpreting Sorel's dialectics by providing a glimpse into its genesis.[22] The early Sorel had clearly identified myth as a motor of action, by situating epic poetry as the source of an Athenian virtue besieged by rationalizing science. While this early myth remained bound to a conception of social harmony rather than dialectical rupture, its opposition to hierarchy and ferocious—if misplaced—egalitarianism nevertheless point toward Sorel's eventual embrace of the class struggle. But absent a dialectical gearing, this mythical motor was bound to serve the cause of unity rather than oppositional combat.

Ironically, Sorel's case against Socrates falls apart at the precise moment that it gains social traction by pointing toward the socioeconomic transformation underway in Athenian society. After all, the savant—not to mention the philosopher who trains him—is a mere symptom of the new balance of class power that the shopkeeper embodies in practice. Recognizing this would eventually spell doom for Sorel's idealized vision of ancient Athens, which itself constantly teeters at the edge of disintegration and points toward class ruptures rippling just beneath an ostensibly smooth surface.[23] But no nostalgic attachment to totalities past, no idealized image of unity lost, could possibly hope to hold up once Sorel turned his gaze to the present.

When he did so, it was through an intensive engagement with contemporary Marxist debates but unsurprisingly, given what we have seen, Sorel turned to Marxism not as a new science. Instead, he found in Marxism a new source of "social poetry" to replace the Homeric epic, but in one sense, these two sources of myth could not be more different.[24] If the latter functioned to uphold the idealized unity of pre-Socratic Athenian society, the former entered history in Sorel's view as a divisive and conflictive force intent on nothing so much as the abolition of the unity of the present. Instead of inculcating a traditional egalitarian virtue in all of society, Marxism as myth recognized that equality could only come through struggle, seeking to mobilize and unify the proletariat—a part, not the whole—heroically toward that end. In short, it is at this point that Sorel's myth, by shifting from Homeric unity to Marxian division and from nostalgic stasis to revolutionary change, becomes properly *dialectical*.

In the process, the concepts of revolution and the absolute, moving in tandem with one another, gain a dialectically dual aspect that Sorel would then embrace. Revolution escapes the overbearing historical weight of *The* (French) Revolution, at the same time that the absolute slips the yoke of its Jacobin prototype. From being against all revolutions, Sorel would now craft an anti-Jacobin revolutionary dialectics in which the mythical absolute claimed a central place, not in upholding the existing but abolishing it. This shift toward a dialectics of class combat would only fully emerge once Sorel himself had relocated to Paris, where he ironically came to be known as the "Socrates of the Latin Quarter."[25]

A Frozen Dialectic

Marx and Engels famously wrote that "the epoch of the bourgeoisie . . . has simplified the class antagonisms. Society as a whole is more and more splitting up into two great hostile camps, into two great classes directly facing each other: Bourgeoisie and Proletariat."[26] It is from this increasingly clear opposition that the dialectic of class struggle spirals irrepressibly forth. But when an already middle-aged Georges Sorel surveyed the Parisian political scene fewer than five decades later, this was not what he saw at all. Instead of the progressive clarification of class oppositions through the unbridled logic of capital—and the unfolding historical dialectic leading to inevitable proletarian victory—he saw only blockage and stasis, a frozen dialectic. Instead of "directly facing each other" in a relation of unmitigated enmity, Sorel discovered with no small amount of revulsion that bourgeoisie and proletariat confronted one another in a far more mediated way, through the blurry lens of a social harmony to which even self-professed Marxists were contributing.

While Sorel therefore remained suspicious of dialectics and especially *the* dialectic as deployed by his contemporary socialists, he nevertheless pressed forward in a struggle over the meaning of a dialectics that would remain faithful to the spirit rather than the occasionally misleading word of Marx.[27] His reformulated dialectic of class struggle contains three essential moments, each marked profoundly by his own stamp. First, Sorel diagnoses the frozen immobility of the present, becoming in the process one of the first substantial theorists of ideology and of what would later come to be known as hegemony.[28] Second, confronted with a dialectical impasse, Sorel set about theorizing how the proletariat might—shoulder to the wheel of history—set historical oppositions into dynamic motion, deploying mythical violence to reestablish those oppositions whose sharp edges had been worn down by ideology. Finally, in a third moment, Sorel embraced the profound open-endedness of this dialectic by rejecting the determinism of his contemporary Marxists and foregrounding the unpredictable creativity of a radically transformative revolutionary violence.

Sorel's Marxist contemporaries were divided into two broad camps. Revisionists, buoyed by the unprecedented electoral success of socialist candidates, generally argued that evolving economic conditions unforeseen by Marx had undermined the relevance of the class binary. Without a sharp class opposition, revolutionary overthrow was unlikely, and so they proposed a range of reformist, gradualist, and even "evolutionary" strategies.[29] On the other side, self-professed orthodox Marxists clung to revolutionary rhetoric by insisting both on the existence of class antagonisms and the inevitability of the socialist revolution, despite all evidence to the contrary. Sorel's own peculiar approach rejected both the blind fatalism of the orthodox position and the reformist consequences of revisionism. Instead, he revealed deep complicities between the two.

Both positions exaggerated "objective" economic factors at the expense of "subjective" political and ideological factors. Both, as a result, appealed to broad notions of unity: the reformists reinforcing the essentially perfectible unity of the present, and the orthodox Marxists the future unity of communism. Both, in their own way, fell prey to a Jacobin attachment to scientific truth and state worship. The fatalist blind spot of orthodox Marxists, their faith in the automatic movement of history, prevented these professed revolutionaries from grasping how ideology and concrete reforms were making the revolution less likely by the day. Both, in short, contributed to what Foucault would have understood as a "recentering" of previously oppositional Marxist doctrines, shifting these from the terrain of class rupture to the terrain of unity, even to the point of "becom[ing] the discourse of power itself . . . the discourse of a centered, centralized, and centralizing power."[30]

Sorel fought a war on two fronts against what he saw as the complicities between revisionists and reformists, embracing a paradoxically unorthodox orthodoxy in the process. On the one hand, he insisted on the need to "complete and improve" Marxism by "abandon[ing] many formulas to better penetrate the spirit of the master," while driving a wedge between this revisionist imperative and any reformist implications by insisting that Marx's "spirit" was a resolutely revolutionary one.[31] This revolutionary revisionism, this unorthodox orthodoxy meant confronting the fatalist dialectics and "old aphorisms" of Marxist orthodoxy head on.[32] According to Sorel, the fatalist determinism of the orthodox camp—which presumes to grasp the inevitable movement of history—was grounded in an exaggerated and even "false idea of science" that threatens to "divest historical materialism of its mysterious and paradoxical character."[33]

Properly understood, science is for Sorel a modest endeavor constrained by its experimental setting and with *ceteris paribus* as its byword. Without the ability to hold conditions constant, in particular when we leave the laboratory setting for the social world, science quickly loses its power to predict the future.[34] It is only in this limited sense that Marxism should aspire to the status of a science, and for Sorel, a proper historical materialism seeks only to draw practical conclusions from the "totality [*insieme*] of facts" at a given moment.[35] Here instead of Hegel's own temptations toward a *pro*spective unity in which "everything has to fit into a fully defined system," all that remains is the *retro*spective unity of the Owl of Minerva: "Science arrived when the debate was already closed, to give a regular shape to results gained gradually and empirically."[36] Consequently, the "dialectical rhythm" should never be understood as a "demonstrated law," but instead merely as an "explanatory hypothesis."[37]

While "Marx never was a slave to the dialectic" in the exaggerated and illusory sense, his "zealous disciples," like those of Socrates before him, were nevertheless waiting in the wings to transform even the most contingent observations into "sacred and immutable" laws.[38] These disciples overstepped the limited bounds of historical materialism, inventing speculative connections in the present—like the inexorable deepening of class conflict—and worse still, projecting these forward to forecast the ultimate revolution. Irony of ironies, it was in an effort to avoid utopianism and idealism that these most orthodox sectors themselves fell into both, turning to an "apparent social physics" that "replac[ed Marx's] *rational idea* about the [contingent and momentary] unity of things with a particular definition of a determined relation between parts."[39] By attempting to explain everything, they lost the capacity to explain anything at all.

Moreover, the mystical connections upheld by orthodox Marxists moved in one direction: from base toward superstructure, viewing the impending political catastrophe as the necessary outgrowth of economic progress. By loosening the bonds of this "absolute determinism" and insisting on a "reciprocal dependence" between base and superstructure, Sorel opened a space for intervention in both directions—recognizing both the ideology that upheld the existing order and the relative autonomy of the violence that would seek to abolish it.[40] On the one hand, this view introduces a dialectical relationship into the economic "base" itself: "the *social mechanism is variable*" because the "industrial struggle" is itself the product of a "tumult of wills" and subject to "an infinity of causes."[41] If scientific prediction requires conditions be held constant, capitalism is rarely if ever constant, subject as it is to "aleatory conditions," contingency, and political intervention.[42] Where Marx famously described force as a "midwife" of history, Sorel carefully insisted that force does not merely "accelerate a movement whose parts are already determined," but can also redirect the movement of history since "it creates these very parts and dominates them completely."[43]

On the other hand, the autonomy of force, on which many decolonial thinkers insist, presents the possibility of conscious intervention. But this is for both better and for worse, since intervention can bring the revolution closer or stave it off indefinitely, and the latter is what most concerned Sorel. Capitalists could conceivably, and indeed *would* logically, intervene to manage the class struggle in ways that benefit their own power. If the playing out of Marx's revolutionary dialectic of class struggle requires class antagonism as its sine qua non, this antagonism is not itself guaranteed: "The conditions which make the revolution the necessary result of a natural process are not in themselves inevitable, as we now clearly see: no one is in a position to say what can result from the attempts at social reform."[44]

It is here that the complicity between orthodox Marxism and reformism lie. At best, assuming an immanent logic of history encouraged a quietist fatalism among the working classes, awaiting the inevitable because it is inevitable. At worst, however, it actively contributed to making revolutionary change less and less likely by overlooking barriers to revolution in the present and, worse still, the active strategies being put into place to shore up the capitalist system. This is because it was not only the capitalists themselves who had intervened in an effort to prevent the playing out of the Marxist dialectic. More dangerous for Sorel were those intermediary elements, in particular parliamentary socialists whom he held responsible for defusing the French class struggle. Where orthodox Marxists at least ostensibly displaced class reconciliation to some future communist horizon—what Jay would call "longitudinal totality"—reformists sought a much more immediate reconciliation in the false universal of social harmony in the present, a "latitudinal totality."

These reformists did more than profess a dangerous ideology of unity; they proved that all ideologies are practical and all practices ideological. Not content to embrace the false universality of the present, they sought to actively construct cross-class unity by erasing class identity and defusing the class struggle through two central mechanisms: education and arbitration. The goal of the first was to educate the proletariat, and indeed the capitalists as well, in the "practices [*mœurs*] of social peace."[45] "The *wise men*" in parliament "think that violence will disappear when popular education becomes more advanced; they recommend, therefore, a great increase in the number of courses and lectures; they hope to drown revolutionary syndicalism in the saliva of the honorable professors."[46] Where popular education once served as the glue of a social harmony lost, for Sorel the Marxist, unity was now pernicious and education its most dangerous weapon.

If education was more ideological than practical, its more practical than ideological counterpart was labor arbitration. As bosses pressed wages downward and workers did the opposite, these socialist mediators stepped in to ensure a golden mean: "To the demands of the workers [the bosses] reply that they have already reached the limit of possible concessions—while the philanthropists wonder whether the selling price will not allow a slight increase in the wages."[47] Through arbitration, parliamentary socialists themselves intervene as a buffer between the two sides of the capitalist class opposition, mediating demands and negotiating the eventual resolution of every conflict over the wage. If parliamentary socialists produced mediation, they were themselves produced by it, since this intermediary role was their very raison d'être. They were "master[s] in the art of utilizing anger," uniquely positioned to simultaneously "make the workers believe that you are carrying the flag of revolution, the bourgeoisie that you are holding back the danger which threatens them, and the country that you represent an irresistible current of opinion."[48]

By cushioning the blows of the class struggle, Sorel worried, these social intermediaries had helped to gradually slow the historical dialectic to a standstill. And by placing themselves strategically in the no-man's-land separating the would-be warring classes, parliamentary socialists—both proponents of mediation and its embodiment—revealed themselves to be the true heirs of Jacobinism. Just as Jacobins past had assumed the mantle of progress as sole possessors of the general will, so too with those reformist socialists—possessors of a new notion of progress—who transitioned seamlessly from opposition to government.[49] These new intellectual oligarchs had risen above the fray, uniquely capable of producing harmony, their goal not to overthrow the state but to incorporate the workers into it and keep it for themselves.[50]

These latter-day Jacobins were as complicit with the "superstition of the God-State" as their predecessors, but the socialist Jacobins entered that state at a qualitatively higher stage of development.[51] Rather than the unity of a Jacobin state standing over society, the unity of the parliamentary socialists had a new meaning that coincided with their own historic role as mediators: the "centering" of Marxism and the reinscription of class within the state, a conservative resolution of class antagonisms into harmonious coexistence. For Sorel, this was not the real entry of the workers into government that it claimed to be, but the opposite: a slowing, if not freezing, of dialectical motion, in which inequalities are concealed—indeed legitimated. Parliamentary socialists had incorporated the workers into an enemy totality as a passive force, and by centering the proletarian struggle within the functioning of the state itself, they threatened to destroy it entirely.[52]

In his indictment of parliamentary socialists, Sorel revealed the practical complicity of both fatalist orthodoxy and reformist mediation: as two sides of the same coin, each promises historical closure in its own way: the first through a quietist attachment to the inevitability of the horizon, the latter through a reconciliation with the false universal of the present. Orthodox Marxists were thus more than simply wrong or incapable of prediction, but instead conspired with reformists by denying the autonomy of the political while their opponents proved that autonomy in practice: deploying force, however gently, to slow the dialectic to a standstill.

From Duty to Violence

This incorporation of the workers into the state was more than simply an attack on working-class autonomy; for Sorel, it represented the death of class itself, and with it, the death of dialectics as well. The effectiveness of an ideology of social harmony and of practices of labor arbitration had made it perfectly clear that class identity (Marx's class-for-itself, *Klasse für sich*) does not emerge automatically from the infrastructural conditions of the class-in-itself (*Klasse an sich*).[53] But Sorel presses this observation further: we may be able to speak of the existence of undeniable class *positions* under capitalism, but without class *identity*—without any individual workers understanding themselves to be part of a class—proletariat and bourgeoisie as broad and opposing groupings cease to exist entirely.

In the words of Ernesto Laclau and Chantal Mouffe, for Sorel once the "*totality* as a founding rational substratum has been dissolved . . . social classes . . . no longer play the role of structural locations in an objective system." The dialectic frozen, what was a revolutionary to do? Mouthing the empty mottos of an impending revolution was not an option for Sorel, but nor was abandoning the revolution entirely. Again, Laclau and Mouffe: "[Sorel] is compelled to displace the constitutive moment of class unity to the political level . . . the possibility of a dichotomous division of society is given not as a datum of the social structure, but as a construction."[54] Rather than simply rejecting any automatic connection between class-in-itself and class-for-itself, in which workers necessarily and gradually gain consciousness of objective conditions, Sorel actually *reverses* this formulation, and in so doing renders it an active projection. Absent any objective basis for the existence of class, this basis must be *created* by a political act.

The class-for-itself, in other words, *precedes* and *produces* the class-in-itself, pressing history into motion subjectively through a "dialectics of ideological warfare."[55] From this point forward, Sorel set about reestablishing those conditions under which revolution would be necessary: deepening oppositions, reinforcing class identity through the "social poetry" of the revolutionary myth, and pressing the dialectic of class combat into motion. But Sorel knew full well that ideology could destroy class by dulling its oppositions just as easily as it could reconstitute those oppositions. His first gesture was therefore a sort of negative one, a ground-clearing exercise that hacks unceremoniously through the solemn ideological ties binding the social totality, and more specifically, the ethics of social duty.

He did so by posing a rupture not *within* but *against* ethics, diagnosing an ethical impossibility in which social duty does not exist because the relation between the classes is one of incommensurability and irreconcilability bordering on nonrelation. Boss and worker, for Sorel, speak different languages entirely: "While the boss will always be convinced that he has done the whole of his duty, the worker will be of the contrary opinion, and no argument could possible settle the matter."[56] If anything, the practice of labor arbitration can inadvertently drive this point home: the bosses insist that they cannot "objectively" raise wages, only to later do so upon negotiation, revealing their objectivity—and the limits to growth—to have been a lie.

"Duty has some meaning in a society in which all the parts are intimately connected to one another," for Sorel, "but if capitalism is inexhaustible, solidarity is no longer founded upon the economy and the workers think they would be dupes if they did not demand all they could obtain; they look upon the employer as an adversary with whom one comes to terms after a war."[57] Social duty relies on the assumption that there exists an overarching framework—or better, an underlying totality—on which to ground that duty. Without such a foundation, the basis for ethics dissipates, and what remains between workers and bosses is a military relationship, not an ethical one. Prefiguring Foucault's insistence that the binary relation of social war renders any ethics merely "perspectival" and "one-sided," Sorel's "ethical diremption"—in the words of Axel Honneth—clears the way for the one-sided assertion of a "class-specific morality."[58]

Given Sorel's hostility to unity, it is no surprise that he would bend the stick toward utter incommensurability, but doing so pushes his dialectics to the very brink, to the point at which an internal class relation threatens to become an external nonrelation. It is therefore no surprise that, like Foucault—another thinker treading at the very edge of dialectics—Sorel openly compares this social war to the ungovernable anarchy of the international arena, insisting pointedly that *"social duty no more exists than does international duty."*[59] But where his contemporaries in parliament would seek to impose order on this anarchy, negotiating treaties between warring peoples in what Sorel derisively deemed "socialist diplomacy," Sorel instead positioned himself as a practitioner of socialist *Realpolitik*, a sort of Marxist Machiavelli penning a guidebook not for *The Prince* but for *The Proletariat* (this metaphor only underlined by Gramsci's deep appreciation for both).

The (non)relation prevailing between boss and worker thus consists not of ethics, but of pure force. Or, to put it more precisely, Sorel would drive home the incommensurability of this relationship by insisting that the class opposition is constituted by distinct and incomparable substances entirely: bourgeois *force* and proletarian *violence*. The two are not only qualitatively distinct, for Sorel, but even diametrically opposite: "the object of *force* is to impose a certain social order in which the minority governs, while *violence* tends to the destruction of that order. The bourgeoisie have used *force* since the beginning of modern times, while the proletariat now reacts against the bourgeoisie and against the State by *violence*."[60] Force upholds hierarchy; violence destroys it. Force is Jacobinism incarnate; violence draws its content from an anti-Jacobin egalitarianism. While Sorel treats the bourgeoisie and the state as synonymous, his point is about content rather than form: the "absolute opposition between revolutionary syndicalism and the State" derives from the state's role as an *institution of minority governance*.[61] Given the ferocity of the opposition between the two, we must "adopt a terminology which would give rise to no ambiguity" in which "the term 'violence' should be employed only for . . . acts of revolt."[62]

In formulating violence in such a way as to call into question even the totality underlying and giving meaning to dialectical oppositions, Sorel broke not only with the object of his critique—the mediating impulse of parliamentary socialists—but even exceeds some of the radical dialecticians he would later influence. This was not, for example, the violence of Georg Lukács, which draws its legitimacy and ethical character from the "imperative of the world-historical situation" and in particular, the "historico-philosophical mission" of the proletariat (which Jay describes as an "expressive" totality).[63] Rather than violent means being justified by transhistoric ends, Sorel's violence shuns instrumentality, the means not subjected to the ends. Violence, he contended, "escapes all valuation, estimation and opportunism" and thus shares more with Walter Benjamin's Sorel-inspired account of an immeasurable "divine violence" of "pure means" that is in its essence "law-destroying."[64] Similarly, Foucault's description of social war as a "statement of fact" echoes Sorel's insistence that "proletarian acts of violence have no resemblance to" the Jacobin force of the state with its apparatus of justice and judgment; "they are purely and simply acts of war . . . carried on without hatred and without the spirit of revenge."[65]

If violence—the pure revolt against hierarchical institutions— "constitutes the soul of the revolutionary proletariat," "this revolt does not entirely determine the future of the proletariat," which is another way of saying that revolt absent "the revolutionary idea" is wholly insufficient.[66] In other words, disparate acts of resistance are useless without the unifying horizon that Sorel famously characterized as the revolutionary myth: "As long as there are no myths accepted by the masses," he insisted, "one may go on talking of revolts indefinitely, without ever provoking any revolutionary movement."[67] In this, he saw himself as faithful to Marxism's own social poetry, since those moments when Marx overstepped the bounds of science to speak of an "absolute law which governs history," he did so not to analyze or predict, but to inspire action.[68] "If Marxism has had such a great influence on the popular masses, it is above all due to the attractiveness of its myths."[69] By projecting the "abstraction of dichotomous division"—a firm class opposition, workers against bosses—revolutionary myths help to stitch these many microrevolts together into a broader fabric of working-class identity.[70]

But myths do more than simply unify the class; they also intensify its effect by creating "a coordinated picture" that can be grasped "as a whole, perceived instantaneously."[71] Which is to say that they throw people into action: "revolutionary myths," for Sorel, "are not a description of things but expressions of a will to act . . . myths lead men to prepare themselves for a combat which will destroy the existing state of things."[72] Mythical proletarian identity, a projection of the class-for-itself, is not the sum of a laundry list of past accomplishments or even future aspirations, but instead a *"framing of the future"* of dialectical rupture that brings class into being in the very process of its deployment.[73] The myth, then, constitutes the *form* that violent *content* fills, a vehicle for "the development of specifically proletarian forces, that is to say, *with violence enlightened by the idea of the general strike.*"[74]

Barbarian Dialectics

In the absence of an objective basis for the class struggle, Sorel turns to the revolutionary myth to coordinate proletarian forces, to reassert the dichotomous division of society, and thereby to move from a static and fetishized social harmony toward dialectical motion. But it remains to be seen what the *effects* of carrying this rupture forward are or, put differently, how this mythical hardening of class identity at the center of the dialectic of class struggle impacts its playing out. If Sorel makes working-class subjectivity the motor force of movement, the very depth of the opposition he introduces—the incommensurability between bourgeoisie and proletariat—raises the question of just how dialectical this movement would prove. The deeper the class division is projected, the more absolute and hermetic the opposition, the more utterly irreconcilable the two sides, the closer we might seem to a sort of class nationalism and motionless separatism that Fanon would later call Manichaeism. What is the dialectic binding the subjective activity of the proletariat to future unfoldings?

Sorel himself poses the question: "what will result from the introduction of violence into the relations of the proletariat with society"? And, he adds, already hinting toward an answer: what does this violence mean "in relation to the future social revolution"?[75] The interventions of parliamentary socialism had dulled the enmity of class oppositions, thereby robbing Marx's dialectic of its determinism, derailing and even halting the dialectic of history. But while Sorel rejects Marxist determinism writ large, his narrower, ceteris paribus determinism grants historical motion a degree of predictability *if the conditions are put into place*. In other words, capitalism "performs in an almost mechanical manner," but this mechanical functioning depends entirely upon its component parts. A society composed of sharply antagonistic classes will press toward revolution, but "This doctrine [of class struggle] is evidently lacking if the bourgeoisie and the proletariat do not stand opposed to one other."[76]

The result is a strangely indeterminate determinism: an *objectivity* that relies fundamentally on *subjective* interventions. It was on the terrain of this conditional determinism that Sorel understood his own historical role: if the Marxist theory of revolution requires the fulfillment of a number of precise conditions that have been lost, then the task is to reestablish those conditions—that is, the separation of the classes. Then and only then can any sort of "determinism" and "certainty" can be restored to the Marxist system: "Only then is the development of capitalism pursued with that rigor which so struck Marx, and which seemed to him comparable to that of a natural law."[77] Toward this end, proletarian violence intervenes by performing a double function, operating on both sides of the dialectical opposition.

Not only does violence mythically unify the working class in its self-activity, but it also unifies the bourgeoisie in the process. In an irony surpassed only by Marx's own celebration of the revolutionary character of capitalism, Sorel lauds the most warlike elements among the capitalist class, and scorns the "*conservative mediocrity*" of those capitalists who, "led astray by the *tricks* of the preachers of morals and sociology . . . wish to break with the barbarism of their elders." If capitalists back down from their own role in the class struggle, "then one part of the forces which were to produce the capitalist tendency instead functions to its hindrance, an element of chance is introduced, and the future of the world becomes completely indeterminate."[78] "[T]he role of violence in history appears as of the utmost importance," precisely because it counteracts this tendency by providing a sharp lesson in barbarism. While helping to consolidate working-class identity, "in an indirect manner [violence] can [also] operate on the bourgeoisie so as to remind them of their own class sentiment."

Workers are thus encouraged to "repay with *black ingratitude* the *benevolence* of those who wish to protect the workers, to meet with insults the homilies of the defenders of human fraternity, and to respond by blows to the advances of the propagators of social peace . . . [this] is a very practical way of indicating to the bourgeoisie that they must occupy themselves with their own affairs and that only."[79] Capitalists must be reminded that "they have nothing to gain from the works of social peace or from democracy" and that "they have been badly advised by the people who persuaded them to abandon their trade of creators of productive forces for the noble profession of educators of the proletariat." Then and only then will they regain a modicum of what Sorel admits to have been their original, heroic, and creative energy, operating dialectically upon the proletariat in turn. "The two antagonistic classes act upon one other," setting into motion a virtuous cycle of polarization that hardens identities on both sides: "the more ardently capitalist the bourgeoisie, the more the proletariat will be full of a warlike spirit and confident of its revolutionary force, the more certain the movement will be."[80]

In its two-sidedness, this dynamic would seem to share much with the sort of mutual progress toward self-consciousness found in Hegel's master-slave dialectic. But at the same time, Sorel's formulation moves conspicuously beyond Hegel. Not only would Sorel be suspicious of the idea that a Hegelian politics of recognition might emerge from the class war—and indeed would likely fear the danger of a false universalism this might entail—but most fundamentally, Sorel's dialectics, like Fanon's after him, contains no presumption of an automatic movement. If violence has a two-sided impact, it nevertheless finds its source on one pole of the renewed class divide. "Proletarian violence," and only proletarian violence, can "make the future revolution certain"—subjective intervention to re-constitute objectivity. "A growing and solidly organized working class can force the capitalist class to remain fervent in the industrial struggle; if a united and revolutionary proletariat confronts a rich bourgeoisie hungry for conquest, capitalist society will reach its historical perfection."[81]

The future peril faced by the world can only be avoided "if the proletariat attaches itself stubbornly to revolutionary ideas, so as to realize as much as possible Marx's conception": "Everything may be saved if the proletariat, by their use of violence, manage to re-establish the division into classes . . . Proletarian violence . . . appears thus as a very beautiful and very heroic thing; it is at the service of the fundamental interests of civilization . . . it may save the world from barbarism."[82] It might seem ironic that Sorel here invokes the opposition between *civilization* and *barbarism*, after urging capitalists to embrace the "barbarism of their elders" and suggesting that socialism similarly need not be "frightened of its own barbarism."[83]

But *barbarism* here is faithful to the xenophobia of the Greek *barbaros*: to embrace barbarity is to embrace the cultural incommensurably of speaking an entirely different language, the irreconcilable nature of the class divide. That barbarism stands on the horizon as a threat as well is a gesture toward the dialectics such opposition set into motion, the infinitely deferred horizon of which would transcend barbarism entirely.[84] Against the common opposition that Luxemburg and many since have posed between "socialism or barbarism," Sorel's reply would be characteristically provocative: socialism *through* barbarism. A barbarism to end barbarism may seem paradoxical, but no more so than the subjective objectivity of a violence to end violence. It is the civility of the professors of social peace that makes dialectical progress impossible, and the barbarian purveyors of proletarian violence who—momentarily allied with their class enemies through the fury of their antagonism—have become its saviors.[85]

Simply reestablishing the objective movement of Marx's historical system does not tell us much with regard to where we will end up, however. For a thinker as epistemologically skeptical as Sorel, with so narrow a notion of science and a deep-seated hostility toward utopias, all we will know is that we are once again on the path. It is in part due to the sheer generativity he grants to proletarian violence, which "*entirely changes* the appearance of all the conflicts in which it plays a part," that his dialectics remain stubbornly open ended.[86] Proletarian violence merely forces the dialectic of history, now rusty and having ground to a halt, tentatively into motion once again: it tells us little of our destination.

Fascism and Decolonization

By rejecting the natural basis of class antagonisms and setting into motion an open-ended class struggle stripped of determinism and teleology, Sorel's dialectics is a far cry from a sort of separatist class nationalism. But this point only raises in a more urgent way the question of actual nationalisms, a question that moves in two different directions and poses two distinct challenges to this project of a decolonized dialectics and Sorel's relation to such a project. First, there is the persistent suspicion that Sorel himself was a protofascist, which if true would represent a clear threat to his incorporation into a revolutionary—much less a dialectical and decolonial—politics. Second, and from the opposite direction, there is the suspicion that all nationalisms are fundamentally the same, with some extreme arguments suggesting that anticolonial nationalism is itself a form of fascism. Setting aside caricatures on both sides, the real question lies somewhere between the two: How to reconcile Sorel's rejection of unity in favor of rupture with processes of decolonization that center not on class but the nation?

In a fascinating appendix on "Unity and Multiplicity" that Sorel added to the second edition of *Reflections on Violence* published in 1910, he broadened his attack on unity while further radicalizing the open-endedness of his dialectics. Whereas biology "can never consider the function of an organ without relating it to the whole living being," "Social philosophy is obliged . . . to proceed to a *diremption*, to examine certain parts without taking into account all of the ties which connect them to the whole, to determine in some manner the character of their activity by pushing them toward independence. When it has thus arrived at the most perfect understanding, it can no longer attempt to reconstitute the broken unity."[87] While the object of Sorel's critique here is the notion of biological unity, his argument applies equally well to both forms of "recentering" identified by Foucault: "the dialectical and the biological."[88]

For many Hegelians, the inverse of the "aspiration to totality" was and remains a severe anxiety toward the moment of diremption, division, and rupture.[89] By privileging the moment of diremptive rupture and explicitly disavowing efforts to "reconstitute the broken unity," Sorel is distancing himself not only from the predominant, totality-bound Hegelian-Marxist tradition, which privileges the reconstitution of unity over the dialectical moment par excellence—that of division and combat—but also from any plausible suggestion that he was a forerunner of European fascism.[90] To dispel but one powerful example, Zeev Sternhell argues that fascist ideology is "above all a rejection of 'materialism'" that "did not depend on a class struggle" and notably "constituted a totality."[91] Moreover, fascism—for Sternhell—sought to create cross-class "harmony" grounded in the organic nation and embodied in the state. As we have seen, however, Sorel hates nothing so much as social harmony, loathes the biologized unity of the nation, and views proletarian struggles as seeking the destruction of the state. By claiming Sorel as a fascist precursor, Sternhell has miraculously transformed him into his opposite—a prime example of the "shabby exercises in logic" characteristic of many treatments of Sorel.[92]

In the words of one of Sorel's closest collaborators, Édouard Berth, "We must not forget the radical difference that separates *fascist violence* from *Sorelian violence*. The latter is the true violence, that which tends to destroy the traditional state and institute a *free order*. The former is by definition only a *bourgeois force*."[93] While Sorel's political friendships were deeply suspect, there was a deep incongruity—even an outright contradiction—between the radical social war posed by his dialectics of class struggle and the radical nationalism some of his disciples would embrace. Even the sympathy for Sorel exhibited by the reactionary jurist Carl Schmitt bears this out. Whereas Schmitt's attentiveness to the friend-enemy distinction certainly echoes Sorel, Schmitt's ultimate critique, that Sorel neglects that "the energy of nationalism is greater than the myth of class conflict," only serves to sharply underline the vast gulf separating the class struggle from the national struggle.[94]

Any attempt to expand Sorel's radicalized dialectic beyond the realm of the class war must therefore look beyond and away from fascism, but few have been willing to do so. Some have sought Sorelian resonances in the Nation of Islam, for example, but Sorel's dialectical open-endedness points beyond such hermetic separatism.[95] Others fall into the double error of folding Sorel into debates about so-called Black fascism and Black racism—neglecting both the fact that such categories are as nonsensical and imaginary as "reverse-racism" and that Sorel was hardly a fascist to begin with.[96] To accommodate Sorelian dialectics on the global scale requires a far different approach, a more resolutely dialectical view in which division and rupture are foregrounded and combatively insisted upon. It would be, in other words, more Malcolm X than Elijah Muhammad, more Fanon than Marcus Garvey.[97]

But even if Sorel's dialectics of class warfare is acquitted on the trumped-up charge of fascism, what possible relevance could this thinker have for decolonial struggles? After all, some of Sorel's sympathizers threw their weight behind not only Benito Mussolini's fascism, but also the Italian invasion and later annexation of Libya. But the question is the same: what did these disciples *do* with Sorel's thought? What his own "zealous disciples" did—indeed, what they *had* to do—was to transpose Sorel's dialectic of class struggle, the internal rupture of the social totality into two incommensurable sides, onto the framework of the nation. But to do so was an undeniable betrayal of the combative division at its heart and the open-endedness of its dynamic motion. It was only through the most difficult and unconvincing ideological acrobatics that the invasion of Libya could be described as "proletarian nationalism" or, in the words of Robert Michels, "the imperialism of a poor people."[98] Rather than such unfaithful disciples, we would be better advised to turn to those other zealots on the receiving end of the colonial onslaught. Once we do so, it becomes clear that Sorel's radicalized dialectic of class struggle is not already decolonial, but it does nevertheless open some necessary doors toward a decolonized dialectics.

First, and at the broadest methodological level, Sorel's revisionist impulse, his rejection of received dogmas—Marxist or otherwise—in favor of the concrete analysis of social conditions, will prove a sine qua non for decolonial dialecticians. Struggling under the yoke of Comintern orthodoxy, José Carlos Mariátegui would attempt to craft a revolutionary socialism suited to Latin American reality, and generations of Black revolutionaries like George Padmore, Richard Wright, C. L. R. James, and Aimé Césaire were first drawn into and then pushed away from official communist parties unable to respond to the questions facing Black people.[99] While Marx's *words* often became mere props for the most ossified political forms, it was arguably in the colonized and decolonizing world that the combative *spirit* of Marx was best able to flourish and transform. While Sorel's focus was on the historical variability of capitalism in his own context, his insistence that Marx's own historical studies show "different phases [of capitalist development] taking place in a diverse order and in different historical epochs" opens up an important space for contingency, uneven development, and autonomous struggles that points toward decolonization and liberation from orthodox stageism.[100]

Second, in rejecting the inevitability of historical movement and identifying existing blockages to the revolutionary dialectic of class struggle, Sorel was acutely aware of the dangers of false universals masquerading as ethical systems, whether their reference point is an idealized present (latitudinal totality) or a future harmonious society (longitudinal totality). He thereby opened a space for the subjective rupture and struggle that while necessary in his context to jumpstart the class struggle would also prove necessary—arguably more so—for overcoming those same universals that impede a decolonized dialectic. It almost goes without saying that the idea of history moving incessantly forward, propelled by its own internal logic, has rarely been convincing for colonized and enslaved subjects who have endured both the social death of stasis and genuine reversals by brute force.[101] The same could be said for notions of social harmony in the present and, more radically still, for preconceived dialectics of the future.

Third, Sorel was attentive at an exceptionally early stage to the impact of ideology, in part because he had loosened the bonds of economic determinism in a necessary way, allowing him to grasp not only the arresting the dialectic but also the mythical mobilization of revolutionary ideology toward a renewal, a jumpstarting, of dialectical motion. As a result, he could be seen as intervening in long-standing Marxist debates regarding force and as resisting the tendency—in Engels's *Anti-Dühring* and elsewhere—to assert the importance of the economic by downplaying the autonomy of force. These are debates that Fanon would engage with directly, and the foregrounding of force and violence—be they reactionary or revolutionary, freezing history or pressing it forward—would prove characteristic of decolonial dialectics.

Fourth, Sorel's insistence on deepening the ethical diremption between the classes, dividing them to the point of incommensurability and the breaking point of dialectical linkages, both allows for the subjective reengagement of the dialectic of class combat and facilitates its decolonization. By categorically distinguishing bourgeois force from proletarian violence, absolutely condemning the former as he absolutely validates the latter, Sorel's framework legitimizes combative working-class self-activity. But it also crucially builds bridges to the anticolonial struggle by allowing a similarly absolute distinction, a vast gulf, between the nationalism of the powerful (fascism included) and the nationalism of the weak, stoking the suspicion that these, too, differ not in degree but in kind. If Jacobinism is understood as upholding the state as a structure of hierarchical minority rule, moreover, this anti-Jacobin violence will find its resonance in the decolonial realm as well. By pressing the limits of the dialectic, moreover, Sorel points toward the realm beyond dialectical oppositions that Fanon would call nonbeing and Dussel would call exteriority, simultaneously barriers to dialectical motion and its necessary footholds.

Sorel's ethical diremption is arguably epitomized by his subversion of the opposition between civilization and barbarism, and this insistence that the "civilizing mission" of the bourgeoisie must be thrown back in their faces is one that decolonial thinkers would take to new lengths. In fact, this was Césaire's essential lesson: that the civilizers (Europe) were themselves decivilized and brutalized by their own violence, and thereby complicit in the barbarity unleashed when "the bourgeoisie is awakened by a terrific boomerang effect" and "the continent proceeds toward *savagery*" in the European holocaust.[102] Europe's civilizing mission was the "principal lie that is the source of all the others" and colonization itself the "bridgehead in a campaign to civilize barbarism, from which there may emerge at any moment the negation of civilization."[103] For Sorel, moreover, this insight is nested within an antidevelopmentalist rejection of mimicry that will find similar expression in Mariátegui and Fanon as a rejection of the stages prescribed by Marxist orthodoxy and the mimicry of European nations.

Finally, and crucially, by loosening the determinism between the economic and the political, Sorel's framework counterintuitively insists on the reestablishment of a traditional class opposition while simultaneously opening the door to its transcendence. In other words, Sorel's emphasis on class as a mythical construction, especially when paired with his imperative to heterodox revisionism, inadvertently creates space for the sort of reconfiguration of class structure that will prove necessary not only for a concrete analysis of economic conditions in the (formerly) colonized world, but also for a reconceptualization of the revolutionary subject to be constructed. It is this crucial step that allows for a decolonization of dialectical struggles that draws together combative identities from class to race to nation to people to accommodate a move across the "colonial difference."[104]

While these elements, drawn from the internal imperatives of the European class struggle, do not in and of themselves constitute a ready-made decolonized dialectics, such a reworking of dialectical theory is not possible without them. And while this is not to claim Sorel as the origin or necessary source for such a dialectics, it does clearly explain why his work has remained directly influential for decolonial dialecticians from Mariátegui to Fanon.[105] It is no coincidence, then, that when Sorel defended Lenin's attempt to "force history" through a resort to the political will, he did so by turning to Marx's late comments on the Russian *Mir* or *Obshchina* communes. There, Marx began to call into question the linearity and determinism of his own historical dialectic, suggesting that existing communal structures might provide a direct jumping-off point toward communism.

And it was these very same texts that would provide generations of third-world Marxists with the hope that they need not necessarily pass through capitalism as a painful way station toward a communal future. This confirmed Sorel's already well-established suspicion that "true Marxism is not as absolute in its predictions as the enemies of Lenin would very much like to have it."[106] Not least important among these predictions was the idea that the world revolution would be one simply of class against class, a belief that within a few decades of Sorel's death would be relegated to the dustbin of history by the global outbreak of decolonial struggles. No single individual epitomizes more directly this anticolonial upsurge—and certainly none delineates its unfolding dialectic more convincingly—than Frantz Fanon.

CHAPTER 2

TOWARD A NEW DIALECTICS OF RACE

Sartre's Disavowal

The searing venom that Jean-Paul Sartre reserved for Sorel in his preface to Fanon's *Wretched of the Earth* is well known, but less noted is the disavowal that it contains.[1] His nonchalance notwithstanding, Sartre's dismissal of Sorel appears at a crucial moment in the text, where he offers the second of two reasons that Europeans must "have the courage to read" Fanon's book: the world-historic dialectical role of violence. Here both the imperative to disavowal and peculiarity of the gesture become patent: "if you set aside Sorel's fascist utterances, you will find that Fanon is the first since Engels to return the midwife of history to the light."[2] To understand violence, Sartre implies, is to understand—in Marx's and Engels's famous phrase—"the midwife of history," and of the many attempts to grasp this assisted birth of the new, but three figures stand out: Engels, Sorel, and now Fanon.[3] The praise could not be more explicit! And yet the second of these must be "set aside [*écartez*]." Either due to his own sympathies or as a provocative rejection of French intellectual pieties, Fanon would not bother distancing himself from Sorel, even alluding playfully to his intellectual forbear by describing the first chapter of *Wretched of the Earth* as his own "*réflexions sur la violence*."[4] As we will see, however, Sartre had already been combatively pummeled and transformed by the same violent dialectics he now celebrated so infamously, with the unchecked fervor of a new disciple.

Sartre's disavowal, his attempt to drive a wedge between Sorel and Fanon to rescue the latter from the taint of the former, is symptomatic of the overwhelming majority of critics.[5] As a result, reconciling these two thinkers is a difficult and even daunting task, and all the more so when the grounds for this reconciliation is political identity. How to square Sorel's stubborn class-centrism with Fanon, for whom class was always an important but secondary phenomenon and for whom the central category of identification was first blackness, or negritude (in *Black Skin, White Masks*), and later the decolonial nation (in *Wretched of the Earth*)? Further, if what defines Sorel's radicalized dialectic of class struggle is precisely his insistence on pressing class rupture to the breaking point at which the (national) social totality is itself called into question and even disintegrated, then how to reconcile this combative division with Fanonian decolonization, and in particular Fanon's emphasis on a third-world nationalism housed in the state?

For those attempting to draw Sorel and Fanon together, however, one path stands out for its relative ease of travel, the brush having been cleared and the analytic soil tilled by a thinker no less incisive than Sartre's most eloquent critic, Hannah Arendt. In *On Violence*, Arendt draws Sorel and Fanon together *not* according to the underlying structure of their dialectics, but rather according to their shared emphasis on violence and their efforts (heretical, for Arendt) to politicize this essentially antipolitical concept.[6] But Arendt's rigid definition of violence as "incapable of speech," as mute and muting, as mortal threat to power as collective action, is wholly incompatible with what both Sorel and Fanon mean by the term.[7] Hers is a violence that is by definition undialectical, incapable of unleashing a transformative chain of confrontations except toward the certainty of its own increase. By contrast, Sorel's violence, as we have seen (and Fanon's, as we will see), is profoundly "productive" in Foucault's terms, generating political identities and transforming those identities and the world. This is, in short, not a mute violence at all, but a violence that speaks volumes. By reducing violence to its formal characteristics at the expense of its content, Arendt ironically both *does* "violence" (in her understanding) to their formulations—muting the richness of their radical dialectics of identity— and, more dangerously, abandons to the "technicians" a dynamic that even she would have to recognize as profoundly political.

Ours is a more difficult and less-trodden path, that of drawing together Sorel and Fanon not strictly on the basis of violence—and certainly not through such formalistic misinterpretations—but instead by locating violence within the broader chain reaction that binds it to the identities it generates and the radicalized dialectics it sets into motion. By doing so, we can begin to think race, class, and the nation anew by neither reducing one to the other nor separating these identities hermetically from their contexts, but instead by grasping their shared dialectics and even the microdialectics of their mutual interplay. But to do so requires that we begin prior to Fanon's explicit analysis of violence, stepping back to a moment when the gulf between him and Sartre, mutual respect notwithstanding, was considerably wider. It was within the pages of Fanon's earliest work, *Black Skin, White Masks*, that he underwent a process similar to Sorel's in the aftermath of *The Trial of Socrates*, driven by force away from dreams of universal harmony and toward a combative political practice rooted in the decolonization of Hegel's master-slave dialectic and an embrace of black identity.

"As long as the black man remains on his home territory," Fanon wrote, reflecting critically on his own early years, "except for petty internal quarrels, he will not have to experience his being for others."[8] While race was certainly a heavy presence in interwar Martinique, its aspirational reference point—whiteness, Frenchness—was largely held at arm's length, allowing local racial distinctions to flourish and the self-congratulatory illusions of the relatively wealthier and lighter-skinned segments of Antillean society to thrive unchecked. It is only upon crossing the line demarcating metropole from colony—a line which in this case coincided with the vastness of the ocean—that one might experience "being for others," which is to say, racism.[9] One can subsist for many years in the racial daydreams of the colony, but following Sartre's analysis of anti-Semitism, the later the colonial subject experiences colonial racism, "the more violent the shock."[10] It is the lateness of Fanon's own shock—which he documents within the pages of *Black Skin, White Masks*—that rattles Fanon's universal pretensions, driving him for a time away from universal human love and into the dialectical detour of identity, away from the totalizing pretensions of reason and into a mythical irrationalism against unreasonable reason.

Fanon's own biographical and metaphorical crossing to the metropole was a subjective point of no return, after which he had "nothing in common" with the black subject (in the colony and elsewhere) who "wants to be white." Where Fanon had initially approached the world with a spirit of generosity, he was denied access to universal humanity. The fifth chapter of *Black Skin*—the book's centerpiece, on the "lived experience" of the racialized subject—instead "shows the black man confronted with his race . . . striving desperately to discover the meaning of black identity" and the dialectics it sets into motion.[11] The path of the universal foreclosed upon,

Fanon was driven repeatedly backward, forced to seek a new outlet for his humanity in combative rupture. Knowing full well the irrationality of race, he was left with no alternative but to embrace Black identity and to embrace it fully—mythically and violently—in the hope that doing so would provide racialized subjects with the necessary "ontological resistance" to jumpstart the Hegelian dialectic of recognition.[12]

Despite the very different registers Sorel and Fanon deploy, we will see a fundamental correspondence between the two. Fanon's counterontological violence, like Sorel's proletarian violence, is irreconcilable with the sort of repressive, Jacobin force that upholds hierarchical minority rule (class domination for Sorel, racist-ontological disqualification for Fanon). For both, the uncritical unity of the present—social duty and harmony for Sorel, emancipation and formal equality for Fanon—conceals and maintains inequalities by halting dialectical motion, and for both a determinist and teleological dialectics of history serves to contain progress rather than advance it.[13] Both thinkers, as a result, instead throw themselves headlong into combative division as the only possible path toward an eventual reconciliation. But even then, Fanon's misgivings about the dialectic will remain as tangible as Sorel's, and he will push still further, upbraiding even Sartre himself for having betrayed the Black struggle by containing its self-activity within a teleological and Eurocentric dialectic. Against such preemptive closure, Fanon formulates a decolonized and open-ended master-slave dialectic in which universal reconciliation is infinitely deferred, before later projecting this framework outward onto the global movement of decolonization.

Rebuffed from the Universal

Fanon was a reluctant participant in the dialectic of Black identity. Indeed, one would be hard-pressed to find a thinker more universal in aspiration and character. His entire being ached for the universal, for a fully reconciled humanity, and it was for the universal that he himself screamed, wept, and finally, prayed. He begins:

> Toward a new humanism . . .
> Understanding among men . . .
> Our colored brothers . . .
> I believe in you, Man . . .
> To understand and to love . . . [14]

And concludes similarly:

> Superiority? Inferiority?
>
> Why not simply try to touch the other, feel the other, to reveal our-
> selves to one another?
>
> Was my freedom not given to me to build the world of the *You*?[15]

Here was a man for whom race, the ultimate crime against human unity, had no objective standing. "Blacks" only exist as such on the basis of "a series of affective disorders" resulting from a process of racialization in which, paraphrasing Sartre's analysis of anti-Semitism, "*It is the racist who creates the inferiorized.*"[16] Given his explicit and generous *openness* to the world, it would not be easy for Fanon to descend into the conflictive realm of Black identity, since to do so would threaten to rupture the human community as a harmonious totality.

The opening scene of this phenomenological retreat into Black identity, in which Fanon himself was "confronted with his race," is the now-famous "Look! A Negro!" of young child to mother. That even a child could so easily reduce him to an object dealt a crushing blow to Fanon's optimistic universalism, and his response to it contained an embryonic dialectic of revolutionary identity and violence. Desiring only the ethical intersubjectivity of the "world of the *You*," he was instead "fixed" by the gaze of the Other as a slide is "fixed" in preparation for the microscope, and "sealed into . . . crushing objecthood."[17] In an intersubjective world, to lose one's status as a subject is to lose the world as well, and here as elsewhere, Sartre's earlier observations regarding the hostility of the Other's gaze gain for Fanon a burdensome, racialized reality: "I existed in triple: I was taking up room. I approached the other . . . and the Other, evasive, hostile, but not opaque, transparent and absent, vanished. Nausea."[18]

Fanon had offered the (white) world an exchange on the most generous of terms: forgetting (of slavery, a history of racist violence, and even the abuses of the present) for integration, but true integration was not to be had, and his disbelief that such a kind offer could be rejected is palpable: "What? Whereas I was prepared to forget, to forgive, and to love, my message was flung back at me like a slap in the face. The white world, the only decent one, was preventing me from participating. It demanded that a man behave like a man. *It demanded of me that I behave like a black man*—or at least like a Negro. I hailed the world and the world amputated my enthusiasm."[19] Here, in the distance separating "man" from "black man" and "black man" from "Negro," the human universal begins to splinter in tandem with Fanon's own fragmented ego. But even this amputation, this slap in the face, was not enough to dampen Fanon's longing for the universal, and this initial rebuff only sets in motion an elaborate intradialectical dance, a double helix of generosity and rejection by the racist world, courtship and flight, anticipation and trauma.

As rationalist as he was universalist, Fanon's first resort was to turn the "knife blades" of reason against this assault by the unreasonable. He set about gathering the objective proof of his equality, a classic idealist intent on proving whiteness wrong and thus reconstituting the broken unity of humanity: "Reason was assured of victory on every level. I reintegrated the brotherhood of man. But soon I was disillusioned. Victory was playing cat and mouse; it was thumbing its nose at me."[20] Fanon soon realized that he was up against the *irrational*.[21] Or rather, a double irrationality: not only is it irrational to embrace an imaginary system of racial difference, but that difference is itself structured according to the question of reason itself. White Europeans (no matter how irrational) are the bearers of reason, and even the most educated among the colonized are still held to different standards. As Fanon seethingly put it, even for the sympathetic surrealist André Breton, his teacher Aimé Césaire was simply "a great *black* poet."[22]

You cannot reason with the fundamentally, structurally unreasonable, and Fanon soon found racial Manichaeism descending like Du Bois's veil. Neither history nor biology, philosophy nor psychology, would prove the corruption of whiteness to its beneficiaries, and neither love nor language would allow for his own assimilation into it. This discovery, which doomed not only reason but also the human universal it claimed to reflect, was powerfully traumatic for Fanon. Whereas traditional psychoanalysis is attentive to the trauma of the child confronting the rational, Fanon inverts this equation for the colonized and racialized by interjecting a moment of epistemic decolonization: "for a man armed solely with reason," paradigmatically, the colonized, "there is nothing more neurotic than contact with the irrational."[23]

Even Hegelian dialectics—reason inscribed longitudinally in history— was in on the act, conscripted into the work of white supremacy. When Fanon countered claims of Black backwardness by pointing to the accomplishments of African history, he suffered viscerally the sort of dialectical "recolonization" that so worried Foucault. These accomplishments were simply folded with a condescending nod into a long historical progression in which white Europe stands as the pinnacle of civilization: "*you reconcile us with ourselves*." Fanon was cornered: "So they were countering my irrationality with rationality, my rationality with the 'true rationality.' At my every move, I was losing. I tested my heredity. I did a complete diagnosis of my sickness. I wanted to be typically black—that was out of the question. I wanted to be white—that was a joke. And when I tried to claim my negritude *intellectually* as a concept, they snatched it away from me. They proved to me that my effort was nothing but a term in the dialectic."[24] Frozen and fixed by the white gaze, anguished and traumatized by this assault on reason and the impossibility of recourse to it, and seemingly immobilized without dialectical outlet, Fanon saw clearly that white supremacy was not simply a bad idea but a structuring premise of the world.

Faced with this perversely inverted Hegelianism in which only the irrational is real, it would be no surprise to find Fanon initially hesitant to embrace a dialectical framework, and as we will see this would not be his last dialectical betrayal. But like Sorel before him and Dussel after him, Fanon's skepticism toward dialectics led him not to reject the dialectical tradition entirely, but instead pressed him toward the sort of radical reformulation that emerges only at the breaking point. Desperate for any path that might lead toward the universal, or at least beyond the impasse of white supremacy, Fanon crafted a decolonized dialectics that centered the radical assertion of Black identity in the present at the expense of all determinism, teleology, and preemptive reconciliation. Embracing Black identity was not a choice that Fanon made willingly, but no amount of training in existential philosophy with its talk of absolute freedom could withstand brutal collision with the white-supremacist world: "I had to choose. What am I saying? I had no choice."[25]

Decolonizing the Master-Slave Dialectic

It is at the intersection of Fanon's all-too-human curiosity about his own inhumanity—"again I want to know why"—and the condemnation to choose in the absence of freedom, that he forges ahead to reformulate and ultimately decolonize Hegel's dialectic of lord and bondsman, master and slave.[26] He does so in four moments, each pointing toward an aspect of his reformulated dialectic. First, he confronts like Sorel a situation in which dialectical motion is blocked from the outset, although for reasons more ontological than ideological. Whereas Hegel presumed a shared basis for reciprocity and ultimately recognition, Fanon diagnoses the existence of a "zone of nonbeing" inhabited by the racialized, which prevents the dialectic from entering into motion to begin with. Second, confronted with this absence of reciprocity—and lack of dialectical motion—Fanon turns to the one-sided subjective combat set into motion by those disqualified nonbe-ings. This combat takes the precise form of the "violent" self-assertion of Black identity, a "making oneself known" that prepares the basis for fur-ther dialectical movement.

However, in a third moment, this Black self-assertion at the heart of Fanon's dialectics is immediately beset by the risk of a false universalism in the guise of formal emancipation and equality. Like Sorel's much-loathed ideology of social harmony, formal equality enters Fanon's framework as a threat, dulling identity and whittling down the oppositions necessary for continued dialectical motion, something that must be similarly combatted. Fourth and finally, as Fanon's dialectic lunges forward, he confronts the be-trayal of an erstwhile comrade in Sartre, whose subsumption of race to class threatens to foreclose on the open-endedness of Fanon's own approach. It is in fending off this dialectical threat—of the premature enclosure of race within a predetermined dialectic of class—that Fanon is forced to vaccinate his own dialectics against determinism, teleology, and closure in a far more radical manner than most (a critique that Sartre himself would eventually come to embrace).

In its one-sided and mythical projection of Black identity, not to men-tion its radically open-ended deferral of dialectical resolution, Fanon's violent dialectics of blackness shares much with Sorel's own radicalized dialectic of class struggle. But Fanon's dialectic sets out from a different location, the zone of nonbeing, which is specific to decolonial thought and serves as a fulcrum for epistemic decolonization. Setting out from the specificity of colonial reality, what Walter Mignolo would term the *colonial difference*, does more than shift the course of this decolonized dialectic: it transforms its every moment.[27]

The name often given to Hegel's master-slave dialectic is misleading, since it begins with neither masters nor slaves. Rather, it envisions two simple self-consciousnesses in pursuit of a truer self-consciousness, autonomy, and self-sufficiency (*Selbstständigkeit*). The path toward self-consciousness passes inevitably through the other, who accordingly appears as if magneti-cally: a threat to be overcome but not avoided. Simple self-consciousness "sees *itself* in the *other*" and, as a result, "must set out to sublate [*aufzuhe-ben*] the *other* self-sufficient essence in order to become certain of *itself*."[28] This attempted sublation—a process of cancelling while also preserving—takes the form of an ensuing "life and death struggle" through which "each *proves his worth* to himself, and . . . both *prove their worth* to each other."[29] The circuit that passes through the other is not a one-way street, however, but is instead strictly two-sided, "the doubled movement of both self-consciousnesses," in which "one-sided activity would be useless."[30]

Self-consciousness begins to develop through confrontation with the other standing before it, and in so doing the progress toward full humanity trumps mere biological existence and even *requires* risking that bare existence for something higher: "The individual who has not risked his life may admittedly be recognized as a *person*, but he has not achieved the truth of being recognized as a self-sufficient self-consciousness."[31] This process of progressing toward true humanity through struggle is more than simply two-sided for Hegel: it is *symmetrical*, albeit counterintuitively so, and even arguably *circular*. During the course of the struggle, one is subjected and becomes a slave, while the other prevails and emerges a master. Despite this apparently unequal outcome, however, Hegel's dialectic presumes equality from the outset: both parties enter into conflict with the same standing (universal *Grund*, or Ground), and either could theoretically emerge as victor or vanquished.[32]

This fundamental symmetry is only underscored by Hegel's famous dialectical inversion, in which it is the slave who—by virtue of labor on and direct contact with the world—ultimately emerges as independent and autonomous.[33] True self-consciousness thus requires struggle, but for Hegel this struggle is a characteristically circular affair, and this circularity is but a different way of grasping the symmetry of his point of departure: one must have ground upon which to stand, and absent the ontological Ground of Being no standing can occur. To lack standing is to lack the foundation on which to make a circular move that defends that very same ground, upholding what one can already rightfully claim. In Hegel's strangely redundant dialectic, all enjoy the ground on which to stand, and this assumption is the weak point at which Fanon would launch his attack, taking Hegel to task for this uncritical circularity.

THE ZONE OF NONBEING

When Fanon, a Black man, sought recognition from the white Other shortly after arriving in France, he discovered something peculiar: that the Black subject suffers what Fanon deemed an ontological "flaw," an absence of access to Being itself. Lacking "ontological resistance" in the eyes of whites—that is, not appearing as fully human or worthy of recognition—Black subjects lack an entry point into the dialectic of recognition itself and are forced to enter into a conflict that differs fundamentally from what Hegel had envisioned.[34] Rather than two abstract and ahistorical subjects confronting one another on the smooth plane of guaranteed Being, Fanon instead found himself "overdetermined from the outside," forced to shoulder the weight of an entire "historical-racial schema . . . woven . . . out of a thousand details, anecdotes, and stories."[35]

When Fanon approached the Other seeking reciprocity, the response was neither reciprocity nor even aggressive interest and attempted sublation, but a shattering objectification: "Locked in this suffocating reification, I appealed to the Other so that his liberating gaze . . . would give me back the lightness of being I thought I had lost. But just as I get to the other slope I stumble, and the Other fixes me with his gaze . . . I lose my temper, demand an explanation . . . Nothing doing, I explode. Here are the fragments put together by another me."[36] Thus "locked into thinghood," he does not appear as a subject to struggle against, much less to recognize, and the slope on which he stumbles is a slippery one that leads directly to the zone of nonbeing.[37] Hegel's dialectic is inaccessible by virtue of a short-circuit, its circularity of standing ground rendered a brutal farce for those lacking the ground on which to stand. Black subjects are seen— indeed, they are hypervisible—but they are not truly seen; they *exist* but they *are* not (human).

According to Fanon, the "absolute reciprocity" of Hegel's dialectic cannot hold beyond the abstract and ahistorical allegory of two simple self-consciousnesses, especially when the history and concreteness providing its content is that of colonization, chattel slavery, and white supremacy.[38] This is because "the White is not only 'the Other,' but also the master, whether real or imaginary," to which we could add that the master is not only the Other, but also white, the standard-bearer of Being empowered to deny it to those classified otherwise.[39] Without reciprocity, the two sides of the dialectic fall back from the necessary struggle at its heart, a double movement that Fanon—somewhat characteristically—addresses most directly in an extended footnote: "For Hegel there is reciprocity; here the master scorns the consciousness of the slave. What he wants from the slave is not recognition but work."[40] The concrete, white master does not recognize the concrete, Black slave's humanity on even the most basic level, and besides, in the very real history of slavery that escapes the simple dyad, the master can seek out recognition elsewhere.[41]

More perversely still, the slave falls prey to an ontological inferiority complex, either accepting subjection as deserved or futilely attempting to sneak into the realm of Being by becoming "white," rather than busying himself or herself with that liberatory activity of laboring in the world or fighting for liberation.

> Likewise, the slave here can in no way be equated with the slave who loses himself in the object and finds the source of his liberation in his work.
> The black slave wants to be like his master.
> Therefore he is less independent than the Hegelian slave.
> For Hegel, the slave turns away from the master and turns toward the object. Here the slave turns toward the master and abandons the object.[42]

And since Blacks are not merely black, but instead always black *in relation to whiteness*, this ontological distinction derails open conflict between self and other, dispersing it into compensatory horizontal struggles with their peers. As for Sorel, both sides of the dialectical opposition fail to play their part, albeit for very different reasons.

In his critique of Hegel's master-slave dialectic, Fanon thereby draws back the curtain to reveal what lies beneath the apparent universality of the Hegelian system, diagnosing a subontological realm *below* Being that renders ontological solutions "impossible."[43] This "zone of nonbeing, an extraordinarily sterile and arid region, an incline stripped bare of every essential" constitutes "a veritable hell" to which racialized subjects are condemned (as in the damnés of Fanon's last book).[44] This "hellish zone," as philosopher Lewis Gordon calls it, is one fundamentally marked by *absence*, "a zone neither of appearance or disappearance." Not only does this "below-Otherness" render politics—as *publicity*—impossible, but paralleling what we have seen in Sorel, the absence of a universal grounding renders ethics impossible as well: "damnation means that the black (or better, the blackened) lives the irrelevance of innocence . . . the absence of a Self-Other dialectic in racist situations means the eradication of ethical relations. Where ethics is derailed, all is permitted."[45]

Fanon's diagnosis of the zone of nonbeing would have a seismic impact on his own reformulation of Hegel's master-slave dialectic, but also far beyond it, operating as a veritable fulcrum for theoretical decolonization even beyond dialectics. Whereas Fanon's work is often pigeonholed within recognition studies, his emphasis on the zone of nonbeing shows him instead to have been a pioneering contributor to a powerfully different approach that might be better understood as "nonrecognition studies." And since one simply does not dialogue or reason with nonbeings, much less justify one's actions or explain oneself to them, Fanon's critique of recognition on the basis of nonbeing can be extended to reveal a similar and parallel circularity running from the Cartesian cogito to Habermasian discourse ethics.

This zone of nonbeing is a realm inhabited by *subterranean* beings who, lacking access to ground, must first struggle to gain steady footing for the climb ahead. The predialectical struggle necessary to gain this ontological footing would not be an easy one, and certainly not the difficult but clear "mountain path to Canaan" of which W. E. B. Du Bois wrote.[46] For equality to be contemplated, for recognition to even appear on the horizon, racialized subjects must first storm the fortified heaven of *Being itself*, but this would entail a mode of action far different from what Hegel had envisioned, one characterized more by backsliding on as-yet unstable ground than progress, testifying to a dialectics stripped of all certainty.

MAKING ONESELF KNOWN

Lacking the reciprocity necessary for the dialectic to enter smoothly into motion, these disqualified nonbeings have no choice but to initiate a one-sided struggle to gain it. "Since the other was reluctant to recognize me [*me reconnaître*]," Fanon argued, "there remained only one solution: to make myself known [*me faire connaître*]."[47] Fanon's predialectical struggle to enforce the basis for symmetry through combat, and the counterontological violence it entails, could therefore be best summarized in these three words: *making oneself known*. It is only through such initial struggle that disqualified nonbeings can crack the surface of ontological Ground from beneath and emerge into the full light of day.

We return to the train in Lyon for a moment, for the concluding act of Fanon's dramatic encounter with white mother and child, and consequently, with himself. What begins with the objectification of "Look! A Negro!" provokes first a tight smile, then feigned enjoyment that immediately collides with its own impossibility, leaving both "Negro" and child trembling:

> I can feel the familiar rush of blood surge up from the innumerable dispersions of my being. I am about to lose my temper. The fire had died a long time ago, and once again the Negro is trembling.
> "Look how handsome that Negro is . . ."
> "The handsome Negro says, 'Fuck you,' madame!"
> Shame flooded her face. At last I was freed from my rumination. I accomplished two things at once: I identified my enemies and I made a scene. Overjoyed. Now we could have some fun.
> The battlefield having been drawn up, I entered the lists.[48]

Why should identifying an enemy, not to mention making a scene, provoke such a seismic ontological shift? Because to discover an enemy, and to discover it clearly, is also to turn away from the master and discover something essential about oneself—to establish one's own identity in opposition to the other, identity and enmity intertwined at the heart of dialectical possibility. Indeed, Fanon's sheer *joy* at the prospect of the battlefield speaks to the predialectical barriers he has already begun to clear from his path: "I had incisors to test. I could feel that they were sturdy."[49]

As we saw above, the blockage that race constitutes for the Hegelian master-slave dialectic is a *double* one, in which the master cannot turn *toward* the slave, and the slave cannot turn *away* from the master. Overcoming this impasse must similarly trace the contours of the two-way street that is self-consciousness. It must somehow *force* the master to open his eyes to the being of the (Black) other, and to *disalienate* the slave, to rid her of her long-cultivated inferiority complex and make possible independence in work (or as we will see, struggle *as* work). On the subjective side, Fanon's outburst creates a euphoric exhilaration whose practical effects could hardly be exaggerated. From being denied the world, he suddenly sits "astride" it, "my heels digging into its flanks, I rub the neck of the world like the high priest rubbing between the eyes of his sacrificial victim."[50]

The *external* impact of Fanon's violent self-assertion of blackness is inextricably tied to its *internal* impact; the very same gesture that frees the Black subject from her self-alienation, that makes possible a "turning away" from the master does not leave the master untouched. What is stolen is not merely the master's property, the runaway slave, but his unquestioned dominance of the world itself. The master, suspicious and fearful, "must have felt an aftershock he was unable to identify." Worried that his slave might have stolen something of value, he stops and frisks her, searches her pockets and interrogates her. "At last I had been recognized," even if only as an object of anxiety. "I was no longer a nothingness."[51] Just as Sorel's proletarian violence seeks to reset the dialectical mechanism by simultaneously projecting working-class identity and provoking bourgeois ferocity, Fanon's combative self-assertion has the same dual function.

Fanon's presence before white eyes lacks ontological weight, his arguments lack rational weight, and this "weightlessness"—this lack of *gravity* in both its senses—leads him to explode, an explosion that is simultaneously violent and mythical. Fanon's outburst on the train is *mythical* in that it projects identity and enmity, but also in the enthusiasm it entails.

If Fanon had earlier insisted that zealousness [*l'enthousiasme*] is the untrustworthy weapon of the powerless, then this is the moment that he embraces his own ontological powerlessness.[52] And if he had been and remained deeply suspicious of Black identity, this was the moment in which he gave himself over to that as well, projecting the firmness of an absolute identity—not merely "making himself known" as an individual, as an enlightened rational subject suited for formal citizenship, but rather asserting himself "as BLACK."[53]

Conceding to the double irrationality of the world, Fanon assumes the mythical identity imposed upon him enthusiastically, as a mantle for struggle. "I had rationalized the world, and the world had rejected me in the name of color prejudice. Since there was no way we could agree on the basis of reason, I resorted to irrationality. It was up to the white man to be more irrational than I . . . I am made of the irrational; I splash about in the irrational. Irrational up to my neck."[54] Forced into a corner, Fanon had thrown himself desperately into Césaire's "black hole," embracing the absoluteness of identity in the fraught but unavoidable hope that it might lead somewhere else.[55] But the double irrationalism of the world grants Fanon's response, however desperate, a particular relation to reason. Forced into unreason by the very architecture of a world that was irrational down to its cracked foundation, to cling to reason would have been the most irrational of responses.

Faced with unreasonable unreason cunningly disguised as reason itself, Fanon was forced against every generous shred of his being to dive headlong into the momentary absoluteness of Black identity. "The fact remained that it was an unfamiliar weapon," however, and Fanon's flight to the irrational—a flight not chosen but forced—would be marked by a palpable ambiguity that had profound implications for his dialectic, one which would never sacrifice "the present and future in the name of a mystical past."[56] From there on out, his path was chosen for him, passing through Black identity but never acquiring the stony completeness of essentialism. Instead, he walked a fine, if jerkily dialectical, line, keeping his distance from the twin perils of naive universalism and racial essentialism.

With Black identity, the specter of violence inevitably rears its head, but not for the reasons we might initially think. To say that Fanonian self-assertion and making known is inherently violent is not to read into this subjective explosion the concrete violence that was at least partially the subject of *Wretched of the Earth*.[57] The paranoid psyche of the slave owners, transferred almost intact to whites today, is one in which Black freedom and equality bespeak the inevitability of revenge—the fearful specter of a new Haiti. Black identity is violent not because these guilty nightmares are likely to come true, but for the deeper truth they reveal. Fanon's own explosion on the train is a case in point: he does little more than insult a white woman in public, and yet he was fully aware of the fatal results that even a purely verbal outburst might bring, then as now.

Despite the fact that actual, concrete violence lay almost exclusively on the side of whiteness, Black resistance is *always* deemed violent whatever form it takes. For Gordon, "the blackened lives the disaster of appearance where there is no room to appear nonviolently . . . To change things is to appear, but to appear is to be violent since that group's appearance is illegitimate. Violence, in this sense, need not be a physical imposition. It need not be a consequence of guns and other weapons of destruction. It need simply be appearance."[58] For those relegated to nonbeing and condemned to invisibility, to even appear is a violent act—because it *is* violent to the structures of the world and because it will inevitably be treated as such. Black subjects are thereby trapped in a catch-22: condemned to either accept inferiority or be demonized as violent.

Black appearance is "illicit" and Black hyper-visibility, in which racialized subjects stand out as suspicious and objects for surveillance, is itself "a form of invisibility" on the ontological level.[59] When the unarmed Black teenager Mike Brown was murdered in Ferguson, Missouri, for example, the conservative pundit Ben Stein even went so far as to insist that Brown was indeed "armed with his incredibly strong, scary self."[60] As is too often the case, the satirical news outlet *The Onion* offered the best diagnosis of not only Stein's comments, but the broader equivalence between Blackness and violence, when it ran the headline "Our Nation's Unarmed Teens: Are they Armed?" above an image of a young Black man.[61] This apparent redundancy of "Black violence" suffuses all levels of society in the United States, tacitly convicting Mike Brown, Trayvon Martin, and many others as it concretely acquits their murderers who, after all, have merely acted heroically to eliminate an ontological threat. And as similar cases involving Black women reveal, the violence of Blackness transcends and even breaks down gender binaries.[62]

When refraining from violence does not protect, engaging in it does not endanger, and as a result, the objective parameters of white supremacy also destroy any incentive to keep the peace, and indeed demand that it be broken. This is the catch-22 that corners Richard Wright's Bigger Thomas, who "acts" in response, and in so doing "answers the world's expectations . . . in order to break the infernal circle," like Fanon himself, "he explodes."[63] Fanon's reformulated master-slave dialectic is one in which Black subjects struggle impossibly like Sisyphus only to be punished eternally like Prometheus—responding to condemnation with action that will inevitably produce more condemnation, all in the hopes that the transformation set into dialectical motion might outweigh the brutal consequences it inevitably brings. But as a part of this seemingly impossible task, and indeed due to an ethical nihilism that is not chosen but instead foundational to the system, violence itself must be resignified in the struggle. The one bleeds, quite literally, into the next once we realize that the illicitness of black appearance is no accident in a system founded on ontological disqualification of some from full humanity. Black appearance *must* remain illicit because it is violence to the system, and those who oppose that system must sharpen it into a weapon.

This sharpening entails a distinction between violence and force. Whereas for Sorel, force upholds the hierarchical rule of a Jacobin minority, Fanon's understanding of force can be seen as an *ontologization* of Sorel's concept. Ontological force disqualifies the racialized from full access to humanity, erecting thick walls within being itself, or more precisely, between Being and non/sub-being. It is the Manichaean symbolic power that equates whiteness with reason, goodness, progress, and peace, and Blackness with irrationality, evil, backwardness, and violence. This shift to the ontological register, furthermore, moves beyond the question of the political institution of the *state* strictly speaking, to its etymological analogue: the "status" or "standing"—as the position from which one fights—that Hegel had assumed as prerequisite for reciprocity, but which Fanon found lacking.[64]

Against this ontological force—Sorelianizing Fanon while decolonizing Sorel—we could call "violence" anything that attacks or undermines the ontological hierarchy and inequality that this "force" upholds. Fanon's counterontological violence, however, differs in two key respects. First, whereas Sorel voluntarily raises the banner of proletarian violence, Fanon and other racialized subjects are *condemned* (damnés) to violence. The difference between the two is not absolute, but between the voluntarism of John Brown and the condition of Harriet Tubman there nevertheless existed an ineliminable gulf. More important, though, whereas Sorel emphasizes proletarian violence as a mechanism to consolidate collective identities on either side of the class binary, Fanon places more of an accent on the subjective necessity for violence as a transformative tool. This is in part a natural result of his Hegelian register, but it reflects as well the concrete needs of black subjects grappling with an ontological inferiority complex (which that Hegelian framework helps to draw out).

For the racialized subject, self-consciousness *as human* requires counterviolence against ontological force. In a historical situation marked by the denial of reciprocity and condemnation to nonbeing, that reciprocity can only result from the combative self-assertion of identity. It is only through such conflict that Black subjects can transcend the barriers—internal and external—that exclude them from the fullness of Being, at the juncture of the in-itself and the for-itself. The task of this violence is therefore twofold: *internally*, to "disalienate" the Black subject even prior to any physically "violent" act, by turning away from the master; and *externally*, to appear, which will inevitably be perceived as violence to the prevailing system—a perception that is itself necessary for appearance to *become* violence to that system, and for the former master to eventually turn toward the former slave for recognition.

Against the ontological force of white supremacy, Fanon appears to respond in kind: meeting violence with violence. But as with Sorel's proletarian violence, and as will be even more explicit in *Wretched of the Earth*, Fanon's counterontological violence has nothing at all in common with that of its enemies. Rather than establishing hierarchical distinctions that disqualify a part of humanity from access to Being, this is a violence that undoes those very same exclusionary barriers, tearing down the ontological walls separating Being from mere (non)beings, and setting the two once more into dialectical motion. This is a violence, in other words, that operates toward the *decolonization of being*.[65]

AT THE MASTER'S TABLE

But Fanon is writing in the twentieth century, not the eighteenth; how could such an ontological apartheid persist? And if it did, how could such a basic opposition *not* reveal itself as a dialectical division and as the occasion for struggle? Or for that matter, if things were really so bad, how could Fanon have even entertained his universal reveries to begin with? For Fanon, the answer was not to be found outside dialectics, but within the contours of its internal requirements. If his violent outburst on the train had left him momentarily "overjoyed," Fanon would soon discover, with no small amount of revulsion, that he had only cleared the first of many hurdles to come.

If he had discovered—against Hegel—that a decolonized dialectic needs to be jumpstarted to overcome an absence of reciprocity from the outset, he would soon foresee several threats looming on the horizon that threatened to deactivate and short-circuit what had scarcely been set into motion. If the first impasse was the ontological status of the beings in question, the second—still very much plaguing us today—is the false universal posed by formal emancipation and formal equality. The third, which in the next section I distill from his confrontation with Sartre, is the danger of a premature (and Eurocentric) closure of that dialectic. The second reifies the completeness of history in the present (latitudinal totality), while the third dialectically encloses the future into a predetermined progression (longitudinal totality). Each is a form of "recentering" of which a decolonized dialectics must be shorn.

Fanon's master was no longer master in the strict sense, but remained *white* nonetheless. In other words, the emancipation of former slaves in no way corresponded to their ontological promotion to the status of fully human. If anything, Fanon's worry is that the opposite was in fact the case: that emancipation—and formal equality more broadly speaking— *reinforced* ontological hierarchy by masking it beneath a false universalism that became white supremacy's best alibi. From a dialectical perspective, for this alibi to function on both the objective and subjective levels, for it to deactivate struggles and freeze dialectical movement at the level of the merely formal, something essential must have been lacking from the emancipation process itself.

That something was struggle: "the White, *in the capacity of master*, told the black man: 'From now on, you are free.'"[66] Fanon's worry is that emancipation was an overly one-sided affair, a gift bestowed *by masters* (in both the concrete and ontological senses) on the basis of and in a way that consequently reinforced their own capacity for ontological determination. The master *as white, standing above* the master-slave dyad (not within it), decided who would henceforth occupy what position:

> The black man is a slave who was allowed to assume the master's attitude.
> The White man is a master who allowed slaves to eat at his table.
> One day, a good white master, who exercised a lot of influence, said to his friends: "Let's be kind to the niggers . . ." So the white masters grudgingly decided to raise the animal-machine-men [formally] to the supreme rank of men . . .
> The upheaval reached the Black man from the outside. The Black man [le Noir] was acted upon. Values that were not engendered by his actions, values not resulting from the systolic gush of his blood, whirled around him in a colorful dance. The upheaval did not change the negro

[le nègre]. He went from one way of life to another, but not from one life to another.[67]

Absent struggle, the *formal* passage from slavery to freedom did not entail a *substantive* shift in mutual self-consciousness, in either how the former slaves perceived themselves or were perceived by others.

If Hegel's assumption of a universal basis for reciprocity constituted an initial barrier to dialectical movement that needed to be overcome at the outset, Fanon here diagnoses a second barrier similarly masquerading as a universal: a liberal universalism which privileges formal equality and rights, thereby "recolonizing" struggle by relegating it to the past. While Hegel's own view of emancipation remains up for debate—Is it a gradual process? A revolutionary one?—Fanon draws upon the centrality Hegel ascribes to struggle for subjective transformation as leverage to insist that freedom cannot be given, but must instead be fought for.

> "Say thank you to the nice man," the mother tells her little boy . . . but we know that often the little boy dreams of shouting some other, more resounding expression . . .
>
> When the black man happens to look fiercely upon the White man, the White man says to him: "My brother, there is no difference between us." And yet the black man *knows* there is a difference. He *wants* it. He would like the White man to suddenly say to him: "Dirty nigger." Then he would have that unique occasion—to "show them" . . .
>
> The former slave needs a challenge to his humanity, he wants a conflict, a riot. But it is too late . . .
>
> Never certain whether the White man considers him as consciousness in-itself for-itself, he is constantly preoccupied with detecting resistance, opposition, contestation.[68]

The formal is more than merely insufficient; it is a veritable barrier to the substantive, a dangerously false universal that prevents the "life and death struggle" that is prerequisite to any universal future. Former slaves, for Fanon, have been robbed of the chance to fight for and win their equality, lest things get out of hand like they did in Haiti. The false universalism of liberal rights does more than simply halt progress and stunt subjectivities, but—as our own "postracial" present confirms— becomes a real weapon not for combatting but actively reinforcing white supremacy. Formal equality cannot recognize ontological hierarchy and the presence of a subontological zone of nonbeing, and in neglecting ontological difference it conceals and upholds the apartheid of the existing world.

Against the closure of such false universals, Fanon clears the way toward an infinite repetition of the master-slave dialectic as a collective project for substantive disalienation and liberation. In fact, Fanon's anxiety toward formal emancipation—which will resurface in his wariness toward the formal liberation of the colonies—forces him to press forward from the center of the dialectic, constantly foregrounding struggle in the present. But even this liberal attempt to immobilize those struggles was not the final barrier Fanon would confront. One of the most serious challenges to Fanon's decolonization of dialectics would come not only from within the tradition, but from a comrade who—eyes similarly trained toward the future— nevertheless performs a similarly totalizing gesture under the sign of the revolution. The comrade was Sartre, who now enters the picture not as an ally but as an unwitting traitor threatening to enclose this now-jumpstarted dialectic within a limited and teleological historical progression.

SARTRE'S DIALECTICAL BETRAYAL

Fanon had already felt the sting of a white supremacist dialectics of history, in which Blackness is relegated to being merely a prior stage of human progress. He responded with his own radical reformulation of Hegel that foregrounds the centrality of rupture and combat at the heart of a decolonized dialectic rooted in the zone of nonbeing. Sartre's similarly dialectical betrayal would prove even more painful given the source, but would force Fanon to insist all the more resolutely on the radical open-endedness of his own dialectics.

When Sartre penned "Black Orpheus" in 1948, this giant among French intellectuals stepped decisively into the fray in support of the Negritude Movement and the radical assertion of Black identity it espoused. Negritude was, for Sartre, a laudably "anti-racist racism" that aimed not at domination, but rather "solidarity with the oppressed of all colors." But it is the tightness with which Sartre binds the first to the second, the negation of the negation to universal solidarity, that would devastate Fanon. The "subjective, existential, ethnic notion" of black identity must, Sartre argues, "pass" in Hegelian terms, giving way to the "objective, positive, exact notion of the *proletariat*."[69] For Sartre, race and class are utterly incommensurable:

> the notion of race does not intersect with the notion of class: the one is concrete and particular, the other is universal and abstract . . . the first is the product of a psycho-biological syncretism and the other is a

methodological construction emerging from experience. In fact, Negritude appears as the weak term of a dialectical progression ... But the negative moment is not sufficient in itself and the Blacks who employ it well know it; they know that it serves to pave the way for the synthesis or the realization of the human society without race. Thus Negritude is dedicated to its own destruction, it is transition and not outcome, a means and not the ultimate end.[70]

That Sartre cites Aimé Césaire in his own defense already reveals some confusion: a devout communist and party member at the time, Césaire nevertheless already held a far more subtle view of the relationship between race and class that would only deepen with time. Just as Fanon reformulated Hegel to accommodate black experience, Césaire would come to insist on the need to "particularize Communism" to "complete Marx" in a way that would meet the needs of Black revolutionaries.[71]

Fanon's response to this dialectical betrayal is fittingly visceral. Having only just stolen the world from the white master, he now felt robbed in turn. Sartre represented yet another iteration of an old, racist game: the denial of objectivity to Black experience, which he ironically confuses with "race" in an effort to distinguish the transhistorical importance of class. While the proletariat achieves such objectivity—and thereby universal status—from the lived experience on which it is "constructed," Fanon's "lived experience of the black" is granted no such status, relegated instead to mere "psychobiological" superstructure.

This ally had dealt Fanon and other black poets a "fatal [literally: unforgivable] blow":

We had appealed to a friend of the colored peoples, and this friend had found nothing better to do than demonstrate the relativity of their action. For once this friend, this born Hegelian, had forgotten that consciousness needs to lose itself in the night of the absolute, the only condition for attaining self-consciousness. Against rationalism he recalled the negative side, but he forgot that this negativity draws its value from an almost substantive absoluteness. Consciousness committed to experience knows nothing, has to know nothing, of the essences and determinations of its being. *Black Orpheus* marks a date in the intellectualization of black existence.[72]

That Fanon feels slighted as a poet is no accident, nor is the fact that the Negritude Movement largely comprised poets. Just as Sorel viewed

Socrates as intellectualizing—and thereby destroying—the dynamic, mythopoetic source of ancient heroism, so too did Fanon view Sartre as robbing Black struggles of their source of historical motion. Rather than envisioning two dialectics of identity moving according to shared (but not identical) parameters, intersecting and acting upon one another, Sartre had *inscribed* Blackness within a broader, world-historical dialectic, *subsuming* it to the purportedly superior term of class: the teleological completion of *the* dialectical progression, *the* end of history.

If Sorel had rejected the word of Marx to better reclaim his spirit, Fanon similarly responds both within Hegel and beyond him, reformulating dialectics to better grasp its combative content. Sartre, this "born Hegelian," had forgotten that *no* dialectic can operate in a preordained manner without short-circuiting the very process itself.

> And *voila*! I did not create a meaning for myself; the meaning was already there, waiting. It is not as the wretched nigger, it is not with my nigger's teeth, it is not as the hungry nigger that I fashion a torch to set the world alight; the torch was already there, waiting for this historic chance. In terms of consciousness, black consciousness claims to be an absolute density, full of itself, a stage prior to any rupture, to any abolition of the self by desire. In his essay Jean-Paul Sartre has destroyed black enthusiasm [*l'enthousiasme noir*]. Against historical becoming, there necessarily stands the unforeseeable. I needed to lose myself absolutely in negritude . . . *I needed* not to know.[73]

As Sorel had wondered of heroism, Fanon here wonders *how* identity could possibly operate on the basis of anything *but* absoluteness, and *why* someone would embrace an identity already deemed transitory from the outset. Without an appeal to the "absolute density" and mythical fullness of Black identity at the center of the dialectic, which entails unforeseeability rather than predetermined becoming, the combative identities at the heart of a radical and decolonized dialectics fail to harden. "The dialectic that introduces necessity [i.e., determinism] at the fulcrum of my freedom drives me out of myself. It shatters my unreflective position."[74] By virtue of his claim to know the content of this becoming, Sartre is instead the unwittingly condescending parent lecturing the world's children—"You'll change, my boy; I was like that too when I was young"—if not the master inviting slaves to dine at his table.

Beyond Hegel, however, Sartre's insistence that race is subjective and particular whereas only class is objective and universal not only short-circuits the motion of a decolonized dialectic, but even threatens to obliterate its categories entirely. To insist on the centrality of class as *the* universal political identity motivating human progress is to imprison the racialized and colonized of the world within a linear developmentalism that requires them to catch up with Europe. As Fanon, Mariátegui, and others would show, even if this were a desirable path, it is structurally impossible. Fanon does not claim that class—and much less, economics—is irrelevant to the colonized, but Sartre's formulation does the opposite: elevating a particular component of European historical development to the status of world-historic universal.[75] That this is a question of class and not European culture is all that distinguishes Sartre's dialectic from the dialectical subsumption of the racist.

Just as Sartre had undermined the *internal* motion of the dialectic, he also neglected the need for this process to remain open ended, with little more than gestures toward a future, undetermined universal. Fanon's critique of Sartre drives home in the clearest possible way the radical unpredictability of Fanon's dialectics, giving content to his insistence from the outset that his work was "grounded in temporality" and that—somewhat paradoxically—to be an expression of one's time is to build a future that is never complete and always "something to be overtaken."[76] But there is no contradiction—only dynamic tension—between the momentary weight of Black identity and the eventual transcendence of that identity. Instead, this is a transcendence that born only of the temporality of dialectical struggle.

Sartre's dialectical betrayal had snatched away the world, and with it this temporality of struggle: "At the very moment when I attempted to seize my being, Sartre, who remains the Other, by naming me shattered my last illusion . . . I sensed my shoulders slipping from the structure of the world, my feet no longer felt the caress of the ground. Without a black past, without a black future, it was impossible for me to live my blackness. Not yet white, no longer black, I was damned [damné]."[77] Somewhat astonishingly, we can see that it is the devastation of Sartre's undialectical betrayal that provides Fanon with the concept for which he would become most famous: that of the damné, the condemned, or the "wretched" of his last book, for which a repentant Sartre would himself pen the preface.[78]

Sartre had shown, in *The Respectful Prostitute*, how this was a perversely inverted condemnation—one is not condemned for being guilty, one is always-already guilty for numbering among the condemned. Fanon drives home the error of Sartre's dialectical subsumption of Blackness by first reciting his own words back to him, before then translating this "racial allocation of guilt" into ontological terms: "A feeling of inferiority? No, a feeling of nonexistence . . . straddling the crossroads between Nothingness [subontological damnation] and Infinity [black essentialism], I begin to weep."[79] These are not tears of defeat so much as tears of pain from so many betrayals, and tears that anticipate a much longer struggle than Fanon had initially hoped to confront.

But having recognized his time-bound location between nonbeing and the perfection-of-being was the first step toward escape, and he had already identified dialectical, counterontological violence as the "mechanism" that would carry him forward: "I take this negritude and with tears in my eyes I piece the mechanism together again. That which had been shattered is by my hands—these intuitive vines—rebuilt, reconstructed. My shout rings out more violently: I am a nigger, I am a nigger, I am a nigger."[80] But as he had previously described it, "the fragments" of this mechanism are "put together by another me," one already well along the path of the absolute—a path leading in the direction of a fuller self-consciousness.[81] This was a radically decolonial and dialectical path in which the rebuilt "mechanism" of race, the central term, was granted the necessary weight to operate.

But rather than closing in on itself, Fanon's dialectic opens outward onto an unpredictable future in which the horizon of universal reconciliation is infinitely deferred.

> I am not a prisoner of History . . .
> the real *leap* consists of introducing invention into life.
> In the world I am heading for, I am endlessly creating myself.
> I show solidarity with humanity provided I can go one step further.[82]

"A Society to Be Replaced"

Fanon's critique of the ontological circularity of the Hegelian master-slave dialectic—its presumed reciprocity, symmetry, and reversibility—sets the stage not for his rejection of dialectics but instead for the total decolonization and reconstruction of Hegel's approach from the ground up. Or more precisely, from beneath the Ground: diagnosing the existence of a subontological realm to which the racialized are condemned points toward the need for predialectical struggle, for a counterontological violence that creates the basis for truly dialectical opposition. Against Hegel's smooth view of inevitable progress toward universal self-consciousness, Fanon instead sees the need to project blackness subjectively and to do so "violently" in a way that shakes both (Black) slave and (white) master from their respective undialectical slumbers. Fanon does not stop after having set the dialectic into motion anew, however, but instead presses forward, diagnosing the danger that this movement will grind to a halt in the present through the false universalism of formal emancipation, or find its future enclosed in a teleological view that subsumes race to class.

The "untidy dialectic" that emerges from this process is as radically subjective as it is decolonized, building on Sorel's reformulated dialectic of class struggle while also leaping decisively beyond it.[83] Like Sorel, Fanon privileges the moment of rupture, diremption, and division that unleashes dialectical motion, and like Sorel he shuns reconciliation to place weight on the present moment. Like the irrational rationalism of Sorel's myth, which underscores the nonrational aspects of human action, Fanon similarly proposes an unreasonable resort to Black identity against the double irrationality of the white supremacist world. Where Sorel inverts the Marxian formula to pose the primacy of class-for-itself as a projected identity that brings the class-in-itself into being, Fanon turns to Hegel as a source for a dialectic in which the for-itself is already present as a "subjective certainty (*Gewissheit*)" to be transformed through combat into "objective truth (*Wahrheit*)" as one step on the path toward the universal self-consciousness of the in-itself-for-itself.[84] But this unified humanity, away from which Fanon was driven by force, remains an as-yet undefined horizon, orienting while not determining a process of combative rupture that revolutionizes even the structures of the world itself.

Those who would divide Fanon's oeuvre—distinguishing *Black Skin, White Masks* from *Wretched of the Earth*—often do so by neglecting his decolonized dialectical vision. In the next chapter, however, I argue that it is precisely this dialectical framework that Fanon would later transpose in an attempt to understand the Algerian revolution and decolonization more broadly. Both the Algerian context and the historical moment were different, however, and these differences would fill Fanon's dialectics with new content. The Negritude Movement had passed, in his view, from dialectical vanguard to a conservative force in African political life. In its place, Fanon would turn to national consciousness, but despite the unifying or totalizing significance many associate with the concept of "the nation," the basic contours of Fanon's decolonized dialectic—its attentiveness to nonbeing, the violent projection of identity to set frozen history into motion, and a radical open-endedness that foregrounds rupture at the expense of closure—would remain intact.

At least according to its author, *Black Skin, White Masks* was largely concerned with the alienation of middle-class racialized subjects, often those living in the metropole. But as he drew toward a conclusion, Fanon turned his eyes toward Africa and the colonized, recognizing that

> the motivations for disalienating a physician from Guadeloupe are essentially different from those for the African construction worker in the port at Abidjan. For the former, alienation is almost intellectual in nature. It develops because he takes European culture as a means of detaching himself from his own race. For the latter, it develops because he is victim of a system based on the exploitation of one race by another . . . For the black working in the sugarcane plantations in Le Robert, there is only one solution: the struggle . . . because quite simply he cannot conceive his life otherwise than as a kind of combat against exploitation, poverty, and hunger.[85]

Both are condemned, although the parameters of that condemnation may differ. The colonized subject to whom Fanon would now turn was condemned to an exploitative constellation fusing race to class as elements of a global hierarchy, and condemned as well to an unavoidable struggle that would craft of both elements a future nation. Despite Fanon's transposition of race, class, and nation—a shift in his object of dialectical combat—the distance between the two texts is not so great. It is not just any Ivorian who grasps their condition of exploitation, just as not every Caribbean subject is a physician, and whereas the early Fanon diagnosed the Eurocentric escapism of Martinican elites, the later Fanon would identify similar delusions among European-educated African elites.

This criticism was also, moreover, a self-criticism, a tacit concession that his first book was an outgrowth of *his own* reality: between the alienated "physician from Guadeloupe" and the alienated psychiatrist from Martinique, the distance was not so great either. But it would not be long before Fanon came into more direct contact with the broader parameters of colonial reality. In late 1953—less than two full years after publishing *Black Skin*—Fanon found himself running the Psychiatric Hospital of Blida-Joinville in colonial Algeria. But his own philosophy, and in particular the potent theory of *sociogeny* he had formulated in *Black Skin*, according to which social structures are themselves the root cause of many neurotic afflictions, soon drove him to resign.

Fanon's 1956 letter of resignation—penned in the same year that Césaire resigned from the Communist Party—stands as a testament to the insufficiency of not only psychiatry, but indeed of any individualized intellectual endeavor to build a future universal in the absence of constant dialectical struggle: "If psychiatry . . . aims to allow man to no longer feel like a stranger to his environment . . . the Arab, permanently an alien in their own country, lives in a state of absolute depersonalization . . . The social structure existing in Algeria contradicted any attempt to put the individual back in their place . . . The function of a social structure is to set up institutions to serve man's needs. A society that corners its members into desperate solutions is a non-viable society, a society to be replaced."[86] This moment above all others marked Fanon's transition from philosopher to revolutionary, but paradoxically this break occurred as a sort of slingshot effect of his philosophy itself: a philosophy which privileges the generative effects of social structures can only remain in the contemplative mode for so long before it must transcend itself.

And in this transition from philosopher to revolutionary, moreover, Fanon hurdled the barrier that he had so self-critically posed at the conclusion of *Black Skin*. From confronting intellectual alienation, he threw himself into combat as an active participant in the Algerian Revolution. Fanon's practical leap to the armed struggle would not be without its implications for that theory of leaps that is dialectics. From this point on, rather than simply theorizing rupture against ontological apartheid, and certainly beyond attempting to "put the individual back in their place" in a fundamentally broken world, Fanon instead became an active participant in deepening the dynamic oppositions that might one day reconstitute human unity. But in shifting from race to decolonial nation, Fanon also dramatically displaced the unit of analysis grounding these divisions, projecting dialectical combat to the global level.

CHAPTER 3

THE DECOLONIAL NATION IN MOTION

"Under This Banner We Are Marching"

When Fanon appealed to the damnés—the condemned or wretched—in the title of his best-known text, he drove home what was most distinctive about his decolonized dialectics. The term, which had surfaced occasionally in *Black Skin, White Masks*, referred less to the opening line of "L'Internationale" than to its decolonial adaptation at the hands of the Haitian poet Jacques Roumain. Roumain's "New Black Sermon" had also appeared in Léopold Sédar Senghor's volume, for which Sartre's "Black Orpheus" stood as preface. Like Césaire, Roumain was not coincidentally both a founder of his local Communist Party and of the Negritude Movement, and like Césaire and many others, his dual existence was not without its painful complications. The tension between official Communism and Negritude—so blithely erased by Sartre's preface—is palpable in even the most basic comparison of "New Black Sermon" to the "Internationale," as are the fundamentally different dialectical visions they exemplify.

The "Internationale" famously begins with the damned rising to their feet—*Debout!*—driven by thundering reason to transform the very foundations [*changer de base*] of the world in a "final struggle" to reunite a humanity formerly divided by class. Here, the Second International is a peculiarly synecdochical stand-in for the universal in a way that prefigures Sartre's dialectical subsumption of race to class: "The Internationale *will be* the human race." The structure, temporality, and movement of Roumain's version shares little with such a triumphal dialectic. It begins with the condemnation to race as a quasi-religious fall from grace, before passing through the lynching of John—a union organizer—notably echoing Du Bois's own version of the same.[1] More striking still is the infinite deferral of any final struggle and the human reconciliation it promises: Roumain's damnés revolt not at the beginning but at the end and, "like the cry of the storm bird over the lapping waters of the stinking swamps," promise nothing but a continuous struggle couched stubbornly in the present progressive tense:

> We will spread our red flags
> Stained with the blood of our just
> Under this banner we will march
> Under this banner we are marching.[2]

The truly condemned cannot simply "arise" as the "Internationale" exhorts them to do, imprisoned as they are to a subontological hell that itself lies *beneath* the foundation (*base*) to be changed. And even once they do, the classically Hegelian determinism of reason in history is hardly convincing as a motor force for progress; for this, there is only the long and interminable struggle of the "we" who "are marching."

This was hardly the first time a Haitian had seized upon the liberatory symbols of Europe to put them to new, decolonial use: think of the dumbfounded French soldiers hearing Toussaint's troops—their own "barbarous enemies"—singing the *Marseillaise* and wondering if they might not be the ones with justice on their side; or think more generally of the concrete content with which the rebels of Saint Domingue had filled abstract values like liberty, equality, and fraternity.[3] Whereas Slavoj Žižek reduces this moment to an "underlying *sameness*," Césaire himself is much closer to the point: "To prevent the development of all national consciousness in the colonized, the colonizer pushes the colonized to desire an abstract equality. But equality refuses to remain abstract. And what an affair it is when the colonized takes back the word on his own account to demand that it not remain a mere word!"[4]

Given such precedents for the reappropriation and symbolic decolonization of the European tradition of which the idea of the "wretched" was a part, it is perhaps unsurprising that Fanon's methods and his dialectic share so much with what can be gleaned of Roumain's. That Fanon's relation to the universal had changed between 1952 and 1961 is evident from the very structure of *Wretched of the Earth*, which without an introduction lacks the elegiac bookends of *Black Skin, White Masks*. Certainly, the conclusion appeals to a universal, but it is ever more infinitely deferred, and explicit paeans to human reconciliation are fewer and further between. This displaced universal, after all, was far distant from the world Fanon himself confronted in 1961, when he lay dying of leukemia, dictating much of *Wretched of the Earth* as a tortured but stubbornly optimistic last will and testament.

If we rewind from the conclusion to the first pages, we find Fanon taking his prior self directly to task for the naive universalism and rationalism of which he had been disabused within the pages of *Black Skin*: "Calling into question the colonial world is not a rational confrontation of viewpoints. *It is not a discourse on the universal*, but the frenzied [*échevelée*] affirmation of an originality asserted as absolute."[5] You can't argue your way out of colonialism, Fanon now told himself and the world, and nor can celestial dreams of universal love dissolve the heavy concrete walls and barbed walls separating colonized from colonizer. Now a professional militant instead of a practicing psychiatrist, Fanon himself stood amid a dialectic in which—as he put it in his 1956 letter of resignation—individual disalienation meant little in a profoundly sick world where "everyday reality is a tissue of lies, of cowardice, of contempt for man."[6]

Much did remain the same however: Fanon still longed for an end to this contempt while convinced that the groundwork must first be laid; he still confronted a static and immobile present; and he still sought to provoke an oppositional movement that can only be described as dialectical. But he no longer viewed negritude, or Black identity per se, as the central vehicle for setting the world into motion. Instead, he pivoted, largely under the weight of his moment, to the rapidly emerging decolonial nation as the relevant identity that would occupy the center of his newly formulated decolonial dialectic—notably without abandoning the idea that those comprising it remained condemned to the ontological disqualification of the zone of nonbeing. In the process, he crafted a theory of decolonial national consciousness as radically distinct from that of Europe's Westphalian nation-state, something more constantly in motion and grounded not so much on force monopolized from above as on violence dispersed from below.

This bifurcation of force and violence—and with it, the specter of Sorel—had also become more evident, as with Fanon's playful suggestion that his famous first chapter of *Wretched of the Earth* constituted his own "réflexions sur la violence."[7] But Fanon's more literal turn to violence also coincided with his transcendence of the Sorelian framework through a displacement of the relevant totality to the global level. He arrives at the global not through an uncritical and undialectical leap, however, but by tracing and conforming to the internal dynamics of colonialism and anti-colonial resistance. The Manichaean division of the colonial world begged the question of the nation, but stitching that nation together required an intricate dialectic-within-a-dialectic that would only momentarily unify a dynamic decolonial nation—the stepping-stone toward an eventual liberation that could only be global.

A World Cut in Two

When Fanon turned to describing and theorizing colonial reality in Algeria, however—the lived experience of the colonized damnés—the register he adopted was far from dialectical. Instead of dynamic motion, the scene was of a hopelessly frozen nonmotion that he famously deemed Manichaean (a concept, which like the damnés, had made a brief appearance in his earlier work).[8] This was a "world of statues," a "petrified zone, not a ripple on the surface, the palm trees sway against the clouds, the waves of the sea lap against the shore, the raw materials come and go," in which the colonized themselves—nonbeings in an ontologically divided system—constituted an "almost mineral background."[9] The very structure of colonialism aspires to an internally "motionless" social death, a reification (*substantification*) that would seem to militate against dialectical motion entirely.[10] After all, Manichaeism denotes a paradigmatically absolute opposition in which pure good and pure evil maintain a tense but permanent standoff. To describe the colonial relation as Manichaean might therefore be seen as granting the permanence toward which one side, the colonizer, works. But despite Fanon's recent influence on what has come to be known as "Afro-Pessimism," he was never a very good pessimist, instead stubbornly prying agency from the clutches of structure. His turn to the absoluteness of Manichaeism momentarily conceals what would emerge as a powerfully optimistic—too optimistic, in fact—dialectics, in which decolonization is itself coterminous with a setting-into-motion.

The geography of the colonial world is fundamentally segregated and "cut in two," its border marked by police stations and barracks, embodied by police officer and soldier, and guaranteed by "rifle butts and napalm."[11] Even the phenomenology of these two worlds is dramatically opposed: one of well-lit streets, strong walls, paved roads, sturdy shoes, and sated residents; the other tightly packed, starving, "a sector that crouches and cowers, a sector on its knees, a sector that is prostrate."[12] Discrete quantities are transformed almost alchemically into their opposite when viewed through this Manichaean veil—garbage in the one appears as tempting food to the other. Here, as with Fanon's early critique of Hegel's master-slave dialectic, there is no symmetrical interaction, and colonizer and colonized "confront each other, but not in the service of a higher unity . . . they respond to the principle of mutual exclusion: there is no conciliation possible, one of them is superfluous."[13]

Rather than lament this absence of reciprocity, Fanon almost seems to go out of his way to embrace it, describing this ontologically divided world in the most extreme terms he can muster. The colonial world, he tells us, is populated by two "different species," those from here and those "from elsewhere . . . the others."[14] Two species standing opposed with nothing in common, much less a future: if Fanon is being consciously provocative by taking on the absolute Manichaeism of the colonizer, this is not without reason, in both senses of the word. Fanon had previously realized, confronted with the fundamental irrationality of white supremacy, that he had "no choice" but to adopt the racial identity imposed upon him, a rational resort to the unreason at the heart of the world. He was now confronted with a similar realization, that "colonialism is not a machine capable of thinking, a body endowed with reason," not something that the colonized could simply argue their way out of.[15]

Instead, it was by only embracing and inverting this Manichaeism that the decolonial dialectic might enter into motion. This was in no small part because to embrace Manichaeism was to cleave through the ethical bonds superimposed in bad faith on the colonial world; to embrace the sort of "ethical diremption" Sorel had established and the impossibility of ethics under white supremacy that Fanon had previously emphasized, as a way of *freeing* the colonized from ethics. The colonial divide is not devoid of ethics, but is in fact suffused and laden with the ethical imposition of the colonizer, who "fabricates" the colonized, not as insufficiently ethical or even nonethical, but as utterly *anti*-ethical, "impervious to ethics . . . not only the absence of values but also the negation of values . . . absolute evil."[16] But, in driving the ethical division so deep, the colonizer plays a dangerous game, and the ethical disqualification of the colonized becomes a loaded weapon.

It is difficult to bind the embodiment of evil to any system of ethics, and by constructing the natives as so thoroughly anti-ethical, the settler unwittingly slashes through any mutual obligations, freeing the natives' hands in the process. The native "has always known that his dealings with the colonist would take place in a field of combat," in the realm of the martial rather than the ethical, "So the colonized subject wastes no time lamenting and almost never searches for justice in the colonial context."[17] Justice as a shared system of arbitration gives way to a one-sided reformulation of not only the good, but the true as well: "For the people, only fellow nationals are ever owed the truth. No absolute truth, no discourse on the transparency of the soul can erode this position. In answer to the lie of the colonial situation, the colonized subject responds with a lie . . . Truth is what hastens the dislocation of the colonial regime, what fosters the emergence of the nation. Truth is what protects the "natives" and undoes the foreigners . . . And good is quite simply what hurts *them* most."[18] Rather than refuse the Manichaean division undergirding the colonial system, the colonized *takes hold of* that rupture, and indeed radicalizes it.

In so doing, the colonized drives the wedge of difference as deeply as possible, to the brink separating Hegel's internal difference from external diversity. While there exists (between colonizer and colonized) an *internal* relationship of exploitation in which "the raw materials come and go," there also exists (between settler and native) an *external* relationship between two "different species," hailing from and inhabiting two different worlds that find themselves crashing against one another. This coexistence of internal and external difference, however, does not mean a retreat into the meaningless difference of nonrelation. Instead, its meaning is that of the one-sided imposition of colonial domination, and what's more, the promise of an equally one-sided response that has little to do with reciprocity.

"To explode the colonial world," Fanon writes, "does not mean that once the borders have been eliminated there will be a right of way between the two sectors. To destroy the colonial world means no more and no less than abolishing one of the zones, burying it deep within the earth or banishing it from the territory."[19] Explosion, expulsion, abolition, interment, and the "total, complete, and absolute substitution" of one species by another—these are not the terms that first come to mind when contemplating a dialectics oriented toward reconciliation.[20] But the one-sided response of the colonized is the only source capable of turning frozen oppositions dynamic, and the leap to the global this poses would prove the only possible way to square this basic reality of decolonization with a reconciled human future.

This paradoxical assumption and inversion of the Manichaean opposition clears the way for a shift from Manichaeism to dialectics, from frozen opposition to dynamic combat, from stasis to motion. Temptations to unity—assimilation, mimicry, cooperation—fall away, and one-sided resistance seems to be written into the structures of the colonial system.

Whereas Fanon previously confronted the false universalism of formal equality, resorting to the irrational reason of Black identity to *create* division and rupture in the world as the precondition to dialectical motion, here he discovers that the colonized enters the dialectic at an advanced position. Division *already* exists and *is undeniable*; it is embedded in the architectural markers of everyday life in the colony and the Manichaean construction of the colonized. This division is upheld more by force than by ideology, "life and death struggle" simply waiting in the wings to be unleashed: one need only invert Manichaeism, harness its energy, and tether it to the drive toward national liberation.

The Manichaean division of the colonial world therefore counterintuitively undergirds both Fanon's optimism—the apparently self-starting and self-propelling nature of his dialectics—and the apparent simplicity of its two stages. The first stage (dialectical reversal through the simplification of identities) lays the groundwork for the transformation and eventual dissolution of those identities (in a second stage that begins with formal liberation) toward a new and truly universal, if unforeseeable, revolutionary humanism. But the deceptive simplicity of Fanon's two-stage process testifies to the dynamic at play, in which—as his searing critique of Sartre put it—"consciousness needs to lose itself in the night of the absolute." Any attempt to foreclose on the absoluteness of national identity could run the risk of disarming the source of motion itself.[21] It is only through the absoluteness of the Manichaean inversion of the first (national) stage that the decolonial dialectic can gain the momentum necessary to catapult *beyond* that stage (toward social revolution).

But the tension is this: the simplicity of that Manichaean starting point—however convincing Fanon is about its necessity—is difficult for even him to sustain, dissecting itself instead in the complexity of the revolutionary subject that would bear it. If the colonizer carries out a Manichaean simplification of the colonized, the would-be nation remains powerfully divided nonetheless. The distinction between a Manichaean nationalist stage and a more nuanced social revolutionary stage thus disintegrates almost immediately, disrupting the clean division of the world, first from within (in a Manichaeism-within-a-Manichaeism dividing the embryonic nation) and later from without (in a crumbling of this Manichaeism *prior* to formal liberation, and permanent struggle thereafter).

The imperfection of this most perfect of oppositions should not surprise us: while aspiring to a permanent frozenness, *all* Manichaeism, according to Jameson, carries within it a "secret conceptual and even dialectical weakness," and colonial Manichaeism more than any other. Even this most "mythic" of dualisms is unsustainable, for Jameson, because it contains a built-in contradiction: claiming pure goodness on one side while the very existence of an opposition steals away part of its purity.[22] As a result, rather than simply existing, it must attack evil, but cannot destroy this enemy without destroying what defines it as good to begin with. In the colonial context, this powerful logical paradox is exacerbated by a potent clash between the psychic and socioeconomic parameters of the colonial project: colonialism aspires to the total elimination of the natives, but to kill them all *"would amount to the immediate destruction of colonization."*[23]

Instead, the embodiment of evil fights back, and, like a planet out of orbit, the opposition tips and swings, asymmetrical and off kilter, gaining destabilizing momentum from the weighted motion of each of its parts. But this disintegration is a saving grace of sorts, preventing the Manichaean *division* of the colonial world and the *unity* of the decolonial nation from achieving a perfection that would halt motion. It is in this shifting space between perfect rupture and perfect unity that Fanon's radical dialectic emerges, confounding in the process the charges of totalization frequently leveled against him and against decolonial nationalism more generally.

Decolonization's Only Work

Fanon insists that studying the "lines of force" upholding the Manichaean architecture of the colonial world is not simply an exercise in knowing one's enemy, but of knowing oneself and one's future as well. This divided colonial geography, he suggests in an overlooked passage, contains "the backbone according to which decolonized society will be reorganized."[24] For Fanon, in other words, there is something about this Manichaean world that will be extended and projected into the foreseeable future. Colonialism bears within itself not merely contradictions and the seeds of its own destruction, not merely its own gravediggers, but also the parameters of the dialectical path that this destruction and its eventual replacement will take.

By insisting that decolonization emerges from an inversion of colonial Manichaeism, Fanon seems to be doing his best to confound any attempt to distinguish colonial force from the violence of the colonized. In fact, he even seems to say the exact opposite: "the violence which governed the ordering of the colonial world . . . *this same violence* will be vindicated and appropriated" by the colonized.[25] Not only is this the "same violence," but moreover "the violence of the colonial regime and the counterviolence of the colonized balance each other and respond to each other in an *extraordinary reciprocal homogeneity.*"[26] How to square this straightforward insistence on a Manichaean homology of opposing violences with Sorel's categorical distinction between repressive force and liberatory violence, and Fanon's earlier adoption of the same distinction in ontological form?[27] More important, how to avoid the inevitable charge that Fanon's homologous formulation yields either an eternally recurring "cycle" of violence or a self-contained and essentialist nationalism?

The answer, for Fanon, lies both in the constituent parts of the future nation and the role of violent struggle. The concrete point of departure for both is the same: the rural peasantry, which constitutes the only truly revolutionary sector, in no small part because they alone know that "only violence pays."[28] The "old granite foundation" of the anticolonial struggle, the peasants represent the original kernel of the nation because they are both relatively external to the colonizer and relatively impermeable to colonial ideology.[29] If colonialism seeks to inculcate a sense of inferiority in the colonized, it does so unevenly: as Fanon had recognized in the final pages of *Black Skin, White Masks*, there was a vast gulf separating the more educated classes and the poorest, for whom the only solution was to struggle. Those sectors less susceptible to internalizing this sense of inferiority "roar with laughter every time they hear themselves called an animal by the other."[30] Where ideology fails pure force reigns, but at some point both elements begin to lose traction among those populations that will set the rebellion into motion.

Violence becomes "atmospheric," and every effort to deploy brute force only heightens tensions, reminding the colonized who their real enemy is: "This smell of gunpowder which now fills the atmosphere does not intimidate the people. These bayonets and heavy gunfire strengthen their aggressiveness. A dramatic atmosphere sets in where everyone wants to prove he is ready for anything. It is under these circumstances that the gun goes off by itself."[31] The countryside rebels spontaneously, but the existing political leadership of nationalist parties proves incapable of harnessing this violence. Instead—much like Sorel's socialist parliamentarians—they use violent rhetoric merely as a cynical ploy to increase their own political capital as indispensable mediators. Their posture is rooted in self-interest, but also rests upon what Fanon views as a defeatist "preoccupation with objectivity" when it comes to violence: when they think of violence, colonized elites can only picture "the colonizer's tanks and fighter planes," making them "losers from the start."

Fanon locates his argument within longstanding Marxist debates about the autonomy of force, by insisting that the nationalist leadership tends to maintain the "puerile position" that Engels had adopted against "that mountain of puerility," Eugen Karl Dühring.[32] Whereas Dühring foregrounded force as a political phenomenon, Engels devastatingly revealed the economic preconditions for force itself. While "the revolver triumphs over the sword," for Engels this triumph was the triumph of the entire economic structure capable of furnishing revolvers: "the producer of more perfect instruments of force, *vulgo* arms, vanquishes the producer of the less perfect instrument," and as a result "force is no mere act of the will."[33] Without rejecting the undeniable truth in Engels's position, Fanon nevertheless asks, with a mixture of sarcasm and seriousness: "What aberration of the mind drives these famished, enfeebled men lacking technology and organizational resources to think that only violence can liberate them faced with the occupier's military and economic might?"[34]

Fanon's response to what he sees as Engels's narrow understanding of force opens outward from three short words that had by then gained the status of a decolonial mantra—Dien Bien Phu—and from the knowledge that those boasting advanced weaponry do not always win. Rather than siding with Dühring's emphasis on the primacy of force, however, Fanon responded to both him and Engels by dialectically complicating force and will alike: not only is force irreducible to its instruments, will is similarly irreducible to a pure act of consciousness. Rather, just as the economic forces of production contain a subject/object dialectic, Fanon shifts from the cold objectivity of *rapport de forces* to the more ambiguous terrain of *rapports de masse*—if the instruments of violence matter, so do sheer numbers, knowledge of the terrain, and the determination to protect one's own. In the process, force is subjectivized by the rebellious masses and transformed alchemically into its opposite: violence, capable of generating excess and immeasurable surplus effect that is both ideological *and* material, and beyond both, ontological.[35]

This is a guerrilla violence that exudes political effects in an expansive swirl from its hard, Manichaean center. It is this violence that hardens decolonial-national identity and makes possible the leap from a frozen Manichaeism to a properly dialectical logic of dynamic oppositions, generating not merely the rupture of the existing, but also a process of open-ended transformation toward a new decolonized universal. For a lyrical expression of the creative potential of decolonial violence in the calloused hands of the masses, Fanon turns as is so often the case to Césaire—and to a poem he had already quoted at length in *Black Skin, White Masks*:

REBEL: My family name: offended; my given name: humiliated; my profession: rebel; my age: the stone age.

MOTHER: My race: the human race. My religion: fraternity . . .

REBEL: My race: the fallen race. My religion . . . but it is not you who will prepare it with your disarmament . . . it is I with my revolt and my poor clenched fists and my bushy head . . .

The mother, stand-in for the false universal, insists on humanity and fraternity in the present through "disarmament" in the face of force, but only the violent revolt—the "clenched fists" of the fallen—holds out this possibility, the religious origins of diremption again ringing true. The full potential of this violence only emerges once the rebel kills his master, a "good master," for having speculated that his infant child "will make a good" slave:

REBEL: Killed . . . I killed him with my own hands . . . Yes: a *fecund and copious death* . . .

MOTHER: . . . O my son . . . an evil and pernicious death.

REBEL: Mother, an enduring and sumptuous death.

MOTHER: From too much hate.

REBEL: From too much love . . . I struck, the blood spurted: it is the only baptism that today I remember.[36]

Here, force and violence speak directly to one another, which is to say that they speak past one another.

But this fecundity of violence is not guaranteed by the act in-itself, a first necessary but merely "spontaneous" step in what will be a long struggle for national consciousness. This is why Sartre dramatically oversimplified when he penned his famously provocative words, "killing a European is killing two birds with one stone, eliminating in one go oppressor and oppressed: leaving one man dead and the other man free," even with the rarely cited supplement: "for the first time the survivor feels a *national* soil under his feet."[37] Yes, there is hatred, and while this feeling is real, the nation is that but little more: a shared sense, a series of interconnected relay points that only densifies through a long and arduous process extending through an entire chain of identities and intradialectical twists and turns. And more important still is the fact that it is violence itself that helps to transcend hatred and division, launching the decolonial nation toward the universal while guarding incessantly against premature closure.

In other words, where Fanon had initially insisted on the fundamental *sameness* of colonial force and decolonial violence, this insistence counterintuitively serves to drive home the depth of the chasm separating the two. And whereas Fanon had previously lamented the difficulty with which the real, historically racialized slaves turn away from the master and toward labor on the world, he now argues in a powerfully Hegelian fashion that violence itself—directed against the colonizer—"constitutes their only work." In turning toward this new, world-creating labor, decolonial violence gains a "positive, formative" aspect: "cleansing" the individual of "their inferiority complex" as it collectively "unifies the people" through a mythical projection in which "the future nation is already indivisible."[38] Consistent with its decolonized Hegelian foundations—and echoing Sorel's dialectics of class combat—this creative function of violence also impacts the opposite side of the colonial divide: striking fear into the heart of the colonizer, and thereby creating the basis for a symmetrical struggle. In other words, violence, the essential precondition for national identity, stands at the very center of the dialectic of decolonization as its only source of motion.

The Expanding Circle of the Nation

The fact that the decolonial nation emerges in a fragmentary way from but a single part—the peasantry—and the generativity of the violence that brings it into being point toward the imperfect, mobile, and dynamic character of that nation. But these are not enough to fully allay fears that the decolonial nation—as nation—*aspires* to wholeness, to closed unity. Fanon makes the task even more difficult when he repeatedly describes this violence as "totalizing," and even more so when he suggests—with a sort of playful brutality—that the first task of that violence is to establish a unity of the most troubling sort. If colonization "inflicts" a "dichotomy" on the world, the first stage of decolonization not only inverts this division, but furthermore "unifies this world by a radical decision to remove its heterogeneity, by unifying it on the grounds of nation and sometimes race."[39]

Fanon immediately presses outward with both hands, however, in a surprisingly deft two-sided critique of both vulgar Marxism and the essentialist understanding of race that this simplification might suggest: "In the colonies the economic infrastructure is also a superstructure. The cause is effect: You are rich because you are white, you are white because you are rich. This is why Marxist analysis should always be slightly stretched when it comes to addressing the colonial issue."[40] Here begins the dialectical spiral that will characterize much of *Wretched*: if, on the one hand, distinguishing who resides on either side of the Manichaean division couldn't be easier, in another sense it could scarcely be more complex. If Fanon is here insisting that race matters (richness depends on whiteness), he is also simultaneously insisting on an antiessentialist understanding of race as codetermined by class (whiteness depends on richness) and further complicated by the global geography of the "elsewhere."[41]

On the surface of things, decolonization consists of two stages: the "national" stage characterized by inverted Manichaeism, followed by a subsequent "social" (or social*ist*) stage, with the two bound together by the transition from force to violence. This elegant simplicity is visible even in the structure of *Wretched of the Earth*: from violence and spontaneity, Fanon moves to national culture and national consciousness, opening out toward the universal in his conclusion. But even here we find hints that all is not so simple. Spontaneity has its "weakness" and national consciousness its "pitfalls." Even the *need* to unify the nation in such a way testifies to a foundational lack at its heart, and the progress of the dialectic appears littered with obstacles, makeshift barriers strewn across our path and dangerous shards of the world we are leaving behind.

No sooner does the nation begin to emerge, solidify, and unify in the oversimplistic first stage of decolonization then the stages themselves disintegrate, and this collapsing unity reveals its intractable imperfections and the openness of the dialectic at its heart. The first obstacle to be overcome manifests above all geographically. Whereas Fanon had in his first few pages described the simplicity of the Manichaean world, the disconcerting first moments of the decolonial struggle immediately test this simplicity. Not all join in the struggle from the outset, and there exists a deep mutual suspicion between component parts of the future nation, a Manichaeism-within-a-Manichaeism—no longer colonized versus colonizer but rural versus urban—that poses an intradialectical struggle before the colonizer can successfully be confronted. Many educated urbanites bring their Eurocentric education to an unaccommodating reality, seeing the peasantry in essentially the same terms as had Marx, that is, as a fundamentally reactionary "brake on the revolution."[42]

The existential reaction of the peasantry to these Europeanized elites is the correspondent inverse: viewed as essentially European, the urban population is always-already suspected of treason to the not-yet nation.

"Dressed like a European, speaking his language," the rural masses see in this figure "a defector who has given up everything which has constituted the national heritage" to reap the benefits of colonialism.[43] Fanon even goes so far as to suggest that "each side" of the urban-rural divide "evolves according to its own dialectic."[44] But like the broader dialectic within which it is inscribed, the subaltern side—here the peasantry—bears within itself the kernel for overcoming this division: in their anticolonial and proton-ational traditions, the rural masses carry the future nation embryonically within themselves as "the gestation of the national consciousness."[45]

The first stage of decolonization consists in overcoming this apparent division between town and country, but this opposition is not transcended simply through conversion or the suspension of hostilities in the face of a common enemy. Rather, this division can only be overcome through an in-tradialectical struggle that centers a concept of nation irreducible to geo-graphical territory: the splintering of urban-based nationalist parties by colonal repression drives the more radical and uncompromising militants underground and into the interior. It is there, far from the cities, that these militants retreat "deep into the rural masses," whose embrace "wraps him in a mantle of unimagined tenderness and vitality." With this fusion, the rural "masses" enter into struggle as a "coherent people" ready to "sharpen their weapons."[46] By becoming a proto-"people," these revolutionaries are pre-pared to forge "the nation" wherever they go. But while the nation is born in the heart of the countryside, it is only the invasion of the cities that "com-pletes [consacre] the dialectic" by overcoming the geographical division of (most of) the colonized and expelling the colonizer.[47] In other words, it is not that Westernized native elites are convinced to rejoin the nation en masse, but instead they are subjected to a dialectical *reconquest* of sorts in Fanon's equally controversial description of the semiurban lumpenprole-tariat as the "urban spearhead" of national liberation.

If the unification of the decolonial nation represented the completion of *the* dialectic tout court, however, this would lead to a very different and strictly nationalist vision—and *Wretched of the Earth* would come to a close less than one hundred pages in. If the imperfection of the em-bryonic nation disintegrates the simplicity of the Manichaean stage, the component parts of the future nation fragmented and in need of an in-tradialectical unification in the early stages of the struggle, that struggle then opens immediately onto a similar outward disintegration, toward the universal, which begins to emerge *prior* to the stage of formal liberation. This disintegration—and the radical heterogeneity it entails—is most visible in the peculiarly flexible, mobile, and expansive nature that Fanon ascribes to the decolonial nation. And it is this pre- and postrevolutionary incompleteness of the nation, its sheer mobility and mutability, its dynamic imperfection, that shields Fanon from the surprisingly frequent charge of vulgar nationalism.

This decolonial nation emerges first spontaneously and in a fragmented— even pointillistic fashion—in disparate peasant revolts, before acquiring an expansive dynamic with the constitution of a rebel army.

> The rash of revolts born in the interior testify, everywhere they break out, to the nation's ubiquitous and generally dense presence. Every colonized subject in arms represents a fragment of the nation which is alive from this point forward . . . They obey a simple doctrine: make the nation exist. There is no plan, no speeches, no resolutions, no factions. The problem is clear-cut: the foreigners must leave . . . Initiative is localized. On every hilltop a government in miniature is constituted and assumes power. In the valleys and in the forests, in the jungle and in the villages, everywhere, one encounters a national authority. In their actions, everyone makes the nation exist . . . If the nation is present everywhere, it must then be here.[48]

The simplistic and mythical projection of national unity here glosses over the fragmentary nature of the nascent nation, overcoming that fragmentation through its very projection. That a nation could be described by quality like density, that it could be posed as a project in becoming, that its authority could surge forth from ostensibly isolated hilltops already tells us that it is not a substance at all but a contagious collective will and practice. It aspires to unity, certainly, but while this may seem "clear-cut" in the sense that myth is indivisible, it remains to be seen *what* precisely is being unified, according to what parameters, and *for how long*. For now, what is clear is that this is no merely essentialist nationalism wherein a preexisting quantity functions circularly as both beginning and end of a nondialectical movement.

The circle of the nation, its apparently self-enclosed Manichaean circuit, is nevertheless radically expansive from the outset. From its initial localization in sovereign hilltops, this formerly petrified mass gains a new motion and rhythm as it draws together: old enmities are transcended, intertribal communications are reestablished, and the imperatives of guerrilla warfare force a reevaluation of this rooted and impetuous localism. "The national circle widens and every new ambush signals the entry of new tribes. Every village becomes both an absolute agent and a relay . . . Every new group that is constituted, every new volley of cannon fire signals that everybody is hunting the enemy, everybody is taking a stand."[49] Through the expansive myth of the nation, spontaneous revolts are knitted together into a complex revolutionary tapestry and the people rear up in unison. Localized spontaneity gives way to a "pragmatic realism" that sees a shift from local self-defense to the hypermobility of guerrilla war, in which the sovereign hilltop has been transcended and "every fighter carries the homeland to war between his bare toes."[50] If the nation is "everywhere," then I need not remain "here" to defend it.

But if the nation expands territorially according to the reunification of the rural and the urban, it also expands in a second sense as well that is too often overlooked in caricatures of Fanon as a hermetic nationalist. The simplicity of unmitigated war on an absolute enemy cannot survive if the struggle is to be victorious in the long run, and the transition from rebellious upsurge to revolutionary war requires that the insurgents "rediscover politics." This is no longer politics "as a sleep-inducing technique or a means of mystification, but as the sole means for intensifying the struggle and preparing the people to lead the country lucidly."[51] This new politics stands as a way station between the simplistic inverted Manichaeism of the first stage and a deeper process of education and consciousness that is simultaneously a rediscovery of nuance, multiplicity, and complexity. Unreflective simplicity, the absolute opposition to the colonizer that was the sine qua non of the liberation struggle, now becomes a strategic—not to mention a human—liability.

The "spectacular voluntarism" of the earliest stage of the struggle, "which was to bring the colonized people to absolute sovereignty in a single blow, the certainty one had of being able to carry together all the pieces of the nation at the same pace and according to the same perspective, and the strength grounded in this hope," soon becomes a political liability. "As long as he believed in the mirage of the immediacy of his muscles, the colonized achieved no real progress along the road of knowledge. His consciousness remained rudimentary."[52] We are at the tipping point between the "grandeur" and "weakness" of spontaneity, at which the stages of the revolutionary struggle disintegrate entirely, since the transition beyond simplistic national consciousness both *precedes* and *cuts across* the moment of formal liberation that nominally marked its threshold. Before the enemy is expelled and the nation fully consolidated, the inverted Manichaeism at its foundation begins to itself collapse and fall away, inaugurating an outward motion toward a still-deferred universal.

Violent Enlightenment

The dialectic had been pressed into motion, but as Fanon lay dying he saw new dangers looming that threatened to halt that motion and close off the emergence of national consciousness. If formal emancipation and equality had once served to conceal continued white supremacy, with Black subjects "acted upon" as objects by the white world rather than themselves acting, the same threat loomed on the "post"-colonial horizon. The danger was a dual one: threatening to trap the young nation within the simplistic nationalism that had been its initial motor, while harnessing it globally into the neocolonial continuity of the capitalist world-system. The two faces of this threat are embodied in a single figure, as threatening as it was illusory as a class: the national bourgeoisie.

Fanon is among the best diagnosticians of the particular position occupied by dependent, colonial economies in the world-system, and the danger of the national bourgeoisie as a "class" is rooted in this global constellation. Against the standard Marxist account that Sorel had sought to reinvigorate—in which society was increasingly divided into a civil war between proletariat and bourgeoisie—for Fanon, neither class plays this paradigmatic role in the colonized world. The industrial proletariat, he famously insists, is not only small but "pampered"—a judgment that would earn him much posthumous scorn from the Left.[53] The limited size of the proletariat, moreover, is the direct consequence of the weakness of the national bourgeoisie, which cannot truly accumulate, has little incentive to reinvest profits domestically, and instead is condemned to and embraces its "historical mission as intermediary" in colonial extraction.[54]

The national bourgeoisie cannot, in other words, perform the historic function of a bourgeoisie, and thereby embodies the motionless petrification that its existence threatens to introduce into the dialectics of decolonization. It is bourgeois but not bourgeois, national but not national, and is therefore confronted with a choice or, better put, a challenge: to abandon a full half of its contradictory self and commit class suicide.[55] "In an underdeveloped country, the imperative duty of an authentic *national* bourgeoisie is to betray the vocation to which it is destined, to learn from the school of the people . . . We will see, unfortunately, that the national bourgeoisie often turns away from this heroic and positive path, which is both fertile and just, and unabashedly sinks to the antinational, and therefore abhorrent, path of a classical bourgeoisie, a *bourgeois* bourgeoisie that is dismally, inanely, and cynically bourgeois."[56] Whereas Fanon would famously insist that "each generation must discover its mission, fulfill or betray it," the situation of the national bourgeoisie is more complex, since it is precisely its "historical mission" that *must*, in fact, be betrayed.[57] And yet the national bourgeoisie is unlikely to walk the path of the people, opting instead for the double determination of a "bourgeois bourgeoisie" that is nevertheless an objective impossibility.

For Sorel, it was possible for a revitalized European bourgeoisie confronted with a combative proletariat to drive history forward through mutual enmity. There is no such possibility in Fanon's account: bourgeoisie and proletariat can choose to stand on the sidelines of the national struggle or to join it, but in neither case do they constitute leading sectors. Despite Fanon's quasi-Sorelian nostalgia for the "dynamic, pioneering aspect, the inventive, discoverer-of-new-worlds aspect" of a truly bourgeois bourgeoisie, this desperate gamble would prove futile, because the national bourgeoisie enters the global dialectic at a different stage: "It follows the Western bourgeoisie in its negative and decadent aspect without having accomplished the initial stages of exploration and invention . . . At its outset the national bourgeoisie of the colonial countries identifies with the last stages of the Western bourgeoisie. Don't believe it is skipping stages. In fact it starts at the end. It is already senile, having experienced neither the petulance, the intrepidness, nor the voluntarism of youth and adolescence."[58]

Apparent echoes of Sorel are thus purely hypothetical: the bourgeois phase, for Fanon, is "only justified if the national bourgeoisie is sufficiently powerful, economically and technically, to build a bourgeois society, to create the conditions for developing a sizeable proletariat, to mechanize agriculture, and finally pave the way for a genuine national culture."[59] Since this is impossible for a class that represents not "a replica of Europe but rather its caricature," the question is moot. Against the accusation that he advocates skipping historical stages, Fanon deftly flips the script: it is the latecoming national bourgeoisie itself that hopes to skip stages, and since this is impossible, we must look for something different.

The mere impossibility of the national bourgeoisie's mission does not, however, reduce the danger this class poses as the spearhead of neocolonial continuity and an agent of antidialectical stasis. The national bourgeoisie, lacking the "homogeneity of caste" necessary to rupture the national totality and set it into motion, literally "serves no [dialectical] purpose . . .

the bourgeois phase in the history of the underdeveloped countries is a useless phase."[60] This uselessness is a positive threat, posing as it does the twin—and often complicit—dangers of a simplistic nationalism and neocolonial continuity. It is only by barring the way to the national bourgeoisie that the young nation can avoid preemptive closure and maintain the momentum necessary to transcend the merely national stage of its development and open outward toward the universal.

Explicitly applying Sartre's analysis of negritude in *Orphée Noir* to the travails of the young nation, Fanon assumes a lyricism more characteristic of *Black Skin, White Masks*. Whereas "Antiracist racism, the determination to defend one's skin which characterizes the response by the colonized to colonial oppression, clearly represent sufficient reasons to engage in the struggle," in other words to fuel the first stage of revolt, Fanon nevertheless adds that "Racism, hatred, resentment, and 'the legitimate desire for revenge' cannot sustain a war of liberation. These flashes in consciousness which hurl the body down tumultuous paths, which launch it into a quasi-pathological dreamlike state where the face of the other induces me to vertigo, where my blood calls for the blood of the other, where my death through mere inertia calls for the death of the other, this powerful passion of the first hours [of the struggle], disintegrates if it is left to feed on itself."[61]

There is no better proof than this that Fanon understood his task in *Wretched* as a repetition of his earlier dialectical argument vis-à-vis Black identity in the context of decolonial war. But while it may seem strange for Fanon to cite the very text that had previously cut him to the bone, he clearly maintains both the necessity of this prior "racist" stage and grants it a dialectical weight—a mythical "dreamlike" and vertiginous quality—that exceeds Sartre's formulation. And more important still for this thinker resolutely "grounded in temporality," unlike Sartre's prognosticative subsumption of negritude, Fanon is writing from the center of the dialectic at the cusp of this necessary turning point. The recognition that "hatred does not constitute a plan of action" introduces a new torsion into the dialectic of decolonization that undermines Fanon's own best attempt to cleanly distinguish stages.

In the process, it gives rise to an intradialectical helix, according to which the nation, which cannot emerge except through an initially inverted Manichaeism, here disintegrates outward along the fine dialectical line between uncritical universalism and racial essentialism, an *antiessentialist Manichaeism*. As formal, de jure independence approaches on the heels of the de facto expansion of the nation from the interior toward the towns, nowhere is this disintegration clearer than in the sudden and jarring appearance of "multiple realities" within the young nation. "It was once all so simple with the bad on one side and the good on the other. The idyllic, unreal clarity of the early days is replaced by a penumbra that dislocates consciousness. The people discover that the iniquitous phenomenon of exploitation can assume a black or Arab appearance. They cry treason, but need to correct this cry. *The treason is not national, it is a social treason,* and they need to be taught to cry thief."[62]

The species distinction that had constituted the colonial system and structured the early period of resistance to it begins to devour itself: "The racial and racist level is transcended on both sides . . . One no longer grabs a gun or a machete anytime a colonist appears. Consciousness stumbles upon partial, limited, and unstable truths. All this is, one can guess, extremely difficult."[63] Blacks can be traitors and whites can be comrades, and the shift from national to social treason marks a transition between stages of the struggle, however imprecise these may be: "The people, who had at the outset of the struggle adopted the primitive Manichaeism of the colonizer—Blacks and Whites, Arabs and *Roumis*—realize en route that some blacks can be whiter than the whites . . . At this exact moment in the struggle clarification is crucial as it leads the people to *replace a total and undifferentiated nationalism with social and economic consciousness.*"[64]

As if to hammer the dialectical point home, Fanon insists that this transition toward socioeconomic consciousness—from hermetic nationalism toward universal humanism—can come neither too early nor too late. If it arrives prematurely, that is, prior to the national phase, it runs the risk of short-circuiting national identity before it even coalesces, as Sartre had done to Blackness. "The second phase, i.e., nation building," Fanon insists, "is facilitated by the existence of this mortar kneaded with blood and rage."[65] But the specific threat posed by the national bourgeoisie in power is that social consciousness will arrive late or even not at all: "If nationalism is not clarified, enriched, and deepened, if it is not transformed very quickly into social and political consciousness, into humanism, then it leads to a dead end. Bourgeois leadership of underdeveloped countries confines national consciousness to a sterile formalism."[66]

If this feels like a traumatic shift in direction, one that requires the overcoming of the centripetal stumbling block posed by identity itself, it nevertheless draws upon and is catapulted forward by both the momentum of the revolutionary struggle and the continuity of "collective consciousness in motion." This "enlightened and coherent praxis" is but another name for decolonial violence extended forth in perpetuity, and which is itself a source of Hegelian self-consciousness, clarity, and lucidity: "Violence alone, perpetrated by the people . . . allows the masses to decipher social reality, only it provides the key. Without this struggle, without this knowledge-in-praxis there is nothing but a carnival parade and a lot of hot air. A minimal readaptation, a few reforms at the top, a flag, and down at the bottom the undivided and still medieval mass continues its perpetual movement."[67] Violence, the generative Rosetta Stone of the decolonial struggle, provides the most trustworthy vaccine against both remaining trapped within Manichaeism and the global continuity of neocolonialism.

"To politicize the masses," for Fanon, "is to make the nation in its totality a reality for every citizen . . . to link up with the nation as a whole, to embody the *constantly dialectical truth of the nation*, and to will here and now the triumph of the total man . . . Then, and only then, is everything possible."[68] And in so doing, this praxis opens the decolonial dialectic outward in the "long term" toward the universal, breaking down what divisions remain among the people while also raising them to the same level as their new leaders, whom they relentlessly interrogate, prying open a generative space to ground an interminably dynamic motion. "Enlightened by violence, the consciousness of the people rebels against any pacification. The demagogues, the opportunists and the magicians now have a difficult task. The praxis which pitched them into a desperate man-to-man struggle has given the masses a ravenous taste for the tangible. Any attempt at mystification becomes, in the long term, virtually impossible." Through the struggle, "the people realize that life is an endless combat," and that combat is no more and no less than the motor force of an equally endless dialectics.[69]

"We Have Better Things to Do . . ."

This opening of an interminable dialectics within the nation, between mass and leadership, coincides with Fanon's projection of that dialectic outward onto the global plane. After all, the almost inevitable failure of the national bourgeoisie, its opting for "sterile formalism" rather than filling the eyes of the nation with truly "human things," is above all a failure rooted in its own global condition of impossibility.[70] Here Fanon takes up in many ways the radically comparative task that I derive from C. L. R. James. In *Black Jacobins*, James draws an explicit analogy between the distinct class constellations present in revolutionary France and preindependence Haiti: white colonists are to the metropolitan aristocracy as mulattoes to the French bourgeoisie and ex-slaves to the poor French "masses." The Jacobins, by contrast, were somewhere in-between: driven by those masses in an initial phase but caving to their own very bourgeois class tendencies in a later and more conservative phase.

Wretched of the Earth takes up this comparative task quite self-consciously. The colonized working class is "pampered" and even "bourgeois," the colonizer stands in as a sort of imposed foreign nobility, and the Eurocentric national bourgeoisie—incapable of being a truly "bourgeois bourgeoisie"—floats in the uncomfortable denationalized and classless space between the two, an intermediary class like James's mulattoes, with all of the political instability this implies. It is only the rural peasantry—when fused with intellectuals and with the ex-peasant lumpenproletariat as urban spearhead—who have the potential to shake the "Jacobin" hierarchy of colonial rule.[71] Further, as we have seen, these categories are far from static, and enter almost immediately into a complex dialectical transformation: when the peasant and ex-peasant (lumpen) "masses" enter into motion, they become the "people," who then carry and distribute a mobile and expansive "nation" wherever the struggle leads them.

But this domestic repositioning is only half of the story. According to Ernesto Laclau, Fanon's nation remains one in which "heterogeneity has simply disappeared as the result of the full return to a dialectical reversal," adding—suggestively, for our analysis—that "Jacobinism is just around the corner."[72] But whereas this might accurately describe the initial stage of the struggle, which even Fanon himself suggests is characterized by a conscious elimination of heterogeneity, such a surface reading is simplistic on the face of things and openly negligent of the progression of *Wretched of the Earth*. As with this and other concerns frequently leveled against Fanon—that he glorifies violence, that he uncritically embraces the nation, that he was overly optimistic about the future course of African decolonization—one wonders whether many of the critics even read beyond the book's famous first chapter.[73]

Fanon's pointed insistence that "national consciousness . . . is not nationalism" points us in the right direction, but begs that we go further still.[74] If the radicalized dialectics shared by Sorel and the early Fanon is premised upon the combative rupture of society and the displacement or deferral of unity, then how could *Wretched*, with its embrace of even a mobile national unity, lay claim to such a dialectical vision? Further, and more perilously, if we have seen that it is precisely this commitment to internal rupture that shields Sorel from the accusation of fascism, then how does Fanon avoid the charge of a decolonial fascism? The answer to this question comes in two parts that are, not coincidentally, the two faces of the dialectic itself: the internal and the external.

Internally, we have seen that despite Fanon's description of the first stage of decolonization as homogenizing the nation, this unity remained largely mythical, a horizon for the coalescence of forces—a point of condensation for revolutionary struggle—that masked its own real and persistent heterogeneity. The emergent nation is fractured and fissured from the outset, divided fundamentally into a rural/urban dialectic-within-a-dialectic, and even when it emerges, this is a powerfully mobile nation that is never reducible to the unity of a population or territory. Moreover, even before the national "stage" arrives, Fanon's stages themselves disintegrate, racialist unification giving way to social nuance, and ushering in a proliferation of heterogeneity that the looming threat of a merely formal nationalism—one that is indeed Jacobin—threatens to halt. For Fanon, by contrast, the imperative is to continue to press forward.[75]

The second, external aspect has to do with Fanon's opening of the national—through his diagnosis of the colonial class constellation—outward onto a unified decolonial struggle of global proportions. It is in and through this leap that Fanon's national consciousness gains a compatibility with a dialectics of rupture, precisely because his unit of analysis is no longer the national totality but the global world-system. Within this broader totality, the decolonial unity of the Third World itself constitutes a fracture, a dialectical rupture, an antagonistic frontier dividing the globe in unified resistance against the Jacobin ontological hierarchy of the modern/colonial world.[76]

While Sorel opened a space for the relative autonomy of force, his goal was to set proletarian violence into motion against a stifling ideology of harmony that threatened to halt the dialectic of class struggle. Fanon's description of ideology's role under (European) capitalism echoes almost verbatim Sorel's view: "In capitalist-type societies, education . . . the fostering of love for harmony . . . instill in the exploited a mood of submission and inhibition which considerably eases the task of the forces of order. In capitalist countries a multitude of sermonizers [professeurs de morale], counselors, and 'confusion-mongers' intervene between the exploited and those in power."[77] This description, however, serves as a foil for Fanon to insist that a very different dynamic exists on the other side of the colonial divide.

Without minimizing the importance of ideology, we have seen already how he is nevertheless at pains to insist that in the colonial context, colonized subjects are contained not by sermonizing but "by rifle butts and napalm . . . the government's intermediary uses a language of pure violence. The agent does not alleviate oppression or mask domination. He displays and demonstrates them with the clear conscience of the forces of order. The intermediary carries violence into the homes and minds of the colonized subject."[78] Whereas Gramsci had mapped the relative importance of hegemony onto the unevenness of East and West, Fanon was here performing a similar operation along the "colonial difference."[79] Fanon's proviso that the colonial order targets "minds" as well indicates that the distinction is not absolute, however. And just as domination fails to fully capture the colonial situation—indeed, to argue differently would mean discarding most of *Black Skin* and much of *Wretched* as well—Fanon argues that colonization also *exceeds* domination qualitatively as it exceeds the non-West geographically.

Here the global contours of Fanon's dialectic emerge alongside its decolonial content: "We must remember in any case that a colonized people is *not just a dominated people*. Under the German occupation the French remained human beings. Under the French occupation the Germans remained human beings. In Algeria there is not simply domination but the decision, literally, to occupy nothing else but a territory. The Algerians, the women dressed in 'haiks,' the palm groves, and the camels form the landscape, the *natural* backdrop for the human presence of the French."[80] Mere domination does not colonialism make. Colonial relations are premised upon racial disqualification, but this racism is not reducible—as in many contemporary accounts—to the ideological superstructure, or even to a determination or effect of the economic structure. It is instead *sub*-structural, which is to say, grounded in the subontological zone of colonial nonbeing.[81]

This passage is equally interesting for what is absent, the Jews, who by implication are closer to a colonized population than to a merely dominated European population. The colonial difference cuts across Europe just as European colonization spreads globally under the black feet of the Pieds-Noirs, not to mention in the Eurocentric education instilled in even colonized elites. Following Césaire's view of anti-Semitism as "a terrific boomerang effect" whereby racial-colonial ontological disqualification is revisited upon Europe, Fanon too irreversibly transcends the national as a unit of analysis when he structures his analysis according to the colonial difference.[82] The colonial difference appears, in this view, as a broad rupture cutting across the global itself, one that is reducible to neither the internal (dialectical) difference of mutual relation nor to the external (for Fanon, more Manichaean) difference of meaningless diversity. Instead, the colonial rupture internal to the modern/colonial world-system is one that emerges first from the one-sided domination of the colonial enterprise before coalescing into a combative decolonial resistance that is itself global.[83]

Fanon's leap to the global is therefore not characterized by an immediate embrace of the universal. Far from it: he displaces analysis to the global level at the same time that he defers the universal even further into the future, deepening the oppositions at the heart of a global dialectics while insisting on the indeterminate open-endedness of that process. This is not, in other words, a shift to what Hardt and Negri understand as the "plane of immanence" characterizing Empire as a global order.[84] In their view, the shift to the global entails a concomitant shift in resistance, but one that differs radically from Fanon's view. Dialectics has come to an end, the distinction between interiority and exteriority evaporates, and there remains nothing but Empire as "a regime that effectively encompasses the spatial totality."[85]

While it would be misleading to suggest that Hardt and Negri view this Imperial "totality" as a reconciled universal order, they nevertheless view the dispersed resistances arrayed against this Empire—what they call "Multitude"—as immanent to it: "The struggles to contest and subvert Empire, as well as those to construct a real alternative, will thus take place on the Imperial terrain itself."[86] In Fanon's view, by contrast, the terrain of struggle is not the singularity of Empire but the dividedness of a global Manichaeism that must be transformed through inversion into a combative dialectic of global resistance. It is precisely by forgetting the contours of the colonial difference—with which Hardt and Negri are arguably complicit—that Empire is able to come into being in the first place, and it is by denying the possibility of dialectical oppositions on the global level that one renders such oppositions ineffective.

Against such immobilizations of the dialectic—either uncritical universalism or hermetic separatism—Fanon concludes *Wretched* with a striking condemnation of "mimicry" that has powerfully dialectical implications. His appeal to a build a new humanity "to walk in the company of man, every man" echoes the fraught universalism of *Black Skin, White Masks*.[87] But much had changed during this longest of decades, giving rise to a paradoxical combination of the optimistically exhortative appeal to "comrades" of the "Internationale" with Roumain's more radical displacement of that universal toward which they were called to fight.[88] This is no longer the anguished lament-appeal with which he had drawn *Black Skin* to a close, but rather an exhortative plea to change course in the present, to walk the path of global combat with no easy certainty that the anticipated future would ever arrive.

This was a call to shake off the old night for the new day, but the preparation for this dawn required a very real ruptures: old friendships to be broken, old beliefs abandoned, and above all, mimicry of past efforts to be rejected. And in fact, these imperatives were all one and the same: the old friendships were Old World ties, the old beliefs were Eurocentric articles of faith, and the path refused was the unilinear trajectory to which Europe had condemned the Third World. "We have better things to do," Fanon insisted, "than follow in that Europe's footsteps": "Come, comrades, the European game is finally over, we must find something else. We can do anything today provided we do not ape Europe, provided we are not obsessed with catching up with Europe . . . When I look for man in the technique and style of Europe, I see a series of denials of man, an avalanche of murders."[89] European thought emerged parched, its withering roots desperately seeking an impossible sustenance in arid spaces where the human is not to be found.

Even dialectics, as Sorel had shown, lacked traction in this peculiarly barren space: the European proletariat could have smashed the narcissistic dialogue of European thought, but it refused to step forward, instead demanding inclusion in the totalizing Hegelianism of the "European Spirit." The result was a frozen dialectic: "Comrades, let us flee this motionless movement where the dialectic has gradually metamorphosed a logic of equilibrium."[90] But this European equilibrium was only possible at the expense of a substantive outside beyond its borders, and while Fanon here seems sympathetic to Foucault's denunciation of dialectical "recolonization," he moves beyond mere denunciation by appealing to that outside— that "something else" beyond the barrenness of Europe—as a source for new motion.[91] When he does so, it is neither as a flight to pure exteriority nor a resignation to pure immanence.

In Fanon's dramatic inversion of global Manichaeism, the new human will spring not from the spiritual desiccation of Europe. Instead, it was the global "zone of nonbeing," that apparently "sterile and arid region" populated through condemnation, that would provide the sole source for a new dialectical motion, "from which a genuine new departure can emerge."[92] "No," Fanon insists, "we do not want to catch up with anyone."[93] Instead of a global mimicry in which the wretched would turn once again toward the master and away from the world, the revolutionary Third World needs to "shake off" both its attachment and vengeful opposition to Europe—a sort of decolonial *intifada*—turning away from the master to lose itself in its only true work.[94]

This work, this task is to "grow a new skin, develop a new way of thinking, and endeavor to set afoot a new man," and the fact that this process is undertaken "for Europe, for ourselves, and for humanity" is a succinct indication of its dialectical aims: with Europe as antithesis and humanity marking a distant universal horizon, the only path forward is "ourselves," the revolutionary assertion of decolonial identity emerging from the zone of nonbeing to press the dialectic into motion.[95] This is a decolonized global dialectic that walks the fine line between essentialism and the universal, recognizing both European accomplishments and European crimes. The "most odious" of these crimes being "the crumbling of [human] unity," both in European class divisions and across humanity more generally in ontological hierarchies of racism, colonialism, and slavery.[96]

Fanon's leap to the global is thus irreversible, and therefore his formulation of a decolonized dialectic is not simply complementary to the radicalized dialectic of European class struggle we find in Sorel. Instead, it displaces the narrow European dialectic by way of a "decolonial turn" in which the national unit of analysis is no longer sufficient—if it ever was—while the decolonial nation assumes an oppositional position within the broader unit of analysis that is the global-colonial totality of the world-system.[97] But Fanon's transcendence of Sorel—and decolonization's displacement of the class struggle strictly understood—nevertheless reveals a peculiar compatibility between first-world class struggle and the third-world decolonial "nation": neither is totalizing and unifying, and both instead stand in the middle of the dialectic as combative identities pressing, in their best formulations, toward an open-ended future.

When the national constitutes rupture instead of totalizing unity, it cannot be fascist, and if the decolonial nation can thereby be spared the smear of fascism, its appearance at the heart of global antagonism nevertheless points toward a new, global fascism against which we must guard. Césaire's and Fanon's insistence on the historical homology of colonialism and fascism acquires here a new relevance in the emergence of a new global-colonial order. Sorel's dialectic of class struggle therefore becomes compatible with radically dialectical notions of race, people, and even nation, but only does so on the eve of its own obsolescence. And indeed, as waves of migration into Europe—a new (post)colonial boomerang effect—provoke ever-sharpening existential crises, this obsolescence is undeniable. To paraphrase C. L. R. James's own decolonial *détournement* of François-René de Chateaubriand's description of the French Revolution, we might even say that "the European workers began the revolution: the colonized masses will complete it."[98]

CHAPTER 4

LATIN AMERICAN DIALECTICS
AND THE OTHER

Fanon's decolonization of Sorel's dialectic of class struggle, while arguably indebted to the syndicalist's concept of violence and revolutionary identity, was nevertheless irreversible. While in a certain sense Fanon did with racial and national identity what Sorel had done with class, the national unit of analysis was rendered obsolete in the process, making it impossible to move backward to prioritize *any* rupture—be it of class *or* race—contained entirely within the national framework. Not only is Fanon's decolonial nation dynamic and nontotalizing—in sum, dialectical—but this internal motility opens outward as well, proliferating the broad opposition between a revolutionary Third World and a stagnant Europe stripped of all dynamism.

By locating the decolonial nation within the broader framework of the colonial difference, in other words, Fanon renders Sorel's class-centrism untenable even at the heart of Europe: after all, turn-of-the-century France was and today remains nothing if not colonial through and through. Our progression from class to race to nation, and onward toward the people, is therefore neither a linear nor a contingent one, but one that seeks to approximate with more precision those political identities most relevant to the task of decolonization, a task that concerns us all. If Fanon thus put forth a theory of decolonization as an explicitly dialectical movement, this turn to the language of dialectics nevertheless presents a theoretical challenge once we turn to a different identity: that of the people.

In what follows, I approach popular identity in the specifically Latin American context, doing so through the contributions of another giant of decolonial thought: the exiled Argentinian philosopher of liberation, Enrique Dussel. As we will see, Dussel arrives at his concept of the people (el pueblo) by passing through a similarly dialectical conception of the decolonial nation, which he formulates at the intersection of Hegelian dialectics and Emmanuel Levinas's concept of exteriority—that is, at the border separating internal from external differences. As a result, Dussel's pueblo retains much of the conflictive, heterogeneous, and transformative character of Fanon's nation, while also allowing us to stitch together many of the identities discussed so far (class, race, and nation) into a multiplicity of overlapping microdialectics without displacing any of these, reflecting while also complicating Fanon's transnational scope.

But the theoretical challenge of thinking a decolonized dialectics jointly through Fanon and Dussel is this: by drawing Levinas into the equation, Dussel formulates popular identity in a way that is, at least on the surface, sharply critical of dialectics, and even explicitly *anti*-dialectical. His attempts to decolonize the dialectical framework, in fact, bring him to the cusp of rejecting dialectics tout court in favor of the sort of pure appeal to the Other found in the Levinasian concept of exteriority. And since this appeal to the Other is fundamentally ethical, in courting Levinas, Dussel would also seem to court an ethical approach that is arguably incompatible with the ethical impossibility diagnosed by Sorel and Fanon.

However, I argue that Dussel ultimately pulls back from this antidialectical precipice as a direct result of his own process of decolonizing Levinas. Instead, he situates analectics—the turn toward the Other, the outside, and the beyond, understood in concrete historical terms rather than ethical terms—as a *moment* in a broader dialectical progression. It is this complex and dynamic relationship between dialectics and analectics that will finally come to rest at the heart of Dussel's more recent formulation of the people. By viewing Fanon and Dussel in a sort of productive parallax, drawing the former's zone of nonbeing into conversation with the latter's notion of exteriority, I draw out some important resonances between the two that can function heuristically toward the decolonization of political thought broadly and dialectics in particular. It will be this decolonized dialectics—at the crossroads of rupture and exteriority—that I will then put to the test, in chapter 5, as an interpretive lens for grasping contemporary identity dynamics in Venezuela.

Toward Colonial Realities

Fanon's impact in Latin America, while often overlooked, has been significant.[1] This has been particularly true of Fanon's role as a radicalizing influence on the later waves of dependency theory, where his leap to the global level would prove decisively important. Here Fanon was not alone, however, and his influence dovetailed directly with that of another pioneer of decolonized dialectics: the Peruvian socialist José Carlos Mariátegui. Mariátegui—himself not coincidentally a Sorel devotee—could be considered the founder of a properly Latin American Marxism, one that was not imposed unilaterally by the Soviet Comintern, but that instead developed on the basis of a concrete analysis of local conditions and class structures.[2] Mariátegui's starting point, like Fanon's, was the specificity of his still-colonial reality, and hence the object of study in his *Seven Interpretive Essays* was clearly demarcated as *Peruvian Reality*. This foregrounding of "reality" as the basis for theoretical revision sits at the intersection of two elements that Mariátegui shares with Sorel: his methodological skepticism toward sectarian dogma and totalizing theories on the one hand, as well as an openness toward a spiritualized and heroic Marxism grounded in antagonism on the other.

As Mariátegui himself put it: "I do not think it is possible to imagine the entire panorama of the contemporary world in one theory . . . We have to explore it and know it, episode by episode, facet by facet. Our view and our imagination will always be delayed in respect to the entirety of the phenomenon. Therefore, the best way to explain and communicate our time is one that is perhaps a little bit journalistic and a bit cinematographic." To this he added, elsewhere: "Ideas that are perfect, absolute, abstract, indifferent to the facts, to a changing and moving reality do not work; ideas that are germinal, concrete, dialectical, functional, rich in potential and capable of movement do."[3] In other words, Mariátegui, like Sorel, embraced the openness and mobility of dialectics without falling prey to the predetermined and totalizing "dialectical illusions" that would foreclose even on this mobility itself.

Rejecting such illusions and turning instead to an analysis of concrete reality put Mariátegui on a collision course with the Comintern and one of the most pernicious and intransigent elements of the official Marxian dialectic: the suggestion—later transformed into a dogma—that less-developed countries must necessarily pass through capitalism as an unavoidable precondition for a communist future. As a result, Mariátegui, like Sorel, would have to fight a war on two fronts against a dialectical "bad unity" of orthodox Marxists and reformists. For Mariátegui, however, the part of the reformists was played by the anti-imperialist social democracy of Víctor Raúl Haya de la Torre, who while standing ostensibly opposed to Soviet orthodoxy, nevertheless shared the view that capitalism would play a progressive role in modernizing the class structures of so-called underdeveloped countries.

Here, Mariátegui prefigured Fanon, who tersely dismissed *both* the colonized bourgeoisie (as "useless") and colonized proletariat (as "pampered"). When Fanon was consequently accused of attempting to skip necessary historical stages, he quickly turned the tables on his accusers. Unlike Sorel's dialectic of European class struggle, in which action by one side (the proletariat) could reinvigorate the other (the bourgeoisie), awakening in them a sense of their historical task, Fanon saw little possibility of re-creating the dynamism of the original Marxian binary in the colonized context. The national bourgeoisie is already decadent—incapable of even "skipping stages" because "it starts at the end"—and the miniscule proletariat is both too weak and too strategically important to the colonial system—and thus bought off—to effectively change things.[4]

However, we should be careful not to miss the point: this was not a question of whether "skipping" dialectical stages was possible or desirable, but a more radical rejection of the very idea that such stages even existed to begin with in the context of the hierarchical structures of the global capitalist world-system. Against the linear, developmentalist, and Eurocentric Marxist dialectic—with its politics of stages and Comintern-enforced alliances with the stunted national bourgeoisie—Mariátegui therefore adopted a proto-Fanonian line. For underdeveloped nations, so-called development *is essentially impossible*, because capitalism doesn't fundamentally operate on the national level at all, but instead as a global system of structured inequality that obstructs rather than facilitates development in exploited zones.

As Fanon would later do, Mariátegui immersed himself in the study of the colonial and nominally postcolonial class constellation to discover what developmental "deviations" had been introduced by colonization and what the political impacts of these deviations might be. Having ruled out as potential revolutionary subjects both the middle classes (privileged by Haya) and the traditional proletariat alone (which he viewed in terms similar to Fanon), Mariátegui instead sought to reinfuse Peruvian socialism with a view of class struggle as not purely economically determined, incorporating the cultural, political, and economic legacy of indigenous communism into what he deemed "Indo-American Socialism."[5] Thus if the colonial class structure posed a barrier to dialectical motion similar to that which Sorel had confronted in France—in which proletariat and bourgeoisie failed to face each other directly in a great social war—both Mariátegui and Fanon turned to the antagonistic projection of combative identities to jumpstart historical motion, but did so according to dramatically different parameters than had Sorel.

The influence of this arguably Sorel-inspired decolonial couplet, Mariátegui and Fanon, on Latin American thought would prove significant. Influenced by both, dependency theorists like André Gunder Frank would come to understand capitalism as a global structure, thereby challenging both existing linear (as in Modernization Theory) or purportedly dialectical (as in Stalinist orthodoxy) approaches.[6] According to Ramón Grosfoguel, "*Dependentistas* consider incorrect the assumption that equates development to passing through the same 'stages' of the so-called advanced societies. Since historical time is not—as the modernization theories presuppose—chronological and unilinear, the experience of the metropolitan societies cannot be repeated . . . Development and underdevelopment coexist simultaneously in historical time."[7] It would be from this Latin American crucible—whose rebellious heat fused elements of Mariátegui and Fanon with dependency theory, liberation theology, and indigenous Marxism—that Enrique Dussel's philosophy of liberation would emerge as both a challenge to and a contribution to the project of a decolonized dialectics.

From Totality to Exteriority

If references to Fanon in Dussel's sprawling works are few and far between, there can be little question as to the conceptual and political ground shared by these two giants of decolonial thought. In the preface to his first major work, *Philosophy of Liberation*, Dussel describes his philosophy as surging forth from "the oppressed of the earth, the condemned of world history," a clear nod to *Wretched of the Earth* (in Spanish, *Los condenados de la tierra*).[8] Fanon is mentioned, furthermore, as a pioneer whose work was "already a beginning" of the sort of "substantive, explicit philosophy" of decolonization that Dussel himself sought to produce.[9] Moving toward the question at hand, Dussel even suggests—as had Fanon—that, under colonial conditions, the Hegelian master-slave dialectic "is no longer possible: the slave disappears from the horizon—by death."[10]

Dussel's intellectual trajectory, however, draws him first toward and then away from a dialectical framework. After first sinking his roots into the unperturbed universal ground of Heideggerian ontology, Dussel soon turned to Hegelian dialectics *not* for the universal reciprocity it provided, but for the internal rupture it made possible—cleaving the totality in two and setting it into motion. In the process, "Dussel discovers two valuable aspects of the dialectic: it denies the security and obviousness of everyday life, and it opens out on encompassing ontological structures, which are never exhaustively known."[11] He would not remain long within the realm of the purely dialectical, however. Between roughly 1969 and 1972, as though propelled by the energy of dialectical motion itself, Dussel had shifted from Heidegger, through Hegel, and on to Emmanuel Levinas's radical critique of ontology, which finally awakened him from his "ontological slumber."[12]

What Levinas's ethics of alterity offered Dussel was not merely the sort of theory of internal rupture that he had already found in Hegel, but moreover a rupture that opened *outward* toward exteriority, the beyond, which Dussel would come to understand both philosophically (as internal transcendentality) and geopolitically (as the global periphery). While Dussel teeters on the edge of a total rejection of dialectics, however, he goes no further. Instead, the internal parameters of his decolonial approach press dialectics to the limit, the outer border marked by Hegel's difference-diversity distinction, just as this same decolonial sensibility prevents him from abandoning dialectics entirely. By ambitiously incorporating not only internal but also outward rupture, by fusing Levinas with Hegel and later Marx, Dussel is able preserve the dynamic mobility that dialectics—if given a good push from below—can provide.

By the time Dussel published *Philosophy of Liberation*, in 1976, he had been fully awakened from various slumbers, and not only in the theoretical realm: in 1973, Dussel's home in Argentina was bombed by the far Right, and within two years—with military coup just over the horizon—he was expelled from his university and exiled to Mexico.[13] The impact of the blast was more than merely biographical or even psychological: it was inscribed in the book's *form* as well. While undeniably systematic, *Philosophy of Liberation* is also uncharacteristically terse, due in large part to the fact that Dussel's personal library—including his complete works of Hegel and Marx—had been blown into the street, left "unbound by the bomb."[14] Dussel often holds these bomb-damaged books up before his students—it's hard to imagine a more effective demonstration of the mutual imbrication of theory and practice.

The load-bearing beam upon which *Philosophy of Liberation* rests is a critique of the same paradigm of totality whose interrogation also drives my project, and for Dussel, totality is an inherently colonial concept. Abstractly understood, totality is, for Dussel as for Levinas, openly hostile to alterity and difference, always seeking to incorporate the Other within itself under the category of the same. As a result and by its own intrinsic dynamics, totality is always tinged with the threat of a totalitarianism under which the Other suffers disproportionately: "Totality, the system, tends to totalize itself, to center upon itself, and to attempt—temporally—to eternalize its present structure. Spatially, it attempts to include intrasystemically all possible exteriority. As the bearer of an infinite hunger, the fetish attempts to install itself forever in an insatiable cannibalism [*antropofagía*] . . . Totalized totality, Cyclops or the Leviathan on earth, kills as many alien faces as question it."[15]

Ontology—Dussel continues alongside Levinas—is the form of thinking proper to the category of totality, but as soon as he begins to fill this category with specific practical content, the gap between the two thinkers begins to widen. For Dussel, the ontology in question—like the totality that grounds it—is fundamentally colonial, "the ideology of ideologies, the foundation of the ideologies of empires, of the [global] core," and in a more self-critical vein, this former Heideggerian adds that "classical philosophy of all epochs constitutes the theoretical consummation of the practical oppression of peripheries."[16] Ontology, the study of a universal foundation of Being, is by its very definition bound up in the enterprise of colonization; it is a logic of the same, an ideology that subsumes all that is different to a universal view.

The origin of this universal is, not coincidentally, European and "civilized," and it is from a radical critique of the complicity of ontology with coloniality—the revelation, echoing Césaire, that behind a civilized facade there lies the opposite, an "insatiable cannibalism"—that epistemic decolonization sets out. As with Fanon, Being here stands against its disqualified opposite: in Parmenides's tautological equation of philosophy with ontology, "Being is; non-Being is not." But Dussel immediately recasts this opposition in the practical categories of his own political engagement, drawn not coincidentally from dependency theory: "The center is; the periphery is not." To which he adds, echoing Fanon's distinction between visibility and the violence of appearance, "Being is; beings are what are seen and controlled."[17] The totality cannot admit the other as Other. Rather she *is not*, and if she speaks—or more radically, questions—this quasi-Fanonian appearance of non-Being does violence to the order of things, and cannot be ignored.

The "alien faces" questioning the existing order are themselves guilty of provoking an inevitable massacre, a simultaneously epistemological act that Dussel sarcastically deems heroic: "To speak non-Being is falsehood. Before the other can continue their task of falsification and demoralization of the system, the hero throws himself upon the enemy, the other, and annihilates them, kills them."[18] Colonization itself is what Dussel describes as a "huge dialectico-ontological process of human history" that subsumes the Other to the same: "Clothed in noble, warlike, healthy, Nietzschean virtues, white-skinned and blond-haired like the Aryans, Europe throws itself onto the periphery, onto the geopolitical exteriority . . . In the name of Being . . . it annihilates the alterity of Others . . . violently expands the frontiers of its world . . . The conquest of Latin America, the enslavement of Africa and its colonization, as well as that of Asia, constitute the dominating dialectical expansion of 'the same' that murders 'the other,' totalizing it in 'the same' . . . Tautology takes possession of everything."[19]

Here Dussel's suspicion toward dialectics—whose "proper sphere . . . is the ontological," whose proper category is totality, and whose operational "principle is that of identity and difference"—is already perfectly clear.[20] Dialectical difference, understood as an internally determined relation, is a category of the same. In this view, dialectics is therefore always dangerously colonial, because it is internal to the system and points always toward resolution through the gradual and selfsame expansion of that system. Like Foucault, and arguably Levinas as well, Dussel here presents an oversimplified view in which there is only one possible dialectics: conservative and totalizing, contained within the bounds of a totality that divides cleanly and without remainder, and whose motion—rather than incessant, open-ended, and unpredictable—is a stale and mechanical expansion of the same.

Against this sort of totality-bound dialectics, Dussel follows Levinas toward what he calls "analectics," in which the *ano* refers to the realm of the beyond, to exteriority, to the Other. Whereas dialectics proper, for Dussel, constitutes an ontological dynamic internal to the totality, operating according to the parameters of identity and (internal) difference, "the analectical moment opens us up to the metaphysical sphere . . . Its proper category is that of exteriority . . . Its principle is not that of identity but rather that of separation, distinction," or in other words, something closer to Hegel's external difference or diversity.[21] But while Dussel's rejection of dialectics as essentially colonial seems relatively straightforward and faithful to Levinas, on second glance it becomes clear how radically he breaks with, overcomes, and decolonizes Levinas in the process of formulating an approach which remains in many senses dialectical.[22]

Decolonizing Levinas

If Dussel had truly been faithful to Levinas's outright rejection of dialectics and embrace of an ethics of alterity, this would pose a seemingly insurmountable obstacle to claiming Dussel's place in the project of a decolonized dialectics. But as we have already begun to notice, Dussel is far from the faithful disciple of Levinas he might initially seem: the categories are too concrete, too replete with references to specifically Latin American realities to be fully compatible with Levinas's own deliberately abstract philosophy. Here I argue that it is in fact in Dussel's breaks with Levinas and critiques of the latter's residual Eurocentrism that we can trace and uncover his counterintuitive attachment to a reformulated dialectics that is decolonized in the process.

To begin, whereas Levinas's concept of exteriority is so absolute and so omnipresent as to be equivalent to being itself, Dussel's own concept of exteriority is neither as absolute nor as universally distributed.[23] While every individual bears some capacity for *"interior transcendentality"* on the level of consciousness—to the degree that Dussel even defines metaphysics as "knowing how to ponder the world from the exteriority of the other"—their exteriority exists only *in relation to* specific and concrete systems of oppression.[24] And since these institutional systems are multiple and overlapping, exteriority, too, is expressed in a multiplicity of subject-positions. But what is crucial is that Dussel refuses Levinasian abstraction and instead insists on establishing these positions concretely. Thus for Dussel the paradigmatic case of exteriority is precisely *hunger*, a phenomenon both incredibly concrete and "subversive," in that it entails the need to overcome the existing political reality that is its condition of possibility.[25] Whereas Levinas emphasized the "face" of the other as the absolute basis for a universal openness toward alterity, Dussel's face—consistent with this resolute concreteness—is neither absolute nor universal, but instead "reveals a people before it reveals an individual," its physiognomy etched by centuries.[26] Further, it is no mistake that these are "alien faces [*rostros ajenos*]," a more collective and physical visage of the foreigner than Levinas's abstract "face of the Other [*la cara del Otro*]."

This concretizing move gestures toward an even more fundamental break with Levinas, in which Dussel further maps his quasi-Fanonian category of nonbeing onto global structures of colonialism and dependency in which "the center is; the periphery is not."[27] This is not, however, a resort to simple and undifferentiated nationalism, a fetishized romanticization of the colonized subject, or an exoticist primitivism of a substantial "outside." Instead, Dussel's exteriority is a complex, multiple, and dynamic relation that grows out of the intersection of class with nation: "the oppressed or popular classes of dependent nations" possess "the maximum exteriority," and it is through this "metaphysical alterity" that they "can project a real and new alternative for future humanity."[28] But the expansiveness of exteriority allows this exteriority to incorporate all those groups that are systematically excluded (economically, politically, according to gender, etc.) from the various systems constituting that totality and the global "cultural exteriority" of colonized and formerly colonized spaces, where collective practices predate or coexist with those constituting the global world-system.

Finally, this reformulation of the Levinasian concept of exteriority informs Dussel's own direct critique of the Eurocentrism of a thinker who so inspired him. Dussel recalls a 1971 conversation with Levinas in which it became evident that the latter had never really considered the possibility of an exteriority beyond Europe, in the colonized and formerly colonized global periphery.[29] This was more than a merely coincidental oversight, however, since Dussel would come to identify the metaphysical absoluteness of Levinas's Other as the source of his "equivocation."[30] By formulating exteriority as absolute and equivalent to Being, Levinas had obscured the concrete existence of nonbeing and—worse still from the perspective of a radically combative dialectics—he had run the risk of erecting yet another "false universalism" of the sort that Dussel, like Fanon and Sorel, is so intent on debunking.[31]

Just as Fanon's concretization of the Hegelian notion of alterity in the master-slave dialectic as internal, reciprocal, and reversible allows him to retain and reformulate aspects of the dialectical approach—breathing new life into them by filling them with particular content—so too does Dussel's concretization of Levinasian exteriority allow him to transcend the Eurocentric limitations of that approach without abandoning entirely the generativity of the encounter with the Other. It is in part by concretizing Levinas's own categories and subjecting these to a decolonial critique that Dussel avoids what is perhaps the greatest risk of the Levinasian approach: enthroning the ethics of the Other as yet another first philosophy. Moreover, this temptation constitutes a risk for my project as well: were Dussel a fundamentally ethical thinker—as some would certainly argue—

it would be difficult to reconcile his approach with the ethical impossibility that both Sorel and Fanon had diagnosed under colonial conditions.

Here, however, Dussel draws upon liberation theology's "preferential option for the poor" not to uphold the primacy of ethics, but quite the opposite: a preferential option for decolonization that effectively inverts this relationship, situating the concrete liberation of the global exteriority as the precondition and foothold for philosophical thought itself. In this inverted view, "it is necessary to think what has never been thought before: the very process of the liberation of dependent and peripheral countries . . . The option for this praxis is the beginning of a philosophical protodiscourse. *Politics introduces ethics, which in turn introduces philosophy*."[32] Against all appearances, Dussel is therefore *not* a primarily ethical thinker, but instead one for whom ethics finds its basis in the concrete oppositional political struggles that he seeks to channel.[33] Echoing Fanon's concept of *sociogeny*, Dussel insists that "theory is not sufficient in analectics," and this backhanded critique of Levinas, and the turn toward the concrete face of the historical Other that it entails, prevents him from seeking refuge in the preemptive closure of an ethical universalism, driving him instead back toward a combative popular dialectics.[34]

Dialectics of the Other

Despite the clear complicity that Dussel tracks between totality, ontology, and dialectics, his commitment to decolonization in theory and in practice leads him not to reject dialectics out of hand. Instead, by injecting a decolonial skepticism into his embrace of Levinas, Dussel's commitment to concrete struggles generates an analectically enriched dialectic, one that draws upon exteriority as its source but finds its motive force in the dynamic movement of oppositions. In what he will come to call an "ana-dialectical" method, Dussel insists that, for the concrete "historical-biographical" Other, liberation can only take the form of "relaunching the system as a whole in a dialectical motion that leaves people free."[35] This is a reformulated and decolonized dialectics in which the analectical appeal to the Other figures not as a *method* per se—i.e. as a *replacement* for dialectics—but instead as one "moment" in what he calls a "positive or metaphysical dialectical method," recalling that metaphysical here is essentially synonymous with thinking "from the exteriority of the other."[36]

What Dussel envisions therefore is a "sequence" of moments that begins with a turn toward exteriority in which the "totality is called into question by the provocative (apocalyptic) appeal [*interpelación*] of the other."[37] This "analectical moment" then serves as "the foothold for new unfoldings," a sturdy cornerstone from which a combative dialectical movement can burst forth.[38] The analectical appeal to exteriority is therefore not the denial of the radical potential of dialectical motion that it had initially appeared to be, but instead its re-grounding in a potent and untapped source, a sort of positive and substantive stepping-stone for a dialectical motion that is decolonized by virtue of setting out from "the *affirmation* of exteriority":

> It is not only the denial of the denial of the system on the basis of the affirmation of the totality [i.e. a dialectical negation of the negation]. It is the overcoming of the totality but not merely as the actuality of what is present in the system as potential. It is the overcoming of totality on the basis of internal transcendentality or exteriority, that which has never been within. To affirm exteriority is to realize what is impossible for the system . . . it is to realize the *new*, that which is unforeseeable from the perspective of the totality, that which emerged from an unconditioned, revolutionary, and innovative freedom.[39]

Such an appeal is more than a merely internal and negative critique of the totality, in other words, more than simply dialectical rupture. Given both the colonial tendency of ontology and its violent hostility to difference, as well as the reality of exteriority in the concrete struggles of colonized and formerly colonized peoples, Dussel will insist that "the negative dialectic is no longer enough."[40] A dialectics that instead sets out with one foot in exteriority refers not to the self-enclosed movement of identity and difference, and certainly not to the brutal colonization of the Other, but instead to an open-ended decolonial process that shakes the ontological Ground of Being.

While Dussel's critique of negative dialectics is a bit jarring for those of us steeped in Western Marxism and Frankfurt School critical theory, for Dussel this negativity does not refer strictly to the open-endedness of the process—which he upholds—but instead to the internal nature of its oppositions. He does in fact suggest that those thinkers often associated with negative dialectics "like Marcuse, Adorno, or even Bloch" are "naïve with respect to the positive criticality of the utopia of political exteriority of peripheral peoples, the working-class woman, the oppressed youth, and the dependent societies."[41] But as this quote makes clear, Dussel's point is not that, for example, Adorno's critique of Hegelian identity or dialectical determinism is incorrect—in fact, he largely agrees. His point is instead that a global and decolonial dialectics cannot remain strictly internal to the totality and cannot neglect the positive alterity of non-European struggles without becoming blind to coloniality in the process. Such a totality-bound dialectics, he argues, can neither gesture toward its own radical transcendence nor accommodate our own transcendent desires, and much less can it grasp the "cultural exteriority" that Dussel grants however unevenly to the global periphery.

Against a purely negative dialectics, Dussel responds by injecting exteriority not only at the outset of dialectical motion, but toward its conclusion as well. Rather than simply resolving internal contradictions, then, the effect is to open his dialectical vision outward, with exteriority providing not only the foothold for motion but also the leverage to pry open an indeterminate future. "The pure negativity of contradiction is neither the source nor the resolution of dialectics," Dussel insists, and the emergent rebellious classes that establish the dialectical contradiction itself bring with them an unforeclosable exteriority. As such, contradiction cannot be resolved "in pure negativity," but instead "in the exteriority of internal transcendentality, in the analectical affirmation of the alterity of an emergent class, emerging as distinct . . . The dialectical process as passage to a new totality cannot support itself only in the negative thrust of negation . . . It is because of this that the analectical moment of dialectical movement is the origin and resolution of that same dialectics and its negativity."[42]

While the practical implications of this analectical turn may not be immediately clear, Dussel's essential point is that the overcoming of various systems of oppression cannot emerge—or does not emerge most powerfully—from that system's internal parameters, in part because these are systems built on exclusion as much as oppression. The fact that this exclusion reaches even the ontological level only serves to underscore the blind tautology of an internal dialectics that succumbs to the same parameters of Being it claims to oppose. As with the tense transition from Sorel to Fanon, we are therefore drawn irreversibly toward decolonization; to overcome capitalism, we must first call into question the immanent perfection of the (European) proletariat as revolutionary subject, which even in Europe is crosscut and intersected by oppressions and exclusions. Moreover, *capitalism* as an intra-European phenomenon gives way to a far more complex and global colonial constellation in which the interplay of the internal and external is even more pronounced.

While dynamic, quasi-dialectical oppositions remain the driving force of this process, Dussel's goal is to raise our antennae toward the realm of exteriority in an effort to "detect the dysfunctional appeals that the oppressed continually launch from the exteriority of the constituted system."[43] If the internal logic of the totality tends toward its reification as a perfect unity—in other words, its *fetishization*—then the combative response that assaults the reified walls of the totality simultaneously from within and from without is, for Dussel, a process of *de*-fetishization that shares as much with Fanon's disalienation as with Marx's critique of the fetish as terrestrial religion: "Antifetishism, a negative notion that deliberately tries to veil its infinite metaphysical affirmation, is the guarantee of the *perennial dialectic of history*, of the de-totalization that liberation produces in all fossilized systems. Atheism vis-à-vis the present system is a prerequisite for innovative, procreative, liberatory praxis."[44]

Dussel has a precise name for this antifetishist, anadialectical movement that initiates revolutionary motion according to a logic of outward-oriented difference: he calls it quite simply *liberation*, which he describes in self-consciously Marxian terms as a specter haunting the Global South. To Marx, however, he adds what we might read as subtle echoes of W. E. B. Du Bois in the sort of "second sight" that peripheral thinkers enjoy, by virtue of having a foot in exteriority: "Philosophical intelligence is never so truthful, pure, and precise as when it starts from oppression and does not have any privileges to defend, because it has none at all."[45] The philosophy of liberation—in a gesture toward its own universal status—has nothing to lose but its chains, and a world to gain.

For Dussel as for Sorel and Fanon, this is a dialectics that treads the fine line between internal and external opposition, and even more self-consciously so, since in Dussel's formulation, the question is precisely one of breaking down the apartheid wall separating inside from outside. So it is perhaps unsurprising to find that he too inverts the traditional trajectory of human progress to embrace the image of the barbarian: "From non-Being, nothingness, the Other, exteriority, the mystery of non-sense, it is from here that our thought will set out. It is, then, a barbarian philosophy."[46] Anadialectical liberation is "barbarian" not only in its appeal to the nothingness of what lay beyond the walls—to the banished zone of nonbeing—but also in its "transontological" movement to abolish those walls themselves. Rather than a vestige of the past, today's barbarians are a vision of the impending and ever more universal future.

As a result, Dussel's liberation is literally *an-archy*: it moves beyond the principles governing the present by breaking down the barriers that separate the existing from the beyond. "Liberation is the very metaphysical or transontological movement itself by which the horizon of the world is pierced. It is the act that opens the breach, perforates the wall, and penetrates deeply into an unsuspected, future, and truly new exteriority."[47] This decolonized dialectical motion is itself "rupture; it is destruction . . . detotalizing the system and annihilating repressive frontiers."[48] And (decolonial) liberation is a process whereby the totality is ruptured and the apartheid walls of Being, in a powerfully Fanonian fashion, come crashing down. "Thus philosophy is death—death to everydayness, to the secure naïveté of the system," that unleashes a radically untethered process of decolonial dialectical transformation.[49]

Toward the Decolonization of Being

But how to square Dussel's peculiar formulation of a rupture that is simultaneously internal and outward-oriented with the more explicitly dialectical formulations of Sorel and Fanon? If Sorel and Fanon had formulated a combative dialectics of identity premised upon the *internal* rupture or antagonistic division of the social totality, how could this view in any way be compatible with Dussel's insistence on an *outward*-oriented rupture of the borders of the system itself? And if both Sorel and Fanon explicitly viewed these processes as "dialectical," as composed of and driven by conflictive opposition at the heart of that totality, then what are we to make of Dussel's severe critique of dialectics and embrace of an analectics that arguably shuns internal conflict to face the Other? Here we again confront a tension I posed at the outset: is Dussel's turn to exteriority a shift from the difference that matters to the mere diversity that was, for Hegel, a nonrelation?

While this may seem a more serious challenge for the explicitly decolonial formulations of Fanon and Dussel than for Sorel, whose approach is grounded in that most internal of identities—that is, class—the continuities between the three are as important as the breaks. After all, recall that Sorel pressed class difference to the very breaking point of utter incommensurability, and while this reassertion of class oppositions was clearly internal to French society, it threatened to dispense with society altogether through an all-out assault on social harmony and duty. The dizzying flexibility of Dussel's category of exteriority, which stretches from internal transcendentality to geopolitical exteriority, raises the stakes of the question further by itself *bridging* internal and external. As a result, the distance between the two seems less formidable, and like Sorel, for whom subjective self-activity stands as precondition for world-historical objectivity, Dussel speaks in similarly paradoxical terms: only one-sided praxis that breaches the borders of the totality can "guarantee" something so "perennial" as the dialectic of history.

This apparent gap narrows even further when it comes to Fanon's nominally dialectical formulations. Whereas Dussel appears to reject dialectics, Fanon's own embrace of dialectical motion depends on his radical decolonization and reformulation of Hegel's master-slave dialectic, in which the subontological zone of nonbeing provides the source for subjective action to set history into motion. After all, was not Fanon's description of the Manichaeism of the colonial world—and the absolute division between good and evil that it entailed—not also a question of exteriority and exclusion, the "decision to occupy nothing else but a territory"? Both thinkers, in other words, turn to the ontological register as a way of naming and resisting the characteristically colonial disqualification of certain subjects from humanity. Like Fanon, Dussel foregrounds the barriers separating Being from its disqualified opposite; like Fanon, he seeks to set into motion a dynamic that will tear down those barriers; and like Fanon that movement finds its source and unwritten conclusion beyond them. As Fanon made clearer than most, this process of breaching the bounds of the totality is violent by definition from the perspective of those policing the border between Being and the less-than-human barbarian hordes beyond.[50]

If Dussel is not nearly as antidialectical as he initially lets on, we could—in a sort of parallax—say the opposite of Fanon. While Fanon couches his descriptions in openly dialectical terms, his diagnosis of a zone of nonbeing opens up the possibility of an appeal to exteriority and a "colonial difference" that exceeds an internally dialectical relation. Neither fully external nor fully internal, the division marked by colonialism—and underscored by Fanon's turn to Manichaeism—is something quite different: a one-sided process of imposition that systematically obstructs the two-sided reciprocity of the master-slave dialectic. But while the resonances between Fanon's decolonized master-slave dialectic and Dussel's anadialectical movement of liberation are clear, important challenges remain. In his ambitious effort to draw Fanon and Dussel into a shared orbit, Nelson Maldonado-Torres highlights three difficulties in particular, all of which are ultimately rooted in the category of exteriority.

First, "Dussel (con)fuses . . . the 'beyond Being' with the non-being . . . the trans-ontological with the sub-ontological difference."[51] In other words, we have seen how Dussel's decolonization of Levinas involves the concretization of the latter's necessarily abstract and transcendental Other, which

Dussel supplements with concretely historical and situated subjects. While this gesture is quasi-Fanonian, Dussel is not as ontologically precise as Fanon (who hones in first on racial and then on colonial forms of disqualification), nor does he fully discard the transcendental aspect of exteriority. Taken together, both elements run the risk of erasing the particularity of exteriority, allowing it to slide easily from the concretely colonized and peripheral subject, to a privileged subject who simply maintains a radically critical perspective vis-à-vis the system. Moreover, whereas Fanon mapped the dialectical barriers preventing colonized subjects from turning directly toward the master in struggle—and was thus attentive to internalized inferiority among the oppressed and excluded—Dussel's approach might tend, in a more optimistic vein, to see exteriority everywhere one looks.

Second, for Maldonado-Torres, Dussel's divergence from Levinas is even more radical than his break with Fanon, since in its geopolitical concreteness the Other is robbed of its inextinguishable alterity in a gesture that makes Dussel "radically anti-Levinasian."[52] Finally, and in some ways most problematically, is the fact that in Maldonado-Torres's words, Dussel's flexible but concrete category of exteriority runs the risk of allowing him—a well-educated and light-skinned Argentine—to "portray the role of the other himself," empowered to speak for the subaltern.[53]

While the dangers of concretizing the other are real, it also through this same process that both Dussel and Fanon come into closer conversation and that Dussel's concepts gain practical traction in Latin America.[54] While Dussel's category of exteriority ranges from the internally transcendental to the colonized world, cross-cutting multiple levels in the process, this does not straightforwardly contradict Fanon's particular emphasis on, first, Black identity, and later decolonial-national identity. If anything, the fact that the broadest opposition onto which both thinkers settle is that of colonizer versus colonized—but also that they both do so in dynamic and internally variegated ways—testifies instead to their resonances.

To the claim that the transposition of Levinasian categories onto the global scale—one that closely parallels what we have seen in Fanon—constitutes a dangerous reduction in the alterity that defines the Other, Dussel has at least one defense. As we have seen, his understanding of exteriority is one that is always relative and gives rise to multifaceted subjects, individuals who are each to varying degrees *outside* the system. Put differently, to be "outside" is, at least to some degree, to grasp one's exclusion and to orient oneself in an absolute sense *against* that system of exclusion. The "alien faces" find themselves annihilated not only for their preordained alterity, but also for their interrogation of the system, their active "questioning" of the totality. The fact that this concern and this response are in many ways the direct inverse of the previous one—that, in other words, subjects can both easily slip into and easily slide out of exteriority—speaks to an irreducible tension in Dussel's approach, which only gains relevance and traction to the degree that it sacrifices some internal coherence.

This is not to deny some considerable and problematic slippage in Dussel's account: in an effort to transpose Levinas's ethical categories onto the political world, Dussel attempts to finesse the conceptual trauma of this gesture while insisting on various levels and degrees of exteriority, all of which are deeply interrelated. Hence while it is of course easier to identify the exteriority of precolonial societies that had yet to be incorporated into the modern/colonial world-system, Dussel does not fetishize this sort of exteriority.[55] Instead, he insists that a lesser degree of exteriority persists both in colonized and nominally postcolonial societies, and even within Euro-American societies, but that this collective and geopolitical relationship inevitably impacts the individual's "internal transcendentality" without the latter relying on it.[56] In other words, Dussel only escapes Maldonado-Torres's concern to the degree that he installs this slippage between individual, collective, and global at the heart of his conception of exteriority.

The confirmation that this slippage is worth the trouble it brings lies not in thought, however; it can only be confirmed in practice. In concrete terms, Dussel's exteriority overlaps with Fanon's Third World when transposed into geopolitical terms. In line with Dussel's complex and shifting notion of exteriority, however, this transposition does not lead him to uphold a pure third-world subjectivity that is reducible to all members of colonized societies or to accordingly embrace a simplistic and undialectical third-world nationalism. Before turning to his recent reformulation of the category of the people—which we will discuss in the next chapter— Dussel had put forth a theory of the decolonial nation that was as complex and mobile as Fanon's in *Wretched of the Earth*. This was a nation inflected with multiple variables (class, race, education, culture, etc.), that rather than merely *existing* as a fact must instead be formulated as a political *project*, to be *project-ed* as in the struggle against imperialism and capitalism.

The theoretical kernel of this nation, a conceptual bridge to the concept of the people (el pueblo) that Dussel would only fully formulate three decades later, emerges in the distinction he marks between *two nationalisms*: that of Atatürk, Gandhi, Sukarno, Gamal Abdel Nasser, Lázaro Cárdenas, Juan Perón, and (notably) Senghor on the one hand, versus that of Mao, Ho Chi Minh, Patrice Lumumba, Agostinho Neto, Fidel Castro, Augusto César Sandino, Salvador Allende, and (equally notably) Fanon on the other. Much like Sorel and Fanon's distinction between two "violences," Dussel's distinction between two nationalisms is a dialectical one that foregrounds the differential *content* underlying a seemingly shared *form*. Gesturing toward his later work, Dussel cryptically locates this determining content of the nation in "the very idea of the people within the nation."[57] The radical nationalism with which he plainly identifies depends, in other words, precisely on its relationship to the pueblo as "the perspective of the oppressed classes," including *campesinos* as well as the underdeveloped working class and marginal sectors that stand opposed to dominant classes and groups.[58] This framing forespeaks a decolonial nation that is, like Fanon's, a radically dialectical and shifting terrain of oppositions, and in which those oppositions turn as much outward as inward.

The Latin American people, Dussel will come to insist, is a radical and dynamic historical subject that only comes into being through self-activity and rupture by the (internally) oppressed alongside the (externally) excluded. While shifting and multiple, this popular subject draws its basic parameters from the conceptual distinction-cum-alliance between dialectics and analectics, and thus it functions as a nonobjective identity that must be projected and constructed, stitched together through the patient political work Dussel will call dialogue and translation. This understanding of the people will draw Dussel into conflict with those thinkers who, through an uncritical Eurocentrism, reject popular identity out of hand. But turning to the dynamics of contemporary Venezuelan political identities confirms in practice not only the powerful heuristic value of Dussel's people—one that reflects rather than imposes on revolutionary movements and the combative transformations they unleash—but also the broader decolonized dialectics of which it is a part.

CHAPTER 5

VENEZUELA'S COMBATIVE DIALECTICS

Nowhere in our dialectical present screams out for attention quite like contemporary Venezuela, where combat and violence, nationalism and class-consciousness—not to mention Manichaeism and radical movement—are all on the table. But it would be misleading to excise Venezuela from its context, as an object to which a decolonized dialectics might be applied. Both this book and our contemporary political moment more generally are indelibly marked by the dialectical return swing against neoliberalism that was arguably inaugurated by Venezuela's 1989 Caracazo, a massive popular rebellion against structural adjustment on the model of the Washington Consensus. More than for this single moment more than a quarter-century ago, Venezuela stands out due to the dialectical chain that 1989 unleashed—one which moves through the failed coup by Hugo Chávez in 1992, his subsequent election in 1998, and the development and deepening of a dynamic process that has come to be called "Twenty-First-Century Socialism"—each of these contributing to a seismic transformation of the region and the world.

The process of political change currently underway in Venezuela exploded out of the tense overlap of multiple combative identities in movement—Bolivarian, revolutionary, Chavista, Afro-Venezuelan, Indigenous, feminist—each with their own dialectics. But no political identity has been more central than that which draws them together in a combative whole that is nevertheless far from a singularity: *the people*. To settle on the people is merely to open another can of worms, however, since many view the people—like the nation—with a deep suspicion. Through a narrowly Eurocentric interpretation, philosophers like Michael Hardt, Antonio Negri, and Paolo Virno, for example, have dismissed the people as a closed unity, both homogeneous and homogenizing—the diametric opposite of the radicalized and decolonized dialectics I have sought to distill here. But if we reject this narrow interpretation, decolonizing the concept of the people by anchoring it in Latin American realities and revolutionary movements, we instead find a political identity that is far more dynamic and mobile, one which has borne combative fruit in contemporary Venezuela.

"The Multitude Against the People"

In an attempt to recast the parameters of radical identity today, a series of thinkers have come to champion what they call the *Multitude*, a new historical subject emerging immanently from the contours of the new and decentralized mode of global governance that Hardt and Negri famously term *Empire*.[1] With its multiplicity and radical irreducibility, the Multitude— we are told—is no less than *the* revolutionary identity of our moment, marked as it is by the global saturation of information technologies and the dissolution of both the traditional working class and the sovereign nation-state. The Multitude is thus constituted *not* by the dialectical rupture of the global totality, but instead emerges immanently from Empire itself.

This much is perhaps well known, but less noted is the ground-clearing exercise that makes the Multitude singularly important, as not merely *one*, but *the* revolutionary political subject for the present. For its proponents, the radical potential of the Multitude stands in direct opposition to the idea of the people.[2] As Hardt and Negri describe it, "*The people* has traditionally been a unitary conception. The population . . . is characterized by all kinds of differences, but the people reduces that diversity to a unity . . . 'the people' is one. The multitude, in contrast, is many."[3] Or more strongly, the category of the people reduces all social distinction into an "undifferentiated unity."[4] The people thus understood both substitutes a unitary whole for a differentiated population, and—worse still—actively *unifies*, gathering that multiplicity into a substantive unity: the people is a "constituted synthesis that is prepared for sovereignty," whereas the Multitude characterizes a more dynamic "constituent relation."[5]

Virno calls this gathering effect of the people its "centripetal" function, one that furthermore only buys unity at the cost of reinforcing the distinction between self and other, inside and outside.[6] In a quasi-Schmittian fashion, moreover, inside and outside are given a priori, and the unifying function of the people is thereby complicit with equally unified categories of nation and state. "Every nation must make the multitude into a people," in the words of Hardt and Negri, to which Virno adds that this gathered people is a mere "reverberation" or even a "reflection" of the state: "If there is a State, then there are people. In the absence of the State, there are no people . . . Before the State, there were many; after the establishment of the State, there is the One-people, endowed with a single will."[7]

Here, partisans of the Multitude agree with an ostensible enemy, Thomas Hobbes, for whom the dreadful Multitude similarly stands opposed to both state and people: rebellion against the state is by definition "the *Citizens* against the *City*, that is to say, the *Multitude* against the *People*."[8] Hardt, Negri, and Virno draw much of their rhetorical weight from Hobbes's own anxiety toward the Multitude, and it is no stretch to think that their opposition to the people is fueled by a desire to invert the Hobbesian equation, to befriend an enemy's enemy. In fact, as Virno provocatively puts it, "The best way to understand the significance of a concept—multitude, in this case—is to examine it with the eyes of one who has fought it tenaciously."[9] But this same logic would seem to disqualify Hobbes as the most qualified analyst of the people. The question remains as to whether simply inverting Hobbes is enough, or if in their zeal to celebrate the Multitude, these thinkers have unwittingly remained trapped within the parameters of Hobbes himself.

This suspicion deepens when Hardt and Negri chart the genesis of the "centripetal," unifying effect of the people, which they locate in two essential operations, one external (to Europe) and one internal. The first and "more important" operation is the dialectic of colonial racism that defined Europeans in opposition to their colonized subjects.[10] The European side emerges historically in the conservative, Thermidorian phase of the French Revolution, the moment at which the people as a concept of class rupture collapses into unity, becoming in Foucault's terms "centered" through its alignment with sovereignty.[11] But this apparent two-sidedness notwithstanding, the colonial side of the equation drops out when it comes to assessing the potential of popular identity.

"The entire tradition of political theory," they tell us, "seems to agree on one basic principle: only 'the one' can rule . . . Only the one can be sovereign, the tradition tells us, and there can be no politics without sovereignty . . . The choice is absolute: either sovereignty or anarchy! . . . Someone must rule, someone must decide." The singularity coterminous with the concept of the people thus emerges from a gesture that is doubly Eurocentric: not only does it draw its historical and theoretical content from European sources and experiences, but even where the colonial side of the equation surfaces, it does so as a one-sided phenomenon that erases the agency of the colonized.[12] Popular identity is unilaterally overdetermined by the colonizer to be a unitary prop of sovereignty, regardless of what the colonized themselves have to say about it. The "entire tradition of political theory" is evidently one from which Fanon, Dussel, and many others are excluded a priori. To decolonize Hardt and Negri's concept of the people, we need to reverse this imbalance, allowing the category of the people to travel across the colonial difference to see what new content it acquires in the process.[13]

On the surface, Hardt and Negri are willing to grant the decolonial nation the complex duality that Dussel has proposed and that their formulation of the people conspicuously lacks. Third-world nationalism, they admit, "has often functioned very differently . . . *whereas the concept of nation promotes stasis and restoration in the hands of the dominant, it is a weapon for change and revolution in the hands of the subordinated.*"[14] Like Sorelian and Fanonian violence, this is a weapon whose meaning appears to change depending on who wields it. But here, too, the rug is pulled out from under the colonized, because the "unifying power" of the decolonial nation is "at once progressive and reactionary."[15] These are not separable modalities as with Fanon's national consciousness versus national*ism*, Dussel's radical versus reactionary nationalisms. Instead, "those same structures" that protect the subaltern also smuggle (European) sovereignty in through the back door, and after formal liberation, "all of the oppressive functions of modern sovereignty *inevitably* blossom in full force."[16]

Fanon's entire effort, his intricate account of the "pitfalls of national consciousness," the dangers he rightly glimpsed on the horizon, and all his proposals for how to avoid these—in short, his *monumental effort to produce a nationalism not in the mold of Europe*—these are all dismissed as mere fantasy with the stroke of a pen and the slip of a category across the colonial difference. Citing Jean Genet's declaration that "The day the Palestinians become a nation like the other nations, I will no longer be there," Hardt and Negri conspicuously neglect the conditionality of the statement, which only holds *if* Palestine becomes a nation *like the other* (read: European) nations.[17] All national resistance, all Black and decolonial nationalisms, are thereby collapsed into the same: thus spoke Europe.

Rather than embrace the political categories and identities imposed by the colonial order through an inversion of its dialectic, Hardt and Negri insist starkly that *"reality is not dialectical, colonialism is."*[18] But from a Fanonian perspective, this is entirely backward. First, for Fanon, colonialism is in fact *not* dialectical, but instead characterized by a static Manichaean opposition. But second, and arguably more important, it is impossible to distinguish "reality" from "colonialism," which is after all a monstrous generator of not only wealth but also Being. Hardt and Negri neglect the ontological effects of colonialism, according to which Manichaeism is not simply a political style, but a material division of the world. And, as a result, they neglect the fact that for the colonized, it is not as simple as choosing an ideal political identity like the Multitude out of thin air. The colonized are instead condemned to choose among condemnations, selecting from among the very few tools colonialism itself furnishes the one that will best harness mass struggle.

The erroneous suggestion that colonialism is itself dialectical points toward a caricatured, straw-man dialectics, which becomes most obvious when Hardt and Negri attempt to recruit to the cause of the Multitude not only Fanon, but even Malcolm X, apparently oblivious to the radically dialectical character of both.

> For both Fanon and Malcolm X, however, this negative moment, this violent reciprocity, does not lead to any dialectical synthesis; it is not the upbeat that will be resolved in a future harmony. This open negativity is merely the healthy expression of a real antagonism, a direct relation of force. Because this is not the means to a final synthesis, this negativity is not a politics in itself; rather, it merely poses a separation from colonialist domination and opens the field for politics. The real political process of constitution will have to take place on this open terrain of forces with a positive logic, separate from the dialectics of colonial sovereignty.[19]

As we have seen, it is indeed true that, like Sorel before him, Fanon displaces any "final synthesis" in favor of "a direct relation of force." It is further true that by pressing division as deeply as possible, Fanon unleashes a "positive logic" beyond the direct relation with the settler. But Hardt and Negri fail to ask the obvious question: Why did Fanon appeal so unashamedly to the people, to the decolonial nation, and to dialectics, three categories Hardt and Negri cannot tolerate?

The answer is that each of these mean something fundamentally different from the Eurocentric meaning often imposed upon them: both the people and the nation can and do engender not cold unity but dynamic combat, and Fanon's displacement of "future harmony" in favor of this combat is not a rejection of dialectical movement but its condition of possibility. Given Fanon's decolonization of the Hegelian master-slave dialectic, the violently negative inversion of colonial Manichaeism is not apolitical, but instead the most political act of all. Furthermore, while the reference to a "positive logic" echoes Dussel's critique of a purely negative dialectics, Hardt and Negri fail to recognize that this is a specifically decolonial positivity, Fanon's "old granite foundation" of the rural peasantry, which like Dussel he then ties into a dialectical movement.

By evacuating the agency of the colonized, Hardt, Negri, and Virno can only view the people in its Eurocentrically overdetermined form, as a unifying and homogenizing supplement to sovereignty and the state. But if we set aside such Eurocentric proscriptions and instead open a space for the concrete struggles of the colonized to determine the content of their categories, a very different people comes into view. Even the most superficial attention to ongoing struggles in Latin America—not to mention Dussel's own recent work—attests to the fact that the category of the people is a category of rupture at least as often as it is a category of unity, one that instead of simply upholding the state can also establish a radical constituent relation with and against that state, and one that holds out the same openness to exteriority that Dussel had infused into his dialectics.

More than simply *a* combative identity, moreover, popular identity is *the* combative identity of choice across much of Latin America, in part due to the "historical-structural heterogeneity" that colonialism imposed on the region, in which a complex constellation of class relations and other exclusions coexist—begging the question of how to bring these together in struggle.[20] By contrast, it is not ungenerous to say that the category of the Multitude is largely irrelevant to Latin American struggles. Hardt and Negri's opposition to dialectics notwithstanding, it is through opposing the concrete structures of the world that we forge identities that are both negations but also more than that. Only the most myopic of idealism imagines that we can fight with anything but those theoretical weapons at hand that, in Marx's famous phrase, have become a material force in the process of gripping and being gripped by the masses.

The People as a Category of Rupture

In what follows, I contribute to liberating and decolonizing the concept of the people through ever-closer approximation to concrete political struggles in Latin America, and Venezuela in particular. First, I sketch the contours of combative popular identity in Latin America through Dussel's recent reformulation of the people. I then narrow in on the specifically Venezuelan context, by tracking the mirror images of popular identity provided by, on the one hand, ostensible father of Venezuelan democracy and reactionary critic of the people, Rómulo Betancourt, and on the other, revolutionary folk singer Alí Primera, one of the concept's most radical and relevant proponents for the present moment. Finally, I turn to the contemporary crucible of the Bolivarian process to both shed light on the concrete struggles underway, as well as to gauge the utility of the people as a concept—and the decolonized dialectics of which it is a part.

Nearly three decades after *Philosophy of Liberation*, Dussel published his *Twenty Theses on Politics*, a condensed version of his massive, three-volume *Politics of Liberation*.[21] In this concise handbook for engaged political theory and praxis, Dussel argues that the people—or pueblo—represents not unity but instead the very embodiment of rupture.[22] Even etymology points in this direction: *pueblo* can refer to both the totality of a population or to its "common or humble members," the whole or simply one part.[23] Etymology would be meaningless, however, absent concrete popular practices spanning the centuries, but according to Dussel the continued relevance of Indigenous concepts of community such as the Aztec *altepetl* and the Mayan *Amaq'*—which correspond to Mariátegui's understanding of the Incan *ayllu*—only widens this etymological breach. These continued resonances—which both preceded and exceed the Eurocentric concept of the people—intersect with contemporary practices to reinforce the people as a radical identity that is both dialectical and analectical: as Dussel puts it, "the word *pueblo* means something more profound than merely 'the people' in romance languages."[24]

The radical potential of this decolonial people, moreover, is not simply a question of its current oppositional form or pre-Columbian communal content, but of the interpenetration of the two in dynamic practice. For Dussel, the people is not simply something that *exists*, but instead a political identity that dynamically *comes into being*, "a *collective political actor* rather than a substantial and fetishized 'historical subject.'"[25] The way that the people comes into being thus militates against its purported unifying function, while staving off any future dialectical closure in the process. Not only does the people come into being, but it comes into being *against*, when some members of society or groups—subject to either oppression or exclusion—enter into motion to resist the concrete conditions of their existence.

As a result, the category of the people is neither sociological nor economic, but instead, as Dussel describes it, "strictly political."[26] This is the people to which Fidel Castro added his now-famous qualifier "*si de lucha se trata*": the people only comes into existence "when it is a question of struggle."[27] This *against*, however, is not external and Schmittian, not the consolidation of popular identity against a foreign other that Virno, Hardt, and Negri take to be its essence. Instead, the people, like Sorel's reinvigorated class opposition, marks a rupture *internal to* the prevailing totality, in which "The *pueblo* establishes an internal frontier or fracture within the political community," standing as it does "in opposition to the elites, to the oligarchs, to the ruling classes of a political order."[28] The people is not unity, but division.

And while the people establishes a rupture within society, it does not exhaust itself in a merely internal conflict. Instead, el pueblo embodies Dussel's prior fusion of dialectics with an analectical embrace of exteriority, straddling the bounds of the system by drawing into an alliance those internally oppressed *within* that system and those excluded *from* it. But if Levinas had helped Dussel to transcend the merely internal limits of Hegel, here it is Marx's concretization of internal rupture that "completes" Levinas: "Levinas . . . describes this process of the totalitarian totalization of the Totality 'as the exclusion of the Other,' which Marx completes by adding those oppressed by the system. The *people* therefore maintains a complex position. On the one hand, they are the 'social bloc of the oppressed' within the system (for example, the working class), but they simultaneously comprise the excluded (for example, the marginalized, the indigenous peoples who survive through self-sufficient production and consumption, etc.)."[29]

The heuristic strength of Dussel's category of the people should be clear for the Latin American context and for postcolonial societies more broadly. By breaking with a purely internal relation of oppression, Dussel's people breaks with a narrowly Marxist focus on economic exploitation and the working class as a revolutionary subject, providing a new conceptual framework to accommodate the analyses of colonial economic conditions found in Mariátegui, Fanon, and others. By fusing internal oppression with exclusion, moreover, Dussel seeks to draw together a broad historical bloc that includes not only the poor and the working class, but also women, Afro–Latin Americans, and Indigenous communities, each of which is marked by exclusion as much as by oppression and exploitation. The people thus constitutes not only the (dialectical) rupture internal to the totality and embodied in those oppressed by it, but also the (analectical) penetration into the exteriority of non-Being that the totality excludes.

While this people-as-rupture does not coincide with the totality, it does in fact gather together and unify the oppressed and excluded. But this is a far cry from the "centripetal" effect Virno attributes to the people, both in its means and its ends. For Dussel, the subcategories of oppressed and excluded also proliferate difference internally in their many overlapping subject-positions. For example, women as white can be included ethnically while being oppressed according to strict gender norms, and excluded economically as domestic laborers (which despite its clear centrality to capitalist production nevertheless takes the form of an exclusion, as does unemployment, simple circulation, etc.). "Productive" workers can be included-as-exploited by capital but simultaneously racially excluded as non-Being.

The practical and political question is how to articulate and knit together the many different individuals and groups that enter into motion against the structures of exclusion and oppression that blanket and texture the colonized and formerly colonized worlds. For Dussel, such a vast variety of political identities can only come together as a people through a dual process of what he calls *dialogue* and *translation*. While the first entails a conversation or negotiation between existing subject-positions, the second underlines the radical mutability of those positions themselves, the way particular demands can transform without dissolving into the "undifferentiated unity" that Hardt and Negri fear. For example, a process of translation occurs when white feminists respond to the demands of Black feminists *not* merely with a respectful tolerance of difference, but instead with a self-transformative process of internalizing critique.[30] Such a process seeks to craft "an understanding between movements that nonetheless never represents an encompassing universal" and that "maintains the distinctiveness of each movement."[31]

As these passages make clear, there is significant overlap between Dussel's concept of the people and Ernesto Laclau's efforts to reclaim the concept of populism. However, the two differ above all in the concreteness and contextual content that Dussel ascribes to his concept of the people. While Dussel's people seeks to stretch the limitations of Marxist categories—in particular, the working class as revolutionary subject—he is in no sense post-Marxist. Laclau's populist logic, by contrast, pays a heavy price for its post-Marxism, gaining its universal traction at the expense of all particular content, through an explicit privileging of "political logics rather than social contents."[32] We might therefore be tempted to re-pose the Fanonian critique of Hegelian universalism between Dussel and Laclau, beginning from the insistence that no signifier is ever truly empty, no logic ever truly universal.[33]

Dussel's concept of the people therefore refers to a dynamic and combative political identity that only enters into being as it enters into motion, antagonistically dividing the prevailing social totality in the process. In the process, the people knits together a heterogeneous unity through dialogue and translation, whose internal multiplicity—evocative of Fanon's decolonial nation—gestures beyond the existing order and toward a deferred universal whose only parameters are to be glimpsed in the demands of the oppressed and excluded. Much like his "barbarian" philosophy, Dussel's people is therefore a barbarian force that straddles the borderlands of Being itself, besieging those Jacobin apartheid walls that exclude some from the fullness of humanity, and seeking to open a breach toward alterity and the dialectically better future of a transformed and expanded society.[34]

One concern remains, however: that the people might serve as a mere prop reinforcing state power. Like Virno, Hardt, and Negri, Dussel formulates political power in terms of the distinction between the Latin terms *potentia* and *potestas*, between radical constituent potential and constituted state institutions. But whereas Hardt and Negri tend toward an absolute opposition between these two powers, Dussel insists that institutions are necessary if constituent power is ever to enter into real existence, and his dialectic plays out in the dynamic relation between the two.[35] For Dussel, *potentia*, "while representing the ultimate foundation of *all* power—still lacks real, objective, empirical existence" and is "*indeterminate and in-itself.*"[36]

This potential power-in-itself undergoes an "originary (ontological) disjunction," moving outside itself into the realm of institutions, and "this split—with regard to which we agree with Spinoza and Negri, but simultaneously move beyond them—is necessary, and it marks the pristine appearance of politics while representing at the same time the supreme danger to politics and the origin of all injustice and domination."[37] In other words, noninstitutionalized power-as-potential could do no harm, but only because it could do *nothing at all*. So whereas Hardt and Negri remain allergic to all institutionalization—in theory as in the practice of the Multitude—Dussel is able to formulate a more precise understanding of the dialectical relationship between the people and the state, subjecting institutions permanently and ruthlessly to popular pressure from below, to the demands of this tenuous, variegated multiplicity that is the people.

While rejecting a polar opposition of constituent and constituted powers, however, Dussel's dialectic does not deny the fundamental antagonism between power from below and from above. As a result, the people often appears most clearly and explosively in those moments of rebellion that upend existing orders and demand alternatives. Such moments reflect what Dussel calls *hyperpotentia*, the emergence of the people-in-rebellion, and these moments—in his arguably optimistic view, derived in part from the Argentinian rebellions of late 2001—are capable of subverting and resisting even the sovereign state of emergency.[38] The institutional arrangement toward which this concept of constituent power is oriented, however tentatively, is one that Dussel derives in part from the Zapatista practice of *mandar obedeciendo* (commanding by obeying).

This "obediential power" is *not*, for Dussel, one in which the people serves as a sort of lifeless substrate—or mere "reverberation" in Virno's words—upholding the state. Instead, it is much the opposite: a relation in which the constituent people demands the *obedience* of those delegated to occupy positions of constituted power. Unlike the rigid anti-institutionalism of the theorists of Multitude, Dussel's people instead seeks the practical embodiment of what he had earlier formulated in philosophical terms as "anarchy": to transcend the structures governing the present by appealing to what lies beyond the existing institutional order and even the borders of the system. By drawing together a variegated force comprising all those oppressed by and excluded from the prevailing system, Dussel's people "tears down the walls of Totality and opens a space at the limits of the system through which Exteriority bursts into history."[39]

But here we find some reason to worry: whereas Dussel's previous work had distinguished *two* nationalisms, he tends here toward fixing the meaning of the people rather than accepting its discursive polyvalence, or at least its duality. While he does so not by decontextualizing the concept, but instead by filling it with the contextual meaning given to it by the social movements who claim to represent the people, the risk is the same: to neglect the people as itself a terrain for hegemonic struggle. Ironically, to do so runs the risk of reproducing on the epistemological level the closure he resists on the political level, and thereby of falling into the same error of proponents of the Multitude, albeit in inverted form. If we refuse, against the latter, to grant the people a purely negative content, it would be a mistake—not to mention historically unsustainable—to insist that the people, even in Latin America, is always a progressive or radical identity, always a concept of rupture.

Once we turn to the combative interplay of overlapping and opposed identities that constitutes contemporary Venezuelan political reality, we find confirmed both the profound usefulness of Dussel's concept of the people but also this concern. While popular identity has served the cause of revolution, it has served the cause of reaction as well, and if anything, the past half-century has witnessed a struggle—theoretical as well as practical, in the halls of power and in the streets—to seize the banner of the people. This struggle broke out into open combat now more than twenty-five years ago in the explosive appearance of hyperpotentia known as the Caracazo rebellion. In February of 1989, poor Venezuelans took to the streets en masse, rejecting a government-imposed neoliberal reform by rioting and looting for nearly a week. And it is by tracking the revolutionary opening and subsequent interplay of forces that this rebellion unleashed that we can best approximate the meaning of popular identity in Venezuela today.

"El Pueblo Está Bravo"

In the early 1960s, Rómulo Betancourt—the putative "founder" of Venezuelan democracy—denounced the concept of the people in the most scathing terms, insisting that "the people in the abstract does not exist," but instead only represents "an entelechy which professional demagogues use in seeking to upset the social order."[40] Against this dangerous abstraction—directly evocative of late-nineteenth-century anxieties about crowd psychology—Betancourt offered a corporatist view in which the people is simply the sum of the "political parties, unions, organized economic sectors, professional societies, university groups."[41] It was on the basis of this other conception of the people—not centripetal unification and homogenization but instead the corporatist structuring of difference and the channeling of dissent—that Betancourt spearheaded the establishment of a two-party political system that, while renowned abroad for its exceptional stability, was powerfully antidemocratic and exclusionary.

Betancourt had every reason to fear the people: he had already confronted them in the heady Venezuelan streets. Shortly after representative democracy was established in 1958, the poor and excluded, the workers, peasants, and students—all took advantage of both the radical exuberance of the moment and the new freedoms they had won to press forward, and when they did so, it was more often than not under the banner of the insurgent pueblo. Unwilling to concede, Betancourt increasingly faced what Dussel would term the hyperpotentia of the state of rebellion, and responded with a state of exception that would last much of his presidency. Virno's methodological cue here rings true: having "tenaciously" fought the people in the streets, Betancourt could see even more clearly than Virno himself the revolutionary threat posed by popular identity.

Whereas Sorel and Fanon distinguish between two violences—liberatory versus hierarchical—and Fanon and Dussel distinguish two nationalisms on similar grounds, Betancourt's very fear of the people forces him to mark a similar distinction between opposing forms of the people: one unitary, upholding the social order; the other combative, "seeking to upset" that order. His anxieties allowed him to grasp the fact that the pueblo was indeed protean and amorphous, as divided in itself as it is divisive of society, in short, radically dangerous to men like himself who sought only to control and channel its energies. And in denouncing "the people" as entelechic, Betancourt wore on his sleeve an unmistakable dread that this power might become actualized in a combative unification geared above all toward disrupting the status quo and pressing a new dialectics into motion.

This duality at the heart of the people was nothing new even in the Venezuelan context, and the war of position for its meaning is visible even in Venezuela's peculiarly combative national anthem—"Gloria Al Bravo Pueblo"—which at its most literal means "Glory to the Brave People." Boasting radical phrases such as "Down with chains!" and "Death to oppression!," the anthem is nevertheless open to a multiplicity of contrasting interpretations that have put it historically in the service of both the constituted power of the state and constituent upsurges against that state: "Invoked in official contexts, such as the state ceremonial occasion and the school salute to the flag, the hymn embalmed the *bravo pueblo* in the distant past; to sing it spontaneously in a popular assault on the street was to resuscitate it as a living critique, not a ratification of authority."[42]

As the Venezuelan political system became more rigid and social inequalities—masked temporarily by the oil boom of the 1970s—exploded, the radical resignification of popular identity from below gained pace. This often began with the anthem itself, and as the "virtue and honor" it extolled increasingly gave way to the "vile selfishness" it decried, the peculiar double valence of the pueblo extended as well to that term that most frequently modifies it in Venezuelan discourse: *bravo*. While literally meaning "brave," *bravo* increasingly took on the radical content of the people itself as a combative identity, instead assuming its colloquial meaning—angry, pissed-off, or fed up with a state of affairs. Hence, the simple inversion through which "Gloria al Bravo Pueblo" (Glory to the Brave People) becomes "¡El pueblo está bravo!" (the people are fed up), a radical reappropriation that appeared not infrequently daubed in graffiti as the Venezuelan crisis of the 1980s deepened.

The radical reappropriation of "Gloria al Bravo Pueblo," and the combative notion of the people at its heart, would find no better expression than revolutionary folk singer Alí Primera, whose own vocal texts gained a historical weight among disaffected Venezuelans that was arguably second only to the anthem itself. Appropriately nicknamed "the people's singer," Primera used his music to forge a very different understanding of popular identity than that of Betancourt and the representatives of constituted power, and one that—in its mythical combativeness and attention to structures of colonization and exclusion—shares much with a decolonized dialectics. Despite Primera's own critique of abstraction coupled with exaggerated humility—"You'll have to pardon me, sir, I do not know how to philosophize: I am the one who rises up"—we cannot ignore the real theorizing that he himself does and the kernel of a people-as-struggle that this statement already contains.[43]

In the context of deepening economic and political crisis, Primera turned the national anthem itself into a veritable battle hymn for popular struggles, prefacing his rendition of the anthem to an audience in Barquisimeto with the following words: "To purify it, to purify it among ourselves, to purify it in our hands, in our hearts, in our eyes, in our soul. To purify it for the times they have stained it. Our people's highest song, the song forged in the paths and the battles that gave us the name of Venezuelans, of the homeland. The song of always, the song of the birds, of the children, the song of Venezuelan unity, the song of future combat."[44] In the simultaneous appeal to a dialectics of unity and combat, we find the same ambiguity that makes the people so incomprehensible to Hardt, Negri, and Virno and so dangerous to Betancourt. What may seem a contradiction, however, is only resolved temporally through the constant and open-ended struggle that defines our decolonized dialectics: there can be no unity until after combat, and it is in the assertion of the need for such "future combat" that the universal is continually displaced.

Primera himself was acutely aware of the ambiguities of the people and even the anthem, singing on another occasion: "Our best president sang the national anthem, 'Gloria al Bravo Pueblo,' and the gringo said: *yes!* Why do they call the people brave if they sell them out; why do they say 'bravo pueblo' if they sheath it [*lo envainan*]?"[45] The people here figures as a weapon, whose intrinsic and double-edged sharpness means that those in power must "sheath it" if they are to avoid cutting themselves as well.[46] For Primera, "the verses of the people can be flowers or bullets," and if this were not perfectly clear, he drives this distinction *into* violence itself in a manner similar to Sorel and Fanon by distinguishing between "the bullet that defends [the people], or the bullet that kills [the people]."[47]

Given this ambiguous dualism at the heart of the pueblo, it must—as Dussel similarly argues—be fabricated, constructed, mythically drawn together into a combative unity, in a process that for Primera is akin to the patient sculpting of a hard wood: "We will make of this wood a hand to strike powerfully at those who have always struck and struck, struck at us."[48] This source of this popular unity, moreover, draws upon the structurally irrational Manichaean division of the country and the situation of exclusion and exteriority in which the poorest live: "I come from where you have never gone . . . the other Venezuela, the Venezuela of the poor, the Venezuela with no reason, no reason to exist."[49] Far from indicating any completeness, finally, this popular unity remains a unity *against*, a unity premised on antagonistic rupture. If Dussel described liberation as "the act that opens the breach," it is perhaps no coincidence that Alí Primera's work can be best summarized in precisely those same terms, by the single exhortation with which he named an entire album: *Abrebrecha.*[50]

The Virtues of Polarization

It is only more recently that this war of position over the meaning of the people has broken out into an open war of maneuver. But if this genealogy grants local content to the popular identity at the heart of Venezuelan struggles today, what is the nature of the "local" dialectics—to use Jameson's term—that this reconceptualized people inhabits and propels? Venezuela was for decades assumed to be an island of stability in a tempestuous region, an "exceptional" democracy that some have even retrospectively described in the very terms that would most make someone like Sorel cringe: "social harmony." While most observers today admit that this harmony was mythical, a mere "illusion," even the falsest of universals can constitute real barriers to dialectical struggle.[51] This was not a deterministic or self-propelling dialectics of any sort, then, but instead a one-sided dialectics against all odds, tasked with overcoming frozen unity to set history once again into motion.

Inversely, too, many among the right-wing opposition today maintain the mourning tone of someone who has lost something tangible. There is no better proof of the contradictory attachment to the myth of unity lost than contemporary denunciations of the governments of Hugo Chávez and now Nicolás Maduro as violent, "polarizing," and even "Manichaean."[52] According to such arguments, *despite* the fact that Venezuela's golden age was in reality not so golden, *despite* the fact that it was far from the harmonious whole it is often presented as having been, Chavistas are nevertheless guilty of destroying that unity and paving the way for social conflict, class rancor, and even demonization and hatred. While it might be tempting to dismiss such patently self-contradictory affirmations as the cognitive dissonance of a senile and dying class, I argue that we can *read* in this anxiety toward polarization the concrete effects of a decolonial popular dialectics.[53]

In the words of Íñigo Errejón—a political theorist more recently associated with Spain's radical opposition party, Podemos—when the Venezuelan opposition "accuse[s] the Bolivarian Revolution of polarization, they are accusing it of politicizing the poverty and exclusion" that already existed.[54] The Bolivarian Revolution itself has not divided the country, but merely revealed the divisions that were its own raison d'être, converting these into the basis for a combative and oppositional popular identity. Thus many Chavistas respond to such panicked denunciations of polarization with a viral image showing the sprawling slum of Petare in eastern Caracas sitting just across the highway from middle-class high-rises—the epitome of a segregated landscape and the historical sedimentations of class. The caption reads: "It was Chávez who divided us?" If Errejón echoes the two fundamental components of Dussel's pueblo in his reference to both "poverty and exclusion," this is no accident, because rather than merely revealing an underlying *class* opposition, the revelatory "polarization" of Venezuelan society in recent years has occurred against the backdrop of an exclusion that reaches even the ontological level.

According to one fearful critic, while Chávez's "rhetoric and politics have encouraged social division," "*his very image* has shaken up the beehive of social harmony . . . *His image* upsets the wealthy women of Caurimare," and "*his image* has polarized perceptions."[55] Chávez was guilty, it seems, of being seen in public as an Afro-Indigenous man, and moreover for his meddling in that most public of realms: the political. Here, again, Fanon and Gordon resonate: for the racialized subject to even *appear* constitutes a violent act to the prevailing system and, for our purposes, represents as well that necessarily violent gateway toward Being. According to one Chavista, what happened was not that Chávez himself "sowed hatred among Venezuelans" but instead that the long-standing "contempt" of elites toward the poor and dark skinned "turned into hatred" once he had appeared in public, and that hatred was powerfully ontological.[56] If one of the virtues of open dialectical combat is that it tears back the veil of polite society, nowhere is this clearer than in the brutally honest admission by some of just how ontological their loss has proven. While this ontologized hatred has most often taken the form of an upsurge in racism and classism, the two often indistinguishable, it appears most pointedly (and colonially) in those formulations that lack a subject entirely.

Take, for example, a recent article published by the actor Miguel Ángel Landa who, like a child throwing a tantrum or Hume's famous solipsistic preference that half the world be destroyed before he were to prick his own finger, puts things as clearly as one might hope in his title: "Venezuela Disappeared." Landa's erasure of Chavistas as even marginally human is far from a mere provocation or slip of the pen, however. He goes on to mourn a country that "has become a *landfill* and an insane asylum, inhabited by strange and unpredictable subjects, without *taxonomy*."[57] On display here is an essential aspect of colonial domination that Fanon described as "the decision, literally, to occupy nothing else but a territory," rendering all else— people included—part of "the *natural* backdrop."[58] What is mourned is not undifferentiated uniformity but the structured ontological hierarchy of taxonomy. According to such a view, even total destruction is preferable to the nonhierarchical intermixing of Being with mere beings: as one wealthy Venezuelan put it in an oft-mocked 2013 short film about the travails of young elites, "Caracas would be so perfect without the people."[59]

Not only does this openly ontological hatred point toward the expansive nature of the dialectics in question, but it confirms Fanon's insistence that nothing is worse than "contempt" for humanity and that the transition from this to open hatred was almost always a sign of historical progress. In direct response to Landa's eulogy for a lost Venezuela that was his alone, one organic intellectual of Chavismo replied by agreeing with "this total son of a bitch": "Yes, Miguel Ángel, you cocksucker, of course you lost your country, that infected thing that you dare to call 'Venezuela.' Now the country belongs to us, the poor, those who previously kissed your feet and who today understand that you're no special being, but only a piece of meat and bone like anyone else. Your privileged country is gone, you piece of shit."[60]

It is from the sad laments of such opposition intellectuals that we can perhaps best grasp what is gained when the oppressed shift from being ignored, to being hated, to themselves hating in turn: "The balance has been broken and the Other appears . . . transformed into the enemy . . . Chávez, with increasing belligerency, has identified an Other for them . . . he has given the enemy a face."[61] While many wealthy Venezuelans dismiss the hatred of the poor as mere "resentment," Fanon helps us to see how the identification of an enemy indicates that real progress has been made on the ontological level.[62]

Combative Dialectics

But was the Caracazo and the rupture it marked dialectical or analectical, in the language of Dussel? Did it cleave an internal rupture or one oriented outward, toward the exteriority of non-Being? Was the 1989 rebellion in the streets the action of the "oppressed" or the "excluded"? The answer, unsurprisingly, is *both*. Yes, poor Venezuelans were and continue to be the "oppressed" in Dussel's formulation, but this oppression is not as far from "exclusion" as we might initially assume, and like Dussel's formulation more generally, the distinction between the two also cuts across individual subjects.

Hence an Afro-Venezuelan can be excluded—indeed, invisibilized—on the basis of race while being included-as-oppressed as a member of the working class; an informal worker can be included ethnically within the predominant image of Venezuelan-ness and simultaneously excluded from the aboveground functioning of the economy; a beauty queen of the sort Venezuela is famous for can epitomize beauty standards while being condemned to the occluded sphere of reproductive labor in the home; and anyone not simultaneously white, wealthy, and in possession of cultural capital would likely find herself excluded from the twin pillars—the media and the political system—that upheld the old political system. Not only were poor, indigenous, and Afro-Venezuelans almost entirely absent from the media, beyond heavily stereotyped roles, but barriers to acquiring the identification cards necessary to even vote meant that many poor Venezuelans simply *did not exist* in the public life of the nation (as late as Chávez's election of 1998, the electoral registry contained a mere 47 percent of the population, a number which by 2012 had reached nearly 65 percent).[63]

The political subjects enacting this inverted hatred in the streets were thus not simply those "oppressed" by a prior political system that was cynically dressed up in the language of "social harmony." Rather, the prevailing sense of social harmony was in fact *constituted by* their absence, their invisibility, their exclusion, and their banishment to the realm of exteriority in one or more aspects of life. But beginning above all with the explosive hyperpotentia of the Caracazo, their existence could no longer be denied: the poor and dark skinned—the politically, economically, and "mediatically" excluded members of Venezuelan society—"came down from the hills" and took over the cities in a gesture that could only be interpreted as an *invasion*—the entrance of the barbarian hordes into the realm of Being.

If the Caracazo undeniably constituted a moment of radical rupture *internal* to the social totality—carried out mostly by Venezuelan citizens—it nevertheless appeared to those elites who felt most threatened by it as a rupture at the furthest reaches of Being, a wound through which previously nonexistent poor and racialized subjects poured into the social body, infecting it. This expanding and combative people had come into being in the very moment that they shook the frontiers of Being, shattering the mythical façade of Venezuelan harmony and rushing forward relentlessly, with little attention paid to the sometimes-dangerous shards that remained.

The fact that their appearance has been decried as "polarization," as division rather than invisibility, simply proves that it has worked. In their anxiety toward polarization, therefore, Venezuela's traditional intellectuals—and I use the term as pejoratively as possible—actually help us to see that the motion underway in Venezuela today is indeed dialectical, and in their mourning of the ontological exclusions of lost (false) universals and their desperate, visceral fear of the newly empowered masses, they reveal that this is a truly decolonized dialectics as well. What has come since has only confirmed that a combative and oppositional understanding of popular identity is far more illuminating of the trajectory unleashed by the Caracazo than antidialectical theories of the Multitude.

If the direct and unmediated explosion of the Caracazo might seem initially compatible with the Multitude, this view is misleading even for grasping the 1989 rebellion itself, much less the chain reaction that has come since.[64] Even amid the rebellion, dialectical fibers stretched backward in those organized elements of the postguerrilla struggle who threw themselves into the upsurge, and forward in those who were already conspiring—both inside the military and outside—to overthrow the existing order. Against romantic celebration of the Multitude, in other words, this was a rebellion that contained important organized elements and that moreover couched its demands explicitly in a radical conception of the bravo pueblo.

And if "exteriority burst into history" during the Caracazo, then that same exteriority burst into Venezuelan political life in 1992, when Hugo Chávez—responding to the Caracazo itself—led a failed coup that laid the symbolic groundwork for his winning the presidency six years later.[65] The coalition that propelled Chávez to power was in many ways an expression of the same social subject that had taken violently to the streets in 1989, and while the trajectory since has not been without its complexities, it embodies in many ways Dussel's dialectic of constituent and constituted powers, which has in the process allowed the deepening of the constituent elements of popular identity. This is a process that has never shied away from walking the fine line between *potentia* and *potestas*, a radically dialectical engagement with state power, with political leadership and the party form, and with the difficult process of constructing what has come to be known as Twenty-First Century Socialism in the dynamic interplay of power "from below" and "from above."

Moreover, alongside this state-movement dialectic, recent years have demonstrated nothing so clearly as the thesis often attributed to Marx of the "whip of the counter-revolution," in which the antagonism of anti-Chavista forces, especially during moments of heightened conflict, has often sparked a radicalization of the process itself. This was nowhere as clear as with the brief coup of 2002 that removed Chávez from power for less than two days. In the process of mobilizing to reverse the coup through a massive display of constituent power in the streets, the Bolivarian process gained an unprecedented momentum that allowed—indeed, forced—a radicalization. In the words of Roland Denis, a radical intellectual on the leftist fringe of Chavismo, the Bolivarian process has had the virtue of moving "from event to event"—that is, from 1989 to 2002—and the energy gleaned from resisting this second event helped to fuel the expansion first of directly democratic communal councils, and more recently, a national network of communes.[66]

We have seen the emerging dialectic between Chavistas and the opposition, whose division manifests under the fearful code word *polarization*, and the dynamic dialectic of potentia from below with potestas from above. But it remains to be seen by what subdialectical oppositions the Venezuelan pueblo itself is constituted, and whether as a result it maintains the internal heterogeneity of Dussel's concept. Charting this movement, however, requires bringing popular identity in Venezuela into relation with the many overlapping identities with which it interacts on an everyday basis and which as a result help to constitute it and inform its content.

Soy Chavista, ¿Y Qué?

In an article published as Chávez lay mortally ill in Cuba, former Venezuelan vice president Elías Jaua sketched a genealogy of the multiple political identities at the combative heart of the Bolivarian process. While the category of the pueblo is undeniably central, Jaua emphasized a different and often misconstrued political identity that has arguably come to serve as a local and historically contextual manifestation of that people in motion: Chavismo. Jaua recounts that in the years following Chávez's failed coup of 1992 and even after his election, "very few people identified themselves as Chavista," instead opting for a broad "Bolivarian" identity that had emerged from the process of theoretical experimentation in the 1970s that followed the defeat of the guerrilla struggle.

Chavista identity emerged only later, amid the heightened conflict with the opposition that ultimately led to the failed coup of 2002, and specifically from a sort of dialectical tug-of-war with the opposition over who could rightly lay claim to the legacy of Bolívar himself:

> The moment that the dominant elites decided to put an end to this revolutionary experiment, they used their entire arsenal of social hatred against the poor people who followed Comandante Chávez. That's how they added the new epitaph "Chavista" in the singular and "Chavista hordes" . . . in the plural, to the long and historic list of adjectives used to criminalize the people (lowlife, hordes, bandits, black trash, thugs, etc).
>
> In reality this was an attempt to strip us of our identity as Bolivarians, it was the oligarchy's final attempt to preserve the term Bolivarian within the moldy archives of the academies of history. But not only were they not able to steal from us the conscious name of "children of Bolívar," but we took on the name Chavista as well, resignifying it with dignity . . . "*Soy chavista ¿y qué?* I'm a Chavista, so what?"[67]

The attempt to impose Chavismo as an identity was, in fact, an attempt to saddle radical Venezuelan movements with a pejorative notion of the people as well—what traffics so often under the term *populism*. It was an attempt, in other words, to present the followers of Chávez as mere followers and nothing more, naively beguiled by a charismatic *caudillo*. But rather than rejecting this imposed identity, the movements took it up, inverted its meaning, and sharpened it as a weapon to suit their own purposes.

This failed rhetorical strategy of the opposition allows us to grasp with utter clarity not only the centrality of political identities for the revolutionary process in Venezuela, but also the dynamic movement of those identities: a counterattack on the popular appropriation of Bolívar helped to heat the crucible of struggle in a way that blended and even fused identities, endowing them with new dialectical content. This pattern would repeat often, as when Chávez himself responded to the demonization of his supporters as *chusma*—which translates as lowlifes, riffraff, or even scum—by embracing and even celebrating the term: "Yes, we are the same *chusma* that followed Bolívar!" As though intent on missing the point, one opposition commentator described Chávez's dialectical inversion as "vomiting class hatred."[68]

It was in part through this struggle over identities that the Bolivarian process itself was dramatically radicalized. Once Chavismo was consolidated as a weapon in the arsenal of Venezuelan revolutionaries, it was far from either the personalistic identification of media caricature or the reductive homogenization that Virno and others associate with the people. It instead denotes today a popular subject with a clear class content, but also—in the words of Reinaldo Iturriza—a "common experience of politicization" marked by participation in the Caracazo, supporting the coup of 1992, and resisting that of 2002. Chavismo in this sense—like Dussel's pueblo—is not a sociological category but a dynamic relation, a *becoming* that Iturriza describes in terms similar to those of Alain Badiou's theory of the event: "Rebellion is a political event of the first order. Even before being recognized as such, Chavismo was incorporated into the political in the act of rebellion. It is inconceivable without this collective memory, without this shared notion of rebellion: it is in this rebellion that these men and women come together and are politicized, their baptism by fire." Despite this common experience and opposition to a common enemy, Chavismo nevertheless remains a "vigorous subject of subjects" that, while aspiring toward the universal, never sheds its own particulars.[69]

With his failed coup in 1992 and his televised surrender—during which he promised that the rebels had only failed "*por ahora*, for now"—"Chávez invaded the life of Venezuelans as pure conflict, a head-on and public contestation of the existing order."[70] In the words of one founder of the Venezuelan two-party system, Rafael Caldera: "Venezuela was like a showcase window for Latin American democracy. The inhabitants of the Caracas hills smashed that window when they descended, enraged, in February 1989. Today it has again been broken by the rifle-butts and the weapons in the hands of the revolting soldiers."[71] The "Chávez myth" functioned much like Sorel's revolutionary myth: establishing an antagonistic frontier that both deepened the rupture of social harmony inaugurated in 1989 and provided a combative border along which a popular identity could be stitched together.

Chávez's failed coup provided, in the words of Errejón,

> a symbol around which the unsatisfied demands of different social sectors were able to link with one another, which with Chávez as a catalyst passed from fragments to components of a *people* in gestation . . . His radical boundary position vis-à-vis the Venezuelan political scene allowed Chávez to be a name and an inscription surface for a heterogeneous totality of social positions and aspirations, which were not reducible to any of the previously existing ideological frameworks. This popular field is held together by dates and symbols, emotions, shared descriptions of reality, values, and a common horizon for the country, which allow us to speak of a political identity that, as we have maintained, is not only the majority but also relatively hegemonic: Chavismo.

The emergence of Chavismo "erected a new border ordering the loyalties of Venezuelan society, transforming a privileged minority into a political minority and the dispossessed majorities into a project for the construction of a 'people' demanding representation for the entire community."[72] This gap between the now and the future reflects a Sorelian commitment to subjectively established combat; a Fanonian attentiveness to struggle that is "grounded in temporality," granting weight to dialectical momentum; and a Dusselian insistence on a politics that expands toward exteriority, in which present struggles by a part gesture toward a future whole that is both enlarged and radically reconfigured.

Ociel Alí López similarly describes the emergence of this popular subject from the 1992 coup as an "intellectual *sacudón*," a term that translates as a shock or shakeup, but which also refers obliquely to the Caracazo itself.[73] Echoing Dussel's rebellious hyperpotentia, López describes Chavismo as a "hyperactive subject" that "establishes a historical rupture."[74] Moreover, echoing Sorel, this is a subject capable of acting upon both sides of the dialectical opposition: by confronting what he calls *sifrinaje*, the snobbish cultural identity of historical elites and their attempts to pathologize the poor, "Chavismo gave meaning to both its partisans and its detractors."[75] These two sides, however, do not constitute a society without remainder, and López here echoes Errejón's insistence on an expansive reordering of societal loyalties, in which Chavismo provides "a device [*dispositivo*] for interpellating society as a whole" that "far exceeds those who represent and manage it" and through which "something larger than the country was transmitted virally into the minds inhabiting a territory."[76] And this "something larger" that exceeds the whole is the reemergence of a popular bloc from the realm of exteriority: "Struggling against exclusion and the colonial legacy [coloniaje]," Chavismo breaks with "western modernity," driving forth a decolonized dialectic.[77]

The dynamic and overlapping movement of these multiple identities in Venezuela today preserves the heterogeneity of the popular bloc, the part that aspires ultimately to re-create the whole. This is a people that is many things at the same time: it is poor, it is African descended, it is Indigenous, it is women, it is students; it is the informal sector, the workers, the peasants, and the lumpen—all gradually consolidating what Dussel terms an "analogical hegemon" or a "social bloc of the oppressed" and excluded. And each of these constituent elements of the pueblo, in their struggles and their development, maintain to some degree their own dynamic that operates as a sort of subdialectic or dialectic-within-a-dialectic.

The occasionally decisive function of these subdialectics becomes more concrete through an example—perhaps the most important example— the dialectic of racism and the Afro-Venezuelan movements that have emerged in opposition to it. Afro-Venezuelan movements are flourishing today under the broader aegis of the people, and generally with the support of the Bolivarian Revolution. But until recently, these movements confronted even within Chavismo a stubborn ideology of *mestizaje*, which insists that by virtue of a long history of ethnic intermixture, all Venezuelans are mixed and so racism couldn't possibly exist.[78] As a false universal, this ideology stands as a barrier to dialectical motion much like what Fanon confronted in *Black Skin, White Masks*, and upholds white supremacy in the process.

When Afro-movements began to challenge this ideology, they were opposed even by many high-ranking Chavistas, but when the (sub)dialectics of race began to interact with the broader dialectics of the people, both underwent a qualitative leap. In the crucible of conflict that eventually led up to the failed 2002 coup against Chávez, the heat of political struggles and their sharpened polarization allowed not only the forging and consolidation of identities but also their blending and alloying. As anti-Chavistas became more brazen, their language became more openly racist, with some publicly describing Chávez in racialized terms and graffiti reading, "Out with the vermin" and "Death to the monkey Chávez!"[79] It was this heightened combat that forced Chávez and others to finally recognize the centrality of white supremacy (and colonialism) and to increasingly insist that the Venezuelan pueblo was, at its heart, African and indigenous.

Now, the more Afro-Venezuelans organize and Chavistas identify with their struggles, the more the popular bloc as a whole is racially "overdetermined" (in Fanon's terms)—unified in the eyes of its opponents, for whom racism and class hatred blend effortlessly together. A virtuous subcycle of polarization radicalizes both consciousness and organizing in a dialectical manner, strengthening the internal bonds that draw the people together. The struggle of Afro-Venezuelans thus reflects in microcosm a broader decolonized dialectic of popular identity: combatively struggling around race even against the denials of comrades, the movements were able to push their demands in such a way that through outright combat with the opposition, they were taken up as common currency and as component elements of popular identity as a whole.

In this way, the people functions as an identity of identities, drawing together various subidentities—often with their own subdialectics—into a broader horizon and antagonistic frontier. While the struggles of Afro-Venezuelans confirm Dussel's approach, in which a decolonized dialectics finds its central foothold in the nonbeing of exteriority, the combativity it entails is not reserved solely for the Venezuelan opposition, but also functions within the popular bloc. The subdialectics of race thus appear to share more with Fanonian explosiveness than Dussel's cheery description of "dialogue and translation." As the founder of the Afro-Venezuelan Network, Jesús "Chucho" García once told me, even professed revolutionaries did not always voluntarily embrace struggles over race: "It was only as a result of us fighting them and all of the *coñazos*, the blows that we gave them, that some openness developed."[80] Combativeness even within popular identity, an expression of its persistent heterogeneity, was thus central to its radicalization.

It would be a mistake, however, to raise this radicalized and decolonized concept of the people to the status of a new universal, declaring popular identity *the* relevant category for all struggles, and this would moreover violate the internal multiplicity and heterogeneity of the people itself. However, it must be observed that popular identity seems peculiarly well suited to what Aníbal Quijano, following Mariátegui, terms the "historical-structural heterogeneity" of coloniality, the overlapping multiplicity of relations of production that texture the still-colonial world.[81] As a result, we could say that Jameson's general imperative toward a "multiplicity of local dialectics," while not strictly decolonial, nevertheless opens in a decolonial direction.[82] With the proliferation of multiple dialectics and the mobility of the identities involved, the broader movement becomes more contingent and open ended, less predictable, any particular outcome less certain. With so many factors, identities, and movements crashing and banging around, there can be no ceteris paribus, no scientific holding of constants.

What remains is a modified war of position in which determinism dissipates and even small minorities can force broader dynamics into motion. This is especially true of those emergences that leap forth unpredictably from exteriority, violent shocks to the symbolic order through which external diversity becomes internal difference as the totality itself is radically transformed. As we have seen, however, this multiplicity of dialectics does not preclude their dynamic interaction and even tense unity, and this multiplication of local dialectics in Venezuela—popular, racial, gendered, class based—has also coincided with their progressive unification, stitched together in a combative tapestry that, if singular, disintegrates outward at the edges. In this increasingly unified heterogeneity, in the recognition by popular movements that no path is laid out before them and no victory guaranteed except through their own sacrifice, and in the real progress that has already been made in revealing the nonbeing of exclusion and tearing down the apartheid walls upholding it, we can see that we are in the presence of a powerfully decolonized dialectics.

Of Pigs and Chigüires

Where does Venezuela's decolonized dialectic lead? If we have learned anything, it is that any decisive answer would be hubristic and would risk short-circuiting the very dynamics that have allowed it to emerge. What is clear is that it orients toward that dialectical placeholder that has come to be called Twenty-First-Century Socialism, which both in its content and its self-constitution is an open-ended construction with decolonial inspirations. It was above all that decolonial thinker par excellence Mariátegui who broke with the imposed dogma of official socialism earlier and more firmly than most, all in an effort not to impose another model but to think socialism again, differently. And it is in this same spirit that the Bolivarian process moves forward along the path that Mariátegui had indicated but not trodden, doing so under the sign of another, more local imperative that nevertheless retains the same openness of spirit: that of Bolívar's own teacher Simón Rodríguez, today upheld as one of the "three roots" of Bolivarian ideology, who famously insisted, "*O inventamos o erramos*—Either we invent, or we err."[83]

This future is not guaranteed, of course, although we should not mistake the open-endedness of its dialectics for a weakness, even though a surer design might avoid perilous detours along the way. The greatest weakness of all would be to insist on a singular or preordained path for the many dialectics that—tensely unified—have allowed the Bolivarian process to move forward, sometimes decisively, sometimes hesitantly. Our orientation toward this process cannot therefore be to attempt to leap forward, predicting the parameters of its ultimate reconciliation, but instead to inhabit the center of the dialectic, pressing outward to maintain a space for revolutionary combat to play its unpredictable historic role. Once we assume this position, however, other dangers emerge more clearly, particularly those that threaten to halt the struggle, to preemptively declare its conclusion, and to contain popular demands within a newly established false universal.

Not even the figure of Chávez himself is immune to this threat, especially after his death in early 2013. Just as previous generations of Venezuelan leaders had, in Chávez's words, "sanctified Bolívar" in order to "depoliticize him," so too could we say that in pointing to this sanctification, Chávez was foretelling his own future. According to Errejón, those who were unable to defeat Chávez in life have taken a different tack after his death. They who once yoked their poor enemies with the name of Chávez only to have this strategy backfire are now intent on "depoliticizing Chávez and dispersing Chavismo" in part because they themselves must slip the yoke of being simply "anti-Chavistas." Where Chávez in life stood for "pure conflict" and succeeded by sharpening polarization and rupturing society in a way that revealed underlying oppressions and exclusions, many in the opposition "now aim to erase that border by transforming Chávez into a beautiful historic memento and Chavismo into the non-political act of mourning an individual." The goal is to make of Chávez not a boundary figure, but an "ideological transversal," "a central point of reference in Venezuelan political culture that no longer provokes conflicts," a figure of "consensus."[84]

In other words, they seek to transform this dialectically potent figure into an empty symbol for all Venezuelans, a marker of premature reconciliation. If this practice of emptying Chávez of political content begins with the erasure of that antagonistic frontier he helped to inaugurate, then the task before radical Chavistas is, according to Errejón, much like that faced by Sorel, Fanon, and Dussel in turn: to reestablish and "discursively manage" this combative frontier. "Chavismo is tendentially for (almost) everyone but it is not just anything, and nor does just any content fit within it. As a result, it is fundamental to construct its 'outside' carefully and manage the inclusion-exclusion game with flexibility, seducing immediately while at the same time deploying political pedagogy that will cultivate positions of the future."[85] This carefulness and this flexibility reflect the simultaneous task of maintaining the dialectical opposition that Chavismo marks while also pointing beyond it, in an openness toward the exteriority that Chavismo helped to gather.

The danger of Chavismo becoming its opposite would seem a characteristically dialectical one, but the stakes are all the higher for a decolonized dialectics that guarantees no progress, only the combatively one-sided imposition of a new reality. This is a task that, concretely, requires *both* unity *and* difference, within the people as well as between those people and the institutionalized power of the state. During the last months of his life, Chávez insisted on both, demanding "unity, unity, and more unity!" within the movement while making clear that this was not a "centripetal" unity, and much less the totalizing unity of Venezuelans as a whole. It was instead a tense dialectical unity-in-combat that his most radical disciples have since used as a foothold to press radically forward with the expansively dialectical task of building a truly inclusive revolutionary society that abolishes oppression as it overcomes exclusion.

It would be no surprise, then, that while insisting on unity in his now famous *Golpe de Timón* speech—whose title indicates a sharp change in course, and which has come to represent his last political will and testament—Chávez also insisted on the expansion of the dream of the "communal state." This ambitious multiplication of spaces for popular participation—from communal councils to larger and more ambitious self-governed units such as communes and communal cities—in its own way seeks to encompass dialectical opposition while expanding toward exteriority. According to Iturriza, the communal councils were created not "to domesticate Chavismo, to mold it in the image and similarity of the same." Instead, these local institutions of direct self-governance—established above all in the sprawling slums that were both systematically excluded by previous governments and represent the bedrock of support for Chavismo—grew out of the fact that residents of those *barrios* "are recognized as other, as something different, as a subject that points toward the construction of an-other politics." Such councils thus overcome both the anti-institutionalism of the Multitude and the blindness of its theorists toward the dynamically expansive potential of the people as a political subject, "incorporating those from below, guaranteeing them a space, a place" from which to keep fighting.[86]

In his *Golpe de Timón* speech, delivered just months before his death, Chávez recounted a well-known joke about an Indigenous community and a Catholic priest. It was Holy Week, and the priest—seeing a fattened pig nearby—reminded the community that they were not allowed to eat pork that week, only fish or the large amphibious rodent known as *chigüire*, or capybara. The priest then took several community members to the river to be baptized with Christian names. When the priest returned later that day to find the community dancing and roasting the recently slaughtered pig, he was appalled. Their response, which Chávez playfully recounted to highlight the danger of merely calling things "socialist" while capitalism remains intact, stands also as a testament to both subaltern cunning and a subversively decolonial dialectic: "No, we solved the problem. We baptized this pig and named it *chigüire*."[87]

SPIRALS

LEST THE UNDERLYING CHRONOLOGICAL architectonics of this book be seen as reinscribing the very same linear, deterministic, and progressive teleology that the thinkers in question contest, I conclude without concluding, and prior to where I began. The decolonized dialectics of Frantz Fanon and Enrique Dussel exist independently of George Sorel's dialectics of class struggle; he is not their origin, source, or mandatory point of departure. While global capitalism and coloniality emerged so jointly as to be nearly synonymous, and while many decolonial revolutionaries have turned to Marxism as a weapon, decolonization itself is not an outgrowth of—and much less does it find its "parentage" in—the class struggle.[1] More importantly still, a decolonized (and decolonizing) dialectics—understood as a radical practice and orientation toward struggle—predates, exceeds, and exists independently of even Hegel's own formulations, in the combative self-assertion, the making known, of colonized and enslaved peoples.

Without ever having read a word of Hegel, the slave-turned-abolitionist orator Frederick Douglass would not only enact and delineate the fundamental contours of the Hegelian master-slave dialectic with an astonishing degree of clarity on the basis of nothing but his own lived experience, but he would also preemptively radicalize that dialectic in a way that foreshadowed the thinkers considered here. Douglass was to be broken by the infamous slave-breaker Edward Covey, a fate that he initially accepted as his destiny, his ontological reduction—what he calls his "brutification"—to a level scarcely above the ox that he himself was tasked with breaking: "break and be broken—such is life."[2] A rationalist like Fanon but a Christian moreover, Douglass first took refuge in these falsest of universals, only to find both shaken, and his eventual fight with Covey is only fully grasped in light of the scenes that precede it. Douglass first beseeched his owner to protect him, if only as property worth preserving, but despite being his *"brother in the church,"* Douglass was unable to transcend the innate "guilt of the slave," or what Fanon would come to call "the racial allocation of guilt."[3] He concluded painfully that "I had no friend on earth, and doubting if I had one in heaven," but this diremptive rupture of human and celestial solidarity, Douglass's condemnation to a "fallen state," was also nevertheless a form of liberation: "My hands were no longer tied by my religion."[4]

Where religion failed, so too did reason and education fail when confronted with the institutionalized unreason of white supremacist violence: "My book learning . . . had not kept Covey off me."[5] The cunning of reason would not provide history with an internal motor pressing toward reconciliation. Even when he later dedicated himself to arguing for abolition—as a physical embodiment of the untruth of slavery's reason—it was evident to Douglass, as it would later be to Fanon, that systems built upon the ontological disqualification of certain subjects are not only themselves irrational, but also impermeable to reason. Opposing them therefore requires a rational resort to unreason, the sort of mythical response that Douglass would later counterpose to reason in no uncertain terms: "Scorching irony, not convincing argument . . . a fiery stream of biting ridicule, blasting reproach, withering sarcasm, and stern rebuke. For it is not light that is needed, but fire; it is not the gentle shower, but thunder. We need the storm, the whirlwind, and the earthquake."[6]

What ensued between Douglass and Covey was indeed a life-or-death struggle like that described by Hegel, but one that did not take place between two ahistorical subjectivities. Instead, it exuded historicity: Covey was an agent of inborn masters, Douglass of inborn slaves. The confrontation was overcoded with ontological inequality from the outset as, in Fanon's words, a struggle in which "the white man is not only 'the Other,' but also the master."[7] Against this ontological disqualification that undercut any basis for reciprocity, Douglass pledged "to *stand up in my own defense*" and "*resolved to fight*," his one-sided activity creating the basis for a brawl between equals. "Strong fingers firmly attached to the throat of my cowardly tormentor," Douglass forcibly created reciprocity of a sort, "as though we stood as equals before the law. The very color of the man was forgotten . . . He held me, and I held him."[8]

Were the stark distinction between liberatory violence and reactionary force not perfectly clear, Douglass's largely defensive posture makes it even more so, and when Covey attempts to recruit his cousin, Douglass responds violently only to restore the purity of the opposition. Moreover, when Covey seeks to enlist his own slaves, they refuse at great personal risk to themselves, feigning ignorance and turning away from the master and toward the object of their work, notwithstanding Covey's quasi-Hegelian imperative: "*This is your work.*"[9] While the physical struggle between Covey and Douglass may have ended in a draw, the victory was Douglass's alone. The two-sided effects of his decolonial violence had (externally) transformed not only his relation with Covey, who "never [again] laid on me the weight of his finger in anger," but more importantly had (internally) radicalized his own self-consciousness as a being worthy of dignity:

> This battle with M. Covey . . . was the turning point in my "*life as a slave.*" It rekindled in my breast the smouldering embers of liberty . . . and revived a sense of my own manhood. I was a changed being after that fight. I was *nothing* before; I WAS A MAN NOW. It recalled to life my crushed self-respect and my self-confidence, and inspired me with a renewed determination to be A FREEMAN. A man without force, is without the essential dignity of humanity . . . He only can understand the effect of this combat on my spirit, who has himself incurred something, hazarded something, in repelling the unjust and cruel aggressions of a tyrant . . . After resisting him, I felt as I had never felt before. It was a resurrection from the dark and pestiferous tomb of slavery, to the heaven of comparative freedom . . . I had reached the point, at which I was *not afraid to die.* This spirit made me a freeman in *fact*, while I remained a slave in *form*. When a slave cannot be flogged he is more than half free . . . the case I have been describing, was the end of the brutification to which slavery had subjected me.[10]

While the similarities to the Hegelian account in this passage are remarkable, so too are the evident tensions with Hegel's dialectic.[11] Specifically, is the insistence that one must be willing to die—more than merely risk life—a break with Hegel's conception, which is as much driven by the *avoidance* of death and the submission to slavery as a result?[12] Or is such willingness a necessary step in the collectivization of any such dialectic, in which some struggle and die whereas others submit and live?[13]

Ultimately, however, this question is inextricably bound up with the question of ontological disqualification particular to racial slavery and colonial domination. For those innately condemned to servitude, the promise that there was no escaping such a condition would drive Douglass and so many others to a situation inconceivable for Hegel: preferring death to continued slavery.[14] Douglass's account of one-sided dialectical struggle and existential freedom from concrete, historical slavery culminates with a quotation from Lord Byron's *Childe Harold's Pilgrimage*, penned only a few years after Hegel's *Phenomenology*, but whose implications are arguably more radical, and peculiarly suited to a decolonized dialectics:

> Hereditary bondsmen, know ye not
> Who would be free,
> themselves must strike the first blow?[15]

The *hereditary* nature of Douglass's bondage, and furthermore its deepening to the ontological level of being itself, entailed—for him as for Fanon and many others before and after—specific barriers that could only be confronted with a one-sided, decolonial violence, the subjective, prediaLectical struggle of *"the first blow,"* to lay the groundwork necessary for dialectical motion to emerge.

Douglass would not be the last Black American to approvingly cite Byron's epic as the expression of a one-sided dialectic of liberation. None other than W. E. B. Du Bois—who certainly *had* read Hegel—also turned to Byron in *The Souls of Black Folk* to frame his opposition to those Black leaders whom he perceived as minimizing "the emasculating effects of caste distinctions." But Du Bois notably included an earlier verse, as though to drive home the dialectical importance of grasping the condition of those disqualified from full humanity: "From birth till death enslaved; in word, in deed, unmanned!"[16] The hopelessness of this passage notwithstanding, the Du Bois of *Souls* nevertheless insisted optimistically—and under a more clearly Hegelian imprimatur—that the "mountain path to Canaan" was "steep and rugged, but straight," only to see such optimism disintegrate during the course of his own book, under the crushing weight of essays like "Of the Coming of John."[17]

Despite the ambivalence of Du Bois's dialectic in *Souls*—which still retained a Hegel-inspired faith in progress and a palpable ambiguity toward the "terrible" Maroons, John Brown, Nat Turner, and Toussaint L'Ouverture—he nevertheless went on to rediscover, in *Black Reconstruction*, revolutionary Black agency where it was invisible to master dialecticians, through a transposition of slaves with workers and slavery with capitalism as a global system. And he also rediscovered something else in the process: a tragic dialectic of reversals, defeats, and missed opportunities;

not a long but heroic march toward a brilliant future but "a brief moment in the sun" before retreating, under the weight of white supremacist terror, "back again toward slavery"; the ostensible built-in progress of the dialectic of history folded back onto itself, beaten and bloodied.[18]

Nowhere is this tragedy of history as visible as in the history from which we began: C. L. R. James's *Black Jacobins*. After all, what was the Haitian Revolution if not a dialectical eruption in the last place master dialecticians would have chosen to look? What explains its systematic erasure and "disavowal" if not the fundamental unthinkability of its content?[19] And what was this content if not the self-activity of slaves as revolutionary subjects capable of generating their *own* history outside and against overarching logics of history? The fact that this same disavowed history would—through a feedback loop—come to provide the unrecognized *content* for what would come to pass as *the* dialectic, in the work of Hegel, only drives home the world-historical nature of the rebellion, as well as the ill-fitting straitjacket of Hegel's progressive teleology.[20]

We can find echoes of this decolonized dialectical practice throughout the entire trajectory of Black struggles against slavery, in figures like Malcolm X, who insisted on reciprocity if only in death—"Let your dying be reciprocal. This is what is meant by equality. What's good for the goose is good for the gander"—only to find his own dialectics of Black identity cut down by twin shotgun blasts.[21] The basic contours of a decolonized dialectics, moreover, are not limited to chattel slavery, but are present throughout the history of decolonial struggles more broadly understood. In Latin America, for example, traditional dialectics—of Hegelian reason or orthodox Marxism—have long proved ill-fitting to local realities, prompting instead the heretical irruption of counterdiscourses to dialectical counterdiscourses, radical breaks with orthodoxy, the spiritualization of a dialectics of subjective struggle à la Mariátegui, and a resistance to developmental stages visible as well in the turn to Cuban-inspired guerrilla warfare in the 1960s. In other words, the conditions of possibility for and resonances of this decolonized dialectics precede, exceed, and will long outlast the individual thinkers considered here.

Diagnosing Colonial Difference

But what are the parameters of such a dialectics? From the parallax movement between the thinkers considered here, and in particular Fanon and Dussel, we can sketch out some initial contours. In a negative gesture, we can find good reasons—theoretical as well as political—for the colonized and enslaved to be skeptical of many elements of traditional dialectics, especially where posed as *the* dialectic: the optimistic determinism of a self-starting and automatic movement in the present, the teleological progressivism that leads incessantly along the predetermined path of this motion, and the fully reconciled "end of history" with which such a dialectic inevitably concludes. For those confronting not motion but stasis, the stubborn resistance of the present, and for whom historical motion has been uncertain at best—small victories, major setbacks, all permeated with ontological force—such dialectical illusions are little more than comfort in suffering. And for those pressing forth struggles on the basis of particularly colonial conditions, to be told that they are doing it all wrong has not added to the allure of the dialectical approach.

Most fundamentally, however, the gap—indeed, chasm—between "the" dialectic and a decolonized dialectic*s* emerges from the diagnosis of the systematic ontologicial disqualification of certain subjects, their relegation to what Fanon calls the "zone of nonbeing" and the slightly different space that Dussel formulates as "exteriority." The productive if imperfect overlap of these concepts, I argue, constitutes a potent fulcrum for theoretical decolonization. It is this ontological difference between full Being and subjected nonbeings—between that which is visible and legible as humanity and that which is relegated to the status of less-than-being—that intervenes to block dialectical movement in the present, and it is in the one-sided overcoming of such ontological apartheid that much of history's combative progress can be mapped. It is in the play between inside and outside, moreover, between aboveground and subterranean, that any and all determinism is lost, that "the" dialectic collapses into many combative moments that nevertheless coalesce into broad oppositions, and that the reconciled horizon of the future remains that and nothing more: a horizon toward which to aim but never reach.

But this zone of nonbeing and exteriority poses a distinct challenge from within dialectical thought that some might deem fatal to the project of decolonizing dialectics as a whole. From a strict Hegelian perspective, to reject the symmetry of oppositions is also to reject the internal ties that bind them together in a dialectical relationship to begin with, rendering the parts mere diversity rather than difference, an external rather than an internal relation. Even in Sorel we saw an effort to deepen the class opposition to the point of utter incommensurability, and a rejection of social duty and ethics that profoundly divided the social totality. Fanon's rejection of the symmetry of the master-slave dialectic, and his insistence that the two sides look *past* one another in a sort of missed encounter grounded in ontological difference, would seem to be in this sense antidialectical, as would his later resort to Manichaeism. Dussel's more explicit turn to exteriority, which brought him to the brink of rejecting dialectics entirely, only serves to underline this chasm between internal and external.

But were this objection to hold, we would be left in a strange impasse. Hegel and arguably the entire dialectical tradition would be left simply incapable of accommodating such central world-historical processes as colonization and chattel slavery, themselves inseparable from modern-colonial capitalism. In other words, a restrictive understanding of internal difference already carries within it all the pretensions of symmetrical Being that so characterize the limitations of the Hegelian system, and which Fanon straightforwardly rejected. In this sense, the frequent resort to theories of multiplicity and the Multitude stand as a sort of inverted Hegelianism that can only take the latter on its own unquestioned terms. If we refuse to condemn dialectics as a whole to such pretensions, if we refuse to choose between dialectics and decolonization, we need to loosen and recast this internal-external relation by walking the fine line between the two, inhabiting the borderlands of nonbeing and exteriority. In this way, we might be able to reformulate and give a new dialectical meaning to what Walter Mignolo and others have called "the colonial difference."

Beyond the either/or of internal versus external difference, dialectics versus decolonization, we are instead tasked with grasping a fundamentally nonsymmetrical system of difference, an ontological distinction between Being and nonbeings that does not slide directly from internal difference to the unrelated contingency of mere diversity or multiplicity. After all, colonization and enslavement are not processes in which individuals and groups simply bump haphazardly into one another. Rather, they denote the sort of specifically one-sided operations to which Hegel was characteristically blind, the utterly nonreciprocal oppression of those deemed not even worthy of recognition—those unnecessary for the development of self-consciousness—and from whom only work, land, or simply death is desired as a result. Instead of simply loosening the bond of dialectical opposition to the point of multiplicity, then, *colonial* difference indicates a more concrete and precise way of grasping those oppositions not visible to a traditional dialectics but whose appearance does not mark the impossibility of dialectics entirely.

If the colonial difference is paradigmatic of such one-sidedness, however, the relevance of a dialectics of exteriority is not limited to the realm of coloniality strictly speaking. Instead, such an orientation provides an entry-point into grasping a much broader illegibility that further underlines the global and historical complicity of race and class. In the words of the Chilean novelist Roberto Bolaño:

> In the seventeenth century, for example, at least twenty percent of the merchandise on every slave ship died. By that I mean the dark-skinned people who were being transported for sale, to Virginia, say. And that didn't get anyone upset or make headlines in the Virginia papers or make anyone go out an call for the ship captain to be hanged. But if a plantation owner went crazy and killed his neighbor and then went galloping back home, dismounted, and promptly killed his wife, two deaths in total, Virginia society spent the next six months in fear . . . Or look at the French. During the Paris Commune of 1871, thousands of people were killed and no one batted an eye. Around the same time a knife sharpener killed his wife and his elderly mother and then he was shot and killed by the police. The story didn't just make all the French newspapers, it was written up in papers across Europe . . . How come? The ones killed in the Commune weren't part of society, the dark-skinned people who died on the ship weren't part of society, whereas the woman killed in a French provincial capital and the murderer on horseback in Virginia were. What happened to them could be written, you might say, it was legible.[22]

Until such deaths—and lives—count, until the captains of today's slave ships are all hanged, a dialectics grounded in the illegibility of exteriority and nonbeing will be an indispensable weapon.

The Labor of the Positive

Latent within this first challenge is a second one, visible in all three thinkers considered here, but which I have avoided until this point. Sorel, Fanon, and Dussel are peculiar—albeit not contingently so—for their embrace of what we could call, reversing Hegel, the "labor of the positive." In his *Negative Dialectics*, for example, Adorno insists on the need to "free dialectics" from its "affirmative traits," to which Marcuse adds that, "Dialectical theory . . . cannot offer the remedy. It cannot be positive. To be sure, the dialectical concept, in comprehending the given facts, transcends the given facts. This is the very token of its truth. It defines the historical possibilities, even necessities; but their realization can only be in the practice which responds to the theory, and, at present, the practice gives no such response."[23]

By apparent contrast, Fanon and Dussel each embrace some notion of the positive, with the latter as we have seen even insisting on the naïveté of the Frankfurt School theorists "with respect to the positive criticality of the utopia of political exteriority."[24] Similarly, Fanon insisted in his lyrical bookends to *Black Skin, White Masks* that humans are not only a "no" but also "a yes resonating from cosmic harmonies": "Yes to life. Yes to love. Yes to generosity," an insistence that humans—more "*actional*" than "reactional"—affirm as much as they negate.[25] An actional orientation that opens radically onto a future of endless self-creation, for Fanon, that unleashes "what is most human," passes necessarily through the embrace of the other and the effort to "build the world of *you*."[26] While the brutally negative force of the Fanonian dialectic is undeniable, so too this positive source, which later finds its basis in the reservoir of relative exteriority—to use Dussel's terms—of the Algerian peasantry.

Even a thinker so resolutely negative as Sorel, who like Fanon rejected any overarching system of ethics binding workers to bosses, placed a surprising weight on the one-sided ethics emerging from the underside of this rupture. Not only is there an "ethics of violence" that governs the workers' dialectical attack, but also a quasi-analectical "ethics of the producers" that emerges independently from within the production process, according to which the proletariat "organizes itself in obscurity . . . without the aid of bourgeois thinkers."[27] Such an ethic is unmoored from all calculation, and the free worker "wants to surpass everything that has been done before him," thereby generating an "indefinite progress" that is more artistic than material, grounded in the "*infinite nature of his will*."[28]

But in framing his approach as a critique of a purely negative dialectics, Dussel is not suggesting that the outcome of dialectical motion is "affirmative" or laudable, and much less predetermined. After all, here was a thinker forced into exile by the dialectical blowback of a fascist bombing. Rather, he means something very specific when he calls the Frankfurt School "naïve": that due to the movement of critique, a given discourse can be both "critical" toward prior discourses and "naïve" toward those future discourses that will surpass them. While this may be putting it too strongly, since Marcuse points toward a future liberatory "practice" without claiming to know it, Dussel's point is that such practices do indeed exist in the present: in the concrete praxis of the colonized, itself more than simply a "negation of the negation," but a positive program for the abolition of ontological barriers between Being and its opposite.[29]

The tension between negativity and positivity is often seen as marking a separation between the struggles of former slaves on the one hand and colonized indigenous peoples on the other. For example, Afro-Pessimists such as Frank Wilderson use (some would say abuse) Fanon to emphasize Blackness as "absolute dereliction at the level of the Symbolic, for Blackness in America generates no categories for the chromosome of history . . . It is an experience without analog—a past without a heritage."[30] From such a pure negativity, Wilderson argues, only the "negative dialectic" of Fanon's "complete disorder" can spring forth. For others like Lewis Gordon, however, this is to collapse Fanon's understanding of an anti-Black world understood as an always-incomplete project with the world that we inhabit, in which the persistent gap between the two is precisely the space of resistance.

Similarly, Cedric Robinson insists that the European project of reducing "the African" to "the Negro"—or in other words, reducing slaves to pure negativity—is never a fully accomplished fact. Instead, Robinson supplements the negativity of slavery with its persistently positive remainder, which is again the basis for resistance:

> Black radicalism is a negation of Western civilization, but not in the direct sense of a simple dialectical negation. It is certain that the evolving tradition of Black radicalism owes its peculiar moment to the historical interdiction of African life by European agents . . . This experience, though, was merely the condition for Black radicalism—its immediate reason for and object of being—but not the foundation for its nature or character . . . It is not a variant of Western radicalism whose proponents happen to be Black. Rather, it is a specifically African response to an oppression emergent from the immediate determinants of European development in the modern era and framed by orders of human exploitation woven into the interstices of European social life from the inception of Western civilization.[31]

Robinson, as a consequence, emphasizes the shared legacy of colonialism and slavery rather than drawing too sharp a line between the two—while never denying that the abolition of both would take the form of radical disorder.

We cannot fully address the question of the positive and those concrete, decolonial subjects whose self-activity evades a purely negative dialectics— providing a positive wellspring for dialectical motiom—without directly addressing the fraught question of *tradition*. Some might respond to the decolonized dialectics of Fanon and Dussel by insisting that much of the content these thinkers ascribe to the intersection of nonbeing and exteriority remains *internal*, defined more by (dialectical) resistance to oppression than by properly analectical separation and autonomy.[32] Whereas Dussel is able to slip out of this difficulty by virtue of the inescapable and occasionally frustrating flexibility of his concept of exteriority—which ranges from an individual's "internal transcendentality" to the continued relevance of precolonial communism—Fanon's is a more difficult case, since he is often understood, on the basis of his analysis of Algeria, to be a thinker who was deeply and fundamentally hostile to tradition.

The case is more complex than this, however, since what Fanon assails most are those "traditions" that he does not truly understand to be traditions at all, that is, those tribal distinctions he interprets—rightly or wrongly—as having been "reactivated" by a defensive colonizer.[33] By contrast, he celebrates not only those (dialectical) anticolonial traditions of the Algerian peasantry that make it a historical subject and reservoir of resistance—the (Sorelian sounding) "old warrior traditions [that] resurface" when the struggle erupts—but also those (analectical) traditions whose value is undeniable: indigenous organs of popular democracy, communal anti-individualism, and practices of self-criticism.[34] The *djemaa* and palaver are thus to Fanon what the Incan *ayllu* is to Mariátegui and the Mayan *Amaq'* and Aztec *altepetl* are to Dussel: not remnants of the past but living practices in the present.[35]

This duality of tradition should be evident, moreover, from the fact that the nation itself emerges both on the basis of traditional units and through the transcendence of old rivalries that had divided them, and that disciplined altruism of the peasantry is rooted precisely in their "static society" that clings to a "rigid context."[36] Between bad tradition and good there lies the powerful revolutionary process, the dialectic-within-a-dialectic, the "armed or even political struggle against a merciless colonialism" through which "tradition changes meaning."[37] In fact, Fanon is most severe with those abstractly Jacobin urban intellectuals who can see nothing but "obscurantist traditions" in the countryside and who as a result clash with the "old granite foundation that is the national heritage."[38]

For all these thinkers, traditions must be understood critically, met not with outright rejection or wholehearted embrace. They must be filtered and divided into good versus bad traditions, those that "serve man's needs" versus those inhuman relics "to be replaced."[39] Furthermore, this distinction cannot itself be a static one, but must be contextual and even momentary, according to the needs of the decolonial struggle and the strategic and tactical orientation of the enemy. While this may seem to simply punt the question from tradition to the question of "who decides," it nevertheless marks an essential if difficult middle ground that a dialectical approach to decolonization must walk.

Dialectics of Distance

The liminal position of the Algerian peasantry in Fanon's account, existing as they do on the outskirts of the colonial order, at the border where the dialectical slides into the analectical, tacitly introduces an important dialectics of distance into his account. The space between internal and external in a decolonized dialectics, however, is in some ways sharply distinct from that posed more recently by Grégoire Chamayou who, in his dialectics of exclusion and capture—a "dialectic of hunter and hunted"—in some ways provides its dystopian inverse. The manhunt, for Chamayou, is grounded in what he, like Fanon, understands as an ontological contradiction: "Recognizing the humanity of the prey and at the same time challenging it in practice are thus the two contradictory attitudes constitutive of the manhunt."[40]

In the process, Chamayou mounts a critique of the Hegelian master-slave dialectic that shares many elements of Fanon's view (although notably without mentioning him by name).

> Africans are radically excluded from the Hegelian dialectic—and thus also from political subjectivity . . . the point of departure for the relationship of consciousness that is established in the experience of modern slavery does not correspond to the canonical schema of the Hegelian phenomenology of the master and the slave. The initial situation is in fact not a face-off between two undifferentiated consciousnesses that, through a free confrontation, will establish a relationship of domination, but instead a situation in which domination already exists and in which one party is already running away because the other is pursuing him. A different starting point that inaugurated, as we will see, a quite different dialectic.[41]

The two subjectivities do not enjoy, Chamayou rightly points out, "interchangeable positions," but are instead "dissymmetrical from the outset."[42] Instead of the hand-to-hand heroics of Hegel's life-or-death struggle or the ensuing closeness of chattel slavery, this "quite different dialectic" appears as a mediated relation of distance. As a result, it is not purely two-sided, but also echoes Fanon's insistence on white supremacy as an ever-present

Third: "In the hunting situation the master almost never confronts his prey directly. He uses intermediaries, mercenary hunters or hunting dogs. This is a schema with three terms rather than two."

> Thus we obtain that other deviation from the schema of the *Phenomenology*: the master's consciousness is not that of the one who has proven himself able to face death, but rather that of the one who has the power to put others' lives at risk without ever having to risk his own. If the master is recognized as an autonomous self-consciousness, that is precisely because he does not have to expose himself to death. In order to be the master, he has not risked his life, he has not scorned life in himself as he does in others, but only in others.[43]

While these formulations share much with Fanon's decolonization of the master-slave dialectic—and arguably put a sharper point on the danger of distance as not pure autonomous exteriority à la Dussel but instead as itself a structured manifestation of white supremacy—two concerns emerge.

First, Chamayou prevaricates with regard to the weight of ontology itself, beginning with the ostensible contradiction at the heart of the manhunt: that the prey remains human on some fundamental level. Thus he views ancient Greek formulations about slaves as "bipedal cattle" and "living tools" to be "oxymoronic," and even hints that despite the asymmetry of the dialectic of the hunt, "the hunting relationship is always susceptible to a reversal of positions."[44] While this certainly gets at something deeply repressed in the white supremacist psyche, Fanon would push further by suggesting that this is hardly a contradiction at all: nonbeings are subject to death, period. If Chamayou captures something intuitively true about the manhunt, he runs the risk of neglecting the fundamental and persistent "killability" of those subjects disqualified from humanity.[45]

Second, and seemingly paradoxically in light of his insistence that "the history of a power is also the history of the struggles to overthrow it," Chamayou paints a one-sidedly pessimistic picture in which the concretely historical master-slave dialectic, through its structured mediation and avoidance of risk, offers no potential to the prey themselves, in part because they are reduced to simply that: prey.[46] While understandable given his object of analysis, this approach threatens to minimize the agency of subjects who are far more than merely hunted, who draw upon distance and autonomy in more potently radical ways. This approach, put differently, evades the important question of what potential a recrafted dialectics of tradition, exteriority, and distance holds and why it is that so many subjects ostensibly condemned to the status of "prey" have sought weapons from among the Hegelian arsenal. This one-sidedness leads Chamayou to unfortunately stale conclusions, posing the inversion of hunter and hunted as a simple reversal and thus framing resistance as a "tragic trick," an "impasse," a "nondialectical reversal" that is not properly political.[47]

What is erased in Chamayou's pessimistic rendering of distance is readily apparent in Angela Davis's analysis of the role of women in the slave community, in which distance gains a fuller account as an essential moment in the struggle for liberation. Not only does Davis's analysis of community bring to light the often invisibilized background for confrontations such as that between Douglass and Covey, it also points in the process toward the same tension between dialectics and analectics posed by Fanon and Dussel. More important still, through the question of reproductive labor broadly understood—a crucial subject in recent years and decades—Davis demonstrates the intertwined complicity of gender, slavery, colonization, and the geography of resistance.

According to Davis, the (dialectical) process of slave resistance toward the masters would have been impossible without an (analectical) foothold in the exteriority of communal life, however limited: "The conscious thrust towards its abolition could not have been sustained without impetus from the community they pulled together through the sheer force of their own strength. Of necessity, this community would revolve around the realm which was furthermost removed from the immediate arena of domination. It could only be located in and around the living quarters."[48] It was only at a *distance* from the Marxian class dialectic of production—characterized in this case by utter dehumanization rather than alienation from the object of labor—and from the Hegelian master-slave dialectic of hand-to-hand combat, that the slave community could, as community, provide a space for the expression of freedom and the patient reconstruction of humanity. It was only from this analectical and autonomous community, for Davis, that the frontal and dialectical war of maneuver against slavery might be posed and the forces necessary for it composed and recomposed. Dialectical resistance was thus intertwined with and relied upon practical positive exteriority.[49]

Rather than domestic labor serving here as mere reinscription or doubling of the female slave's inferiority, "she was performing the *only* labor of the slave community which could not be directly and immediately claimed by the oppressor." Women were thereby "thrust by the force of circumstances into the center of the slave community" by virtue of this relative exteriority, making "the dialectics of her oppression . . . far more complex": it was not reason in history or the development of productive forces, but instead "the *sheer force of things*" that "rendered her equal to her man."[50] This was a "deformed equality . . . forged quite undeliberately, yet inexorably" at the intersection of the economic needs of the system and the self-activity of the slaves, and while Davis cites Marx, her account fits comfortably neither in the dialectic of Marx nor that of most Marxists: "Latently or actively it was always a community of resistance. It frequently erupted into insurgency, but was daily animated by the minor acts of sabotage which harassed the slave master to no end. Had the black woman failed to rise to the occasion, the community of slaves could not have fully developed in this direction."

"The slave system," according to Davis, would therefore "have to deal with the black woman as the custodian of a house of resistance."[51] The primary weapon in such dealing was sexual assault as counterinsurgency, itself a spectacular manifestation of a reframed master-slave dialectic of sex against gender: "confronting the black woman as adversary in a sexual contest," the master sought to reduce the female slave "to the level of her *biological* being . . . to establish her as a female *animal*," as an attack on "the slave community as a whole."[52] Whereas Hegel sustained a founding gendered distinction that associated women with mere diversity, Davis here disintegrates this distinction as effectively as could be imagined, recentering women in a powerfully decolonized fashion.[53]

Beyond or alongside predator and prey, then, we find an insistence on the reconfigured exteriority of not only Maroon communities, but even those who sought constantly to generate life and resistance from within the social death of slavery.[54] This is not at all to deny the centrality of structured distance to the colonial and racial project, or the need to reestablish proximity. After all, Fanon insists that "the colonist's feet can never be glimpsed, except perhaps in the sea, but then you can never get close enough," to which Jean Améry adds: "the oppressed, the colonized, the concentration camp inmate, perhaps even the Latin American wage slave, *must be able to see the feet of the oppressor* in order to become a human being."[55] But it is to insist on a more complex, dialectical view of the relationship between colonial distance and autonomous self-activity in the process of decolonization, between the exteriority of nonbeing and the fullness of humanity.

The End of the World

If we began from the fraught relationship between decolonization and dialectics, we conclude with a similarly painful tension between decolonization and another tradition too often mired in an unrecognized Eurocentrism: anarchism. Each of the thinkers considered here maintained a tense and complicated relation with anarchism. Sorel was sharply critical of his contemporary anarchists, whom he deemed "*intellectually entirely bourgeois*," while nevertheless recognizing that they had radicalized the syndicalist movement by infusing it with a laudable wariness of the state.[56] While Fanon was critical of anarchistic adventurism in Algeria, he knew that those seeking to unleash a decolonial struggle grounded in the self-activity of the masses would themselves inevitably be tarred with the same brush and denounced by established leaders as "these upstarts, these anarchists."[57] Dussel is critical of what he calls the "impossible-possibility of the extreme anarchist"—referring to an undifferentiated and noninstitutionalized potentia much like the Multitude—but he echoes Sorel in his insistence that "quasi-anarchists do indeed remind us that institutions become fetishized and always need to be transformed," holding out the "dissolution of the state" as his ultimate political horizon.[58]

The peculiar in-betweenness of these thinkers and others—even Mariátegui was deeply influenced by the anarchist Manuel González Prada—suggests a peculiar if often unrecognized resonance between decolonization and something like anarchism. This relationship is best grasped not as the formal unity of the two, however—by simply adding one to the other—but instead by grasping the *content* these impulses share. Recall Dussel's early formulation of decolonial liberation as "an-arche," beyond the principle of the present, and Fanon's ontological correlation of *state* and *status*—either ontological status or the status quo of the present. The state for Fanon and Dussel is thus similar to that of Sorel—an entrenched "Jacobin" structure of inequality and hierarchy—and where they oppose the state, it is because it is a structure of inequality, not simply because it calls itself a state. Attacking the governing structure of the present is always violent and an-archic by definition, but even more so when that structure is based on the racial-colonial apartheid that separates true Being from substandard nonbeings.

Whereas the *New York Review of Books* once described Fanon as a "Black Rousseau" and a "true Jacobin," just as C. L. R. James had deemed Toussaint and others "Black Jacobins," these cannot be understood as terms of unambiguous praise.[59] Fanon shared Sorel's anti-Jacobin wariness of the cold abstraction of those revolutionary intellectuals and political leaders who would simply occupy the upper echelons of a new hierarchy. Even James—his own title notwithstanding—shows how it was the very Jacobinism of Robespierre and Toussaint that led to their downfall: both eventually attacked their left wing, lost the support of the masses, and thereby sealed their own doom.[60]

In an oft-overlooked footnote to the 1963 edition of *Black Jacobins*, James even seems to share Sorel's equation of Jacobinism with a "principle of hierarchy," citing Georges Lefebvre's Sorbonne lectures to cleave a distinction between Jacobins and sansculottes:

> The Jacobins . . . were authoritarian in outlook. Consciously or not, they wished to act with the people and for them, but they claimed the right of leadership, and when they arrived at the head of affairs they ceased to consult the people, did away with elections, proscribed the Hebertistes and the Enrages. They can be described as enlightened despots. The sansculottes on the contrary were extreme democrats: they wanted the direct government of the people by the people; if they demanded a dictatorship against the aristocrats they wished to exercise it themselves and to make their leaders do what they wanted.[61]

While not strictly opposed to the state as a mechanism, or even to the Jacobins that occupied that state for a time, the sansculottes were indeed hostile to the hierarchy that Jacobinism reproduced. It was this gap, turned yawning chasm, that would doom revolutionary processes from Saint-Domingue to France and beyond. Against the abstract and rationalist freedom of the Rights of Man, to which Toussaint himself remained hypnotically beholden, the popular masses were demanding a concrete freedom that drew upon tradition. And against the authoritarian violence of Jacobinism, they sought to deploy a radically democratic brutality that has much in common with Sorel's distinction between two violences, and whose vehicle in the Haitian context was a proto-Fanonian resort to the rational irrationality of Black identity.[62]

As Césaire put it: "Equality refuses to remain abstract. And what an affair it is when the colonized takes back the word on his own account to demand that it not remain a mere word!"[63] Armed with a substantive view of the state and the Jacobin-sansculotte distinction that it entails—not to mention a concretized understanding of decolonial freedom—we are better prepared to draw together anarchism, dialectics, and decolonization in a

way that does not reduce one to the other or simply add them uncom-
fortably together. Not only can we glimpse in both some anarchisms and
some decolonial nationalisms a ruthless hostility toward ingrained hierarchy, but we can also see the inverse: not only that some nationalisms
are certainly reactionary, but also that some anarchisms are too scornfully
Jacobin and too imbued with Eurocentrism to be of much use toward
decolonization.[64]

What reinvigoration of the "unfinished project of decolonization"
might result from an emphasis on these "an-archistic" insights of Fanon
and Dussel, insights that exceed the theoretical to insist on the dangers
of formal decolonization, the reification of the state, and the closure of
the revolutionary dialectic?[65] What enrichment of anarchism might result
from loosening the formalistic grip of "the state" and embracing decolonization as a means of attacking the most powerful and essential hierarchy of
our times—the ontological apartheid that renders some less human than
others? What potentialities might emerge if we refuse the additive formulation of decolonization + anarchism (or communism, for that matter),
instead allowing the mutual interpenetration of the two in a manner
that—with clear complicity between content and form—is no more and
no less than dialectical?

"Colonization," in the words of Maia Ramnath, "is one of the most
concentrated forms of power in history, incorporating extreme modes of
domination, dispossession, and racial hierarchy." If we can loosen our conception of "the state" to its broadest sense—as status, the status quo, the
existing state of things—we might be able to grasp decolonization as truly
constituting, as she rightly puts it, "the highest form of anarchism."[66] It is
against this state of affairs—this sedimented structure of class, racial, and
colonial inequality—that the thinkers considered here sought to unleash
a radically open-ended dialectics whose liberating violence alchemically
transforms everything and everyone it touches and whose objective is no
more and no less than what Fanon called "the end of the world, by Jove."[67]
The abolition of existing structures, of the white supremacy embedded in
institutions both formal and informal, the tearing down of the apartheid
walls separating Being from its constitutive opposite: *this* is the end of the
world, and for Fanon as for Césaire, it was and remains "the only thing in
the world worth starting."[68]

NOTES

Ruptures

1. For Stephen B. Smith, this concern unified Hegel's theoretical production while justifying philosophy as a project of reconciliation. *Hegel's Critique of Liberalism: Rights in Context* (Chicago: University of Chicago Press, 1989), 17.

2. This is not to reduce Hegel to his disciples on the Right, and while Fukuyama is at pains to defend Hegel from the Marxian critique of civil society, he leans heavily on Alexandre Kojève's "end of history" argument to do so. Francis Fukuyama, *The End of History and the Last Man* (New York: Simon and Schuster, 2006 [1992]), 60–65. On Fukuyama as a characteristically Right Hegelian, see Fredric Jameson, *The Hegel Variations: On the* Phenomenology of Spirit (London: Verso, 2010), 5. To be clear, Hegel is far more concerned with the dangerous tendencies of the market than his conservative heirs, but civil society (*bürgerliche Gesellschaft*) remains nevertheless a space of mediation, its inevitable imperfection resolved through the "police" function of the state. G. W. F. Hegel, *Elements of the Philosophy of Right*, trans. H. B. Nisbet (Cambridge: Cambridge University Press, 1991 [1820]), "Section 2: Civil Society," a subset of which is "The Police." On the tendency of civil society to generate poverty, see §§ 241–45; on its tendency to require colonial expansion, see §§ 246–48. For a nuanced discussion, see Reinhart Klemens Maurer, "Hegel and the End of History," in *Hegel Myths and Legends*, ed. J. Stewart (Evanston: Northwestern University Press, 1996), 199–222.

3. Where Fukuyama would consider such regime changes mere "events," hardly noticeable bumps on the ever-smoother road of "universal civil society," civil society's double-role as both *measure* and ambitious *means* for actively securing the end of history should be enough to reveal the cynical circularity

of his system. This complicity of civil society with power is most evident in the discourses and practices of human rights, which Wendy Brown cautions "are not simply rules and defenses against power, but can themselves be tactics and vehicles of governance and domination." " 'The Most We Can Hope For . . .': Human Rights and the Politics of Fatalism," *South Atlantic Quarterly* 103, nos. 2/3 (2004): 459. Slavoj Žižek characterizes human rights discourse as "a false ideological universality, which masks and legitimizes a concrete politics of Western imperialism, military interventions and neo-colonialism." "Against Human Rights," *New Left Review* 34 (2005): 128–29. See also Alain Badiou, *Ethics: An Essay on the Understanding of Evil*, trans. P. Hallward (London: Verso, 2001), 8–10; and José-Manuel Barreto, ed., *Human Rights from a Third World Perspective: Critique, History, and International Law* (Newcastle: Cambridge Scholars, 2013).

4. On Hegel, see Fredric Jameson, *Valences of the Dialectic* (London: Verso, 2009), as well as Slavoj Žižek's gargantuan *Less Than Nothing* (London: Verso, 2012). On the renewal of communism, see especially Alain Badiou, *The Communist Hypothesis* (London: Verso, 2010); Bruno Bosteels, *The Actuality of Communism* (London: Verso, 2011); and Jodi Dean, *The Communist Horizon* (London: Verso, 2012). On contemporary forms of struggle, see Badiou's more recent *The Rebirth of History* (London: Verso: 2012). On dialectics more broadly, see, e.g., Andrew Douglas, *In the Spirit of Critique: Thinking Politically in the Dialectical Tradition* (Albany: SUNY Press, 2013); John Grant, *Dialectics and Contemporary Politics: Critique and Transformation from Hegel through Post-Marxism* (London: Routledge, 2013); and Brian Lovato, *Democracy, Dialectics, and Difference: Hegel, Marx, and 21st Century Social Movements* (London: Routledge, 2015). Elements of what follows have appeared in George Ciccariello-Maher, " 'So Much the Worse for the Whites': Dialectics of the Haitian Revolution," *Journal of French and Francophone Philosophy* 22, no. 1 (2014): 19–39.

5. Antonio Vázquez-Arroyo, "Universal History Disavowed: On Critical Theory and Postcolonialism," *Postcolonial Studies* 11, no. 4 (2008): 452.

6. Alain Badiou, *Metapolitics*, trans. J. Barker (London, Verso, 2005), 97; Badiou, *Ethics*, 27.

7. Slavoj Žižek, "A Leftist Plea for 'Eurocentrism,'" *Critical Inquiry* 24, no. 4 (summer 1998): 988–1009. For a critique of the latter, see Nelson Maldonado-Torres, "Decolonization and the New Identitarian Logics After September 11," *Radical Philosophy Review* 8, no. 1 (2005): 35–67. Even more troubling has been Žižek's recent call to embrace Western culture and "our freedoms" in the face of an influx of refugees—a partial indication of the dead-end into which such an uncritical universalism leads. "In the Wake of Paris Attacks the Left Must Embrace Its Radical Western Roots," *In These Times* (November 16, 2015), http://inthesetimes.com/article/18605/breaking-the-taboos-in-the -wake-of-paris-attacks-the-left-must-embrace-its. Glen Coulthard similarly maps the tensions between decolonization and the "left-materialist" critique

of so-called identity politics in his excellent *Red Skin, White Masks: Rejecting the Colonial Politics of Recognition* (Minneapolis: University of Minnesota Press, 2014).

8. Glenn Greenwald, "Two Short Paragraphs That Summarize the U.S. Approach to Human Rights Advocacy," *Intercept* (September 13, 2015), https://theintercept.com/2015/09/13/two-short-paragraphs-summarize-us-approach-human-rights-advocacy/.

9. Glen Ford, "Obama's Siren Song," *Counterpunch* (June 14, 2007), http://www.counterpunch.org/2007/06/14/obama-s-siren-song/.

10. The debate surrounding this division was nasty and destructive in many ways. While there might seem to be overlap between the proposal to "decolonize" the Occupy Movement and my objectives in this book, in practice it raised troubling questions about the relationship between nonprofits and the state, race-baiting opportunism, and the role (and indeed category) of white "allies." See the original statement, "Communiqué from Decolonize Oakland" (March 18, 2012), http://unsettlingamerica.wordpress.com/2012/03/18/communique-from-decolonize-oakland/. In retrospect, this marked a turning point, prompting a reverse pendulum swing toward a renewed critique of "identity politics" within post-Occupy political formations that both responds to real conditions while arguably throwing out the decolonial baby with the bathwater in a manner akin to Žižek and Badiou. For the best statement on race in the Occupy Movement, and for a more dialectical understanding of the 99 percent, see Joel Olson, "Whiteness and the 99%" (October 20, 2011), reprinted in *We Are Many: Reflections on Movement Strategy From Occupation to Liberation*, ed. K. Khatib, M. Killjoy, and M. McGuire (Oakland: AK Press, 2012), 46–51.

11. Due to the historical weight of the dialectical tradition, the particular trajectory of thinkers I trace in this book, and my own theoretical limitations, this is not a book that deals substantially with gender identity as a dialectical category alongside class, race, nation, and people. However, some—notably Sina Kramer—have already theorized gender at the border of dialectics, where internal and external relations meet. "Derrida's 'Antigonanette': On the Quasi-Transcendental," *Southern Journal of Philosophy* 52, no. 4 (December 2014), 521–51. However, posing gender as an external incommensurability also runs up against the classed and raced complicity *across* genders, a challenge raised in particular by the decolonial and Black feminisms I return to in the conclusion. See, in particular, Hortense Spillers, "Mama's Baby, Papa's Maybe: An American Grammar Book," *Diacritics* 17, no. 2 (summer 1987): 65–81.

12. Cristina Beltrán, *The Trouble with Unity: Latino Politics and the Creation of Identity* (New York: Oxford University Press, 2010). While I take Beltrán's warning seriously, my approach will tread closer to a radicalized dialectics than the sort of rhizomatics associated with Gilles Deleuze.

13. See M. W. Jackson, "Hegel: The Real and the Rational," in *Hegel Myths and Legends*, 19–25.

14. It should be clear here that I mean *teleology* in the strong and literal sense: not the mere existence of a horizon but the idea that the present anticipates and is structured according to that horizon.

15. Martin Jay, *Marxism and Totality: The Adventures of a Concept from Lukács to Habermas* (Berkeley: University of California Press, 1984). Jay's book expands upon and systematizes his previous fivefold typology of totality discussed in Martin Jay, "The Concept of Totality in Lukács and Adorno," in *Varieties of Marxism*, ed. S. Avineri (The Hague: Martinus Nijhoff, 1977), 147–74.

16. The reference point here is Hegel's very rapid transition through diversity in the *Logic*, greater and lesser. As to the first, in which diversity (*Verschiedenheit*) appears as the "indifference of difference" and an immediate bridge to opposition, see *The Science of Logic*, trans. G. di Giovanno (Cambridge: Cambridge University Press, 2010), 362–67 (II.268–272). For the latter, see *The Encyclopaedia Logic*, trans. T. F. Geraets, W. A. Suchting, and H. S. Harris (Cambridge: Hackett, 1991), 182–93 (§117). For Jameson, the question is whether relations are "so intimate as to fold it back into unity, [or] so distant or external as to break apart into two distinct zones or fields, two different objects." To accommodate this "ambiguous no man's land between . . . internal and external relations, or unity and incommensurability," he insists on stretching the term *contradiction* (*Valences of the Dialectic*, 25, 42–43). Sina Kramer emphasizes Hegel's failed attempt to exclude diversity from the dialectic—an exclusion that founds the distinction between the speculative and the empirical, but which by failing to be fully banished contaminates the former with the latter. Sina Kramer, *Excluded Within: The (Un)Intelligibility of Radical Political Actors* (Oxford: Oxford University Press, forthcoming).

17. Jameson, *Valences of the Dialectic*, 25.

18. Jameson, for example, divides Hegel's oeuvre, defending the radicalism of *Phenomenology*. Some, like Timothy Brennan, argue that *Philosophy of Right* is actually Hegel's most radical text for its concreteness and its political imperative to transform the law. *Borrowed Light: Vico, Hegel, and the Colonies* (Stanford, CA: Stanford University Press, 2014). Many Marxists, following Lenin's *Conspectus*, argue that Hegel's *Logic* is his radical work par excellence. Still more identify ambivalences running throughout Hegel's work, for example what Patchen Markell characterizes as the tension between a "diagnostic voice" that is "most clearly audible" in the *Phenomenology*, one geared toward constantly rooting out contradiction, and the "voice of the *system*," a voice of reconciliation, "the voice that promises us that at the end of this journey there lies the prospect of a homecoming, of finally arriving at a state in which contradiction, division, suffering, and other manifestations of negativity have been not necessarily eliminated, but at least *redeemed* as moments of an intelligible, internally articulated, encompassing whole." *Bound By Recognition* (Princeton, NJ: Princeton University Press, 2003), 92–93.

For a truly stunning recent example that seeks to reclaim despair as a revolutionary and "dialectical passion"—with a specific focus on the *Phenomenology*—see Robyn Marasco, *The Highway of Despair: Critical Theory After Hegel* (New York: Columbia University Press, 2015), 5. For Marasco, "the *Phenomenology* is best read not as a roadmap to reconciliation . . . but as a philosophical staging of despair and its persistence" (29). Despair, "a condition that survives the ruins of the [Hegelian] system," is "the name for that undoing that the dialectic endlessly initiates" (2, 6). The dialectic she unfolds, which holds out "no *rational* hope that a brighter future will repay patient struggle in the present," shares much with my project, for reasons that might be easily guessed (1). And while not a strictly decolonial vision, Marasco's embrace of "forms of hope that survive against all hope" is peculiarly suited to (post)colonial conditions (10).

On Marx, it is worth simply rehearsing the historical debates between those who emphasize the early and late and who centered the notion of the epistemological rupture, but also those breaks undertaken by Marx himself that are central to the discussion at hand, namely, his later interrogation of the linear stageism he had previously associated with historical materialism. In later writings and letters to Vera Zasulich, for example, Marx began to consider the possibility of a noncapitalist transition to communism, and these writings would provide crucial leverage for decolonial Marxists. See Kevin Anderson, *Marx at the Margins: On Nationalism, Ethnicity, and Non-Western Societies* (Chicago: University of Chicago Press, 2010).

19. The lineage that runs through Western Marxism and into the early Frankfurt School and its task of thinking a "negative dialectics" speaks directly to the latter, as do recent efforts to reconsider Hegelian and Marxist thought. Other promising tendencies, notably thinkers such as Antonio Negri and some of the tradition of Italian Autonomia, posed sharp challenges to traditional dialectics before veering sharply off, under the influence of Deleuzian theories of immanence, into professedly nondialectical territory. A recent speech by Negri is nevertheless surprisingly ambivalent on the question of dialectics, and certainly not as hostile as one might expect. Antonio Negri, "Some Thoughts on the Use of Dialectics," trans. A. Bove (June 2009), http://antonionegriinenglish.wordpress.com/2010/11/25/some-thoughts-on -the-use-of-dialectics/.

20. Thus the recent attempt by Susan Buck-Morss to shed the "anticipation of unity" in Hegelian thought by drawing Hegel into open conversation with the unspoken inspiration of the Haitian Revolution is dashed on the stubborn rocks of undialectical Eurocentrism. Not only does Buck-Morss fall directly into this "anticipation of unity" by rejecting divisive political identities outright—race and nation in particular—in favor of the immediate and unconditional assertion of universality as a fact, but the parameters of her universal remain conspicuously Eurocentric as well. Susan Buck-Morss, *Hegel, Haiti, and Universal History* (Pittsburgh: University of Pittsburgh

Press, 2009), x, 149–51. I make this argument more fully in "'So Much the Worse for the Whites.'"

Similarly limited approaches can be found in Brennan's *Borrowed Light*, which seeks to ground decolonial thought in Europe itself, and in Bruce Baum's recent article "Decolonizing Critical Theory," which, notwithstanding the grand claims of the title, provides in reality a very limited and almost wholly immanent critique of the Frankfurt School. *Constellations* 22, no. 3 (2015): 420–34.

21. Frantz Fanon, *The Wretched of the Earth*, trans. R. Philcox (New York: Grove Press, 2004 [1961]), 144, translation modified; *Œuvres* (Paris: La Découverte, 2011), 585.

22. On these ambiguities, see Cedric Robinson, *Black Marxism: The Making of the Black Radical Tradition* (Chapel Hill: University of North Carolina Press, 2000 [1983]), 183–84.

23. Orlando Patterson, *Slavery and Social Death: A Comparative Study* (Cambridge, MA: Harvard University Press, 1982).

24. Brennan, *Borrowed Light*, 99.

25. Jameson, *Valences of the Dialectic*, 26–27.

26. Jameson, *Valences of the Dialectic*, 19.

27. Cited in Raya Dunayevskaya, "On C. L. R. James' Notes on Dialectics," *News and Letters* (1997 [1972]): 4.

28. Such a view clearly conflicts with Robert Pippin's more stripped-down reading of Hegel as a practical philosopher concerned with the concrete, for whom dialectics is above all diagnostic and even heuristic. *Hegel's Practical Philosophy: Rational Agency as Ethical Life* (Cambridge: Cambridge University Press, 2008). See also Brennan, *Borrowed Light*, for a similar reading of Hegel's orientation toward the concrete. Even more than Hegel, of course, Marx threw himself subjectively into the condensation of identities at the same time that he analyzed the play of those identities from above and inserted them into a transhistorical dialectical vision—raising the question of where the center of gravity in the analysis falls, a situation not improved by the incorporation of Marx into the academy.

29. I hope it is clear, here and elsewhere, that simply eschewing a strictly economic language or displacing the centrality of class does not in any way minimize the *materiality* of dialectics. I take a cue here from the "insurgent" dialectics suggested by Iris Marion Young in *Justice and the Politics of Difference* (Princeton, NJ: Princeton University Press, 1990). Young similarly puts poststructural insights to powerfully material use by insisting that, "reducing differences to unity means bringing them under a universal category, which requires expelling those aspects of the different things that do not fit into the category." "Difference thus becomes," she writes, "a hierarchical opposition between what lies inside and what lies outside the category, valuing more what lies inside than what lies outside" (102).

30. Beneath the critique of medical-psychological containment there lies the counterdiscourse of "madness"; to the critique of carceral containment, the counterdiscourse of "prisoners" (this being, in fact, the context for one of Foucault's first uses of the term *counterdiscourse*). See Michel Foucault, *History of Madness*, trans. J. Murphy and J. Khalfa (London: Routledge, 2006 [1961]); *Discipline and Punish: The Birth of the Prison*, trans. A. Sheridan (New York: Vintage, 1979 [1975]). For the reference to the "counterdiscourse of prisoners," see "Intellectuals and Power: A Conversation between Michel Foucault and Gilles Deleuze" (1972), in *Language, Counter-Memory, Practice: Selected Essays and Interviews* (Ithaca, NY: Cornell University Press, 1977), 209.

31. Michel Foucault, *"Society Must Be Defended": Lectures at the Collège de France, 1975–1976*, trans. D. Macey (New York: Picador, 2003 [1997]), 7–8. Despite the informal nature of the lectures, they effectively sharpen themes underlying Foucault's work as a whole. We can read this productively as self-criticism of his own lopsided emphasis on the negative (after all, how many pages are devoted to counterdiscourse in *History of Madness* or *Discipline and Punish*?). Anna Laura Stoler recognized early on the importance of this clarification of genealogy in the 1975–76 lectures; see *Race and the Education of Desire: Foucault's* History of Sexuality *and the Colonial Order of Things* (Durham, NC: Duke University Press, 1995), 60–65. For a critique of those who see Foucault's project as foreclosing on the very possibility of counterdiscourse, see Mario Moussa and Ron Scapp, "The Practical Theorizing of Michel Foucault: Politics and Counterdiscourse," *Cultural Critique* 33 (spring 1996), 87–112. For Foucault's own reconceptualization of the concept of critique, see Michel Foucault, "What Is Critique?," trans. L. Hochroth, in *The Politics of Truth*, ed. S. Lotringer (New York: Semiotext(e), 1997).

32. Foucault, *"Society Must Be Defended,"* 8, 10, my emphasis.

33. This is suggested as well by Richard Terdiman, who speaks of a "dialectic of discursive struggle," *Discourse/Counterdiscourse* (Ithaca, NY: Cornell University Press, 1985), 68–69. See also Grant, *Dialectics and Contemporary Politics*.

34. Foucault, *"Society Must Be Defended,"* 9.

35. Conversely, this explains why some discourses are subjugated while others are not, as the task is to "disinter something that has been hidden," but not only hidden: "carefully, deliberately, and wickedly misrepresented." Foucault, *"Society Must Be Defended,"* 72.

36. Foucault, *"Society Must Be Defended,"* 49.

37. Foucault, *"Society Must Be Defended,"* 51.

38. Foucault, *"Society Must Be Defended,"* 52, my emphasis; 73.

39. Foucault, *"Society Must Be Defended,"* 11. This subject is discussed as well by Moussa and Scapp, who speak of the "insidious" way that "counterdiscourses almost inevitably become discourses." Moussa and Scapp, "The Practical Theorizing of Michel Foucault," 92, 106.

40. Foucault, *"Society Must Be Defended,"* 49, 61.

41. Foucault, *"Society Must Be Defended,"* 58, my emphasis.

42. Michel Foucault, *History of Sexuality*, vol. 1: *An Introduction* (New York: Pantheon, 1978 [1976]), 99, 94.

43. Others have similarly turned Foucault's insights, especially those delineated in the lectures, toward the analysis of race. For a pioneering work in this vein, see Stoler, *Race and the Education of Desire*. For a powerful use of Foucault's lectures on abnormality to understand race in the U.S. context, see Ladelle McWhorter, *Racism and Sexual Oppression in Anglo-America: A Genealogy* (Bloomington: Indiana University Press, 2009). For an account that melds Foucault with Martin Heidegger to understand racializing dynamics, see Falguni Sheth, *Toward a Political Philosophy of Race* (Albany: SUNY Press, 2009). See also Eduardo Mendieta, "'To Make Live and Let Die': Foucault on Racism," published in Spanish in *Tabula Rasa* 6 (2007), 138–52, and available in English at http://www.stonybrook.edu/commcms/philosophy/people /faculty_pages/docs/foucault.pdf.

44. Marxism did not relinquish its dangerous function as a "means of deception," however. Michel Foucault, *Remarks on Marx*, trans. R. J. Goldstein and J. Cascaito (New York: Semiotext(e), 1991 [1978/1981]), 134, 137.

45. Foucault, *Remarks on Marx*, 137.

46. In an interview from 1978, Foucault admits to never having explicitly embraced Marxism, but not because he considers his work anti-Marxist. Rather, he considers Marxism "so complex, so tangled . . . made up of so many successive historical layers" and political interests that the question of connecting to it on a systematic level seems impossible, or at least boring. When it comes to Marx himself, however, Foucault is clear: "I situate my work in the lineage of the second book of *Capital*," in other words, not the genesis of *Capital*, but "the genealogy of capitalism." To openly cite Marx, he worried, would be to shoulder unnecessary baggage in France, and so he opted for "secret citations of Marx, that the Marxists themselves are not able to recognize." Michel Foucault, Colin Gordon, and Paul Patton, "Interview: Considerations on Marxism, Phenomenology and Power. Interview With Michel Foucault; Recorded on April 3rd, 1978," *Foucault Studies* 14 (September 2012): 100–101. I am grateful to Andrew Dilts for bringing this passage to my attention. For a coherent analysis of the Foucauldian project that emphasizes the relevance of Immanuel Kant for Foucault's "critical inquiry into the present" in a way that helps to break down the opposition between genealogy and counterdiscourse, see Colin Koopman, *Genealogy as Critique: Foucault and the Problems of Modernity* (Bloomington: Indiana University Press, 2013), 12.

47. Fanon, *Wretched*, 237, translation modified; *Œuvres*, 675.

48. This phrase, often cited in passing from Benedict Anderson, often serves to conceal the *materiality* he granted the idea. *Imagined Communities* (London: Verso, 1982).

49. In Fanon's words, the relationship between being overdetermined from within and from without. See also Aníbal Quijano, "The Coloniality of Power and Social Classification," trans. G. Ciccariello-Maher, published in Spanish in *Journal of World-Systems Research* 6, no. 2 (2000): 342–86. See also Robert Gooding-Williams's joining of the "first person" and "third person" aspects of racial overdetermination, in "Race, Multiculturalism and Democracy," *Constellations* 5, no. 1 (1998): 18–41.

50. Quijano, "The Coloniality of Power and Social Classification."

51. C. L. R. James, *The Black Jacobins: Toussaint L'Overture and the San Domingo Revolution* (New York: Vintage, 1989 [1938]). On the disavowal of the Haitian Revolution, see Sibylle Fischer, *Modernity Disavowed: Haiti and the Cultures of Slavery in the Age of Revolution* (Durham, NC: Duke University Press, 2004).

52. James, *Black Jacobins*, 47. Alongside the decisive self-activity of the slaves, their economic centrality is the most important takeaway from that other towering example published almost at the same time: W. E. B. Du Bois, *Black Reconstruction in America, 1860–1880* (New York: Free Press, 1998 [1935]).

53. James, *Black Jacobins*, 128.

54. James, *Black Jacobins*, 243, my emphasis.

55. James, *Black Jacobins*, 85–86, my emphasis.

56. Rather than a heroically creative class, the bourgeoisie—like the mulattoes—was a politically unstable "intermediate" class with "an immense respect for royal blood" and a concomitant fear of the masses. James, *Black Jacobins*, 207, 230, 71.

57. James, *Black Jacobins*, 7, 88, 212. This latter point would be made best by fellow communist and Fanon mentor Aimé Césaire in his *Discourse on Colonialism*, trans. J. Pinkham (New York: Monthly Review, 2000 [1956]).

58. James, *Black Jacobins*, 63. David Scott has argued that the revised 1963 edition of *The Black Jacobins* showed a marked shift from a romantic to a tragic emplotment, but he overlooks how this tragic perspective—as the quote indicates—is present from the very outset. David Scott, *Conscripts of Modernity: The Tragedy of Colonial Enlightenment* (Durham, NC: Duke University Press, 2004).

59. Fanon, *Wretched*, repeated on 90, 91, 181; *Œuvres*, 534 [*la guerre dure*], 625 [*la guerre continue*], the latter having previously appeared in *A Dying Colonialism*, trans. H. Chevalier (New York: Grove Press, 1965 [1959]), 27; *Œuvres*, 265 . For an analysis that turns to this phrase to exemplify a dialectic that "resists deliverance at every turn," see Marasco, *The Highway of Despair*, 151. Or, to borrow Alberto Toscano's recent description of Franco Fortini, a "communism without guarantees." Alberto Toscano, "Communism Without Guarantees: On Franco Fortini," *Salvage* (September 18, 2015), http://salvage.zone/in-print/communism-without-guarantees-on-franco-fortini/. For Toscano's call to embrace tragedy, see "Politics in a Tragic Key," *Radical Philosophy* 180 (July/August 2013): 25–34. For a reading of tragedy through Fanon and James, see Lewis R. Gordon, "Fanon's Tragic Revolutionary Violence,"

in *Fanon: A Critical Reader*, ed. L. Gordon, T. Sharpley-Whiting, and R. White (Oxford: Blackwell, 1996).

60. Fanon, *Wretched*, 2, translation modified; *Œuvres*, 452.

61. Hannah Arendt, *On Revolution* (New York: Penguin, 1990 [1963]), 114.

Chapter 1: Jumpstarting the Class Struggle

1. Georges Sorel, *Reflections on Violence* (Cambridge: Cambridge University Press, 2004), 111; *Réflexions sur la violence* (Paris: Marcel Rivière, 1910 [1908]), 159.

2. Bertell Ollman, *Dance of the Dialectic: Steps in Marx's Method* (Champaign: University of Illinois, 2003), 59.

3. Sorel, *Reflections*, 112n3; *Réflexions*, 159n1.

4. Georges Sorel, "Necessity and Fatalism in Marxism," in *From Georges Sorel*, ed. J. L. Stanley (New Brunswick, NJ: Transaction, 1987), 115 (hereafter *FGS*).

5. Rosa Luxemburg, *Reform or Revolution and Other Writings* (Mineola, NY: Dover, 2006).

6. Sorel, "Necessity and Fatalism in Marxism," 115.

7. Walter Benjamin, "Theses on the Philosophy of History," in *Illuminations* (New York: Schocken, 1968), 257.

8. Neil McInnes, "Georges Sorel on the Trial of Socrates," *Politics: Australian Journal of Political Science* 10, no. 1 (May 1975): 40.

9. Georges Sorel, *Le Procès de Socrate: Examen critique des thèses socratiques* (Paris: Alcan, 1889), 171.

10. Enthusiasm was historically considered the "nobler cousin" of fanaticism. Alberto Toscano, *Fanaticism: On the Uses of an Idea* (London: Verso, 2010), xxi. Enthusiasm in both love and war would remain central for Sorel, who decades later wrote that "love, by the enthusiasm it begets, can produce that sublimity without which there would be no effective morality" (*Reflections*, 236; *Réflexions*, 342). In the martial realm, he projected the division inaugurated by Socrates forward onto the degeneration of military virtue under Napoleon: "The best officers of that time fully realized that their talent consisted in furnishing their troops with the material means of expressing their enthusiasm [*élan*]," and by their own (egalitarian) example were "merely the first combatants, like true Homeric kings" (241, 350–51). But by this point, military examples were merely metaphors for the class struggle: "The same spirit is found in the working-class groups who are enthusiastic [*passionnés*] about the general strike" (242, 352).

11. Citing Xenophon's *Symposium* (VIII.9), Sorel accuses Socrates of elevating heavenly love (*Aphroditê Ourania*) at the expense of a more common or vulgar "pandemic" love available to any member of the *demos* (*Aphroditê Pandêmos*) (*Le Procès*, 87), adding that "it is not with his ignorant wife that the Athenian [man] could conclude this union of souls, so vaunted by the phi-

losopher" (*Le Procès*, 95). While Sorel is ostensibly defending material love and the women it includes, he clearly does not escape—and indeed invites—feminist criticism, in the martial embrace of warrior virtue and the deeply conservative imprint that Pierre-Joseph Proudhon left on his thinking.

12. "In the old armies, the distance between the officer and the soldier was not great. A developed military science did not yet exist," and under such conditions, "military organization led [*entrainait*], almost inevitably, to political equality," whereas it was only in the time of Socrates that one began to attack other cities scientifically" (*Le Procès*, 168–70). Sorel refers to the Iphicratean Reform shortly after Socrates's death, which involved both a shift in spear and shield technology, but also and as a result, new patterns of drilling and discipline. See J. E. Lendon, *Soldiers and Ghosts: A History of Battle in Classical Antiquity* (New Haven, CT: Yale University Press, 2006), 413.

13. John L. Stanley, *The Sociology of Virtue: The Political and Social Theories of Georges Sorel* (Berkeley: University of California Press, 1981), 37.

14. Some have noted Sorelian themes in Foucault, notably James Miller, *The Passion of Michel Foucault* (New York: Simon and Schuster, 1993), 171, 177; Stuart J. Murray, "Myth as Critique?," *Philosophy and Social Criticism* 30, no. 2 (2004): 247–62; and George Ciccariello-Maher, "An Anarchism That Is Not Anarchism: Notes Toward a Critique of Anarchist Imperialism," in *How Not to Be Governed: Readings and Interpretations From a Critical Anarchist Left*, ed. J. Klausen and J. Martel (Lanham, MD: Lexington Books, 2011), 30–33.

15. Sorel, *Le Procès*, 207.

16. Sorel, *Le Procès*, 177; *FGS*, 64.

17. Sorel, *Le Procès*, 179; *FGS*, 64–65.

18. Sorel, *Le Procès*, 203; *FGS*, 300n11.

19. Sorel, *Le Procès*, 205–6; *FGS*, 67.

20. Sorel, *Le Procès*, 200–201; *FGS*, 65–66.

21. I. F. Stone, *The Trial of Socrates* (New York: Anchor, 1989), 67.

22. While Larry Portis refers to Sorel's "passing interest" in Bergson, Stanley makes the slightly stronger, but still defensible, claim that "Bergson helped Sorel express the theory of the myth." Portis, *Georges Sorel* (London: Pluto Press, 1981), 12; Stanley, *FGS*, 47–48. By contrast, most commentators erroneously cite Bergson as the source of Sorel's concept, when in reality it originated in Homeric poetry before being translated into the "social poetry" Sorel would later find in Marxism.

23. Even Sorel had to recognize the latent class tensions within the military: due to the extraordinary cost of horses, the cavalry represented "the pressure point of the oligarchs" and severely limited the class mobility of infantrymen, no matter how heroic (*Le Procès*, 167). Furthermore, unlike other positions, Athens's ten generals, or *strategoi*, were not drawn by lot, and their annual elections therefore both reflected and exacerbated prevailing class divisions: the wealthiest of citizens were funneled to the top of the military hierarchy (due precisely to "expertise" in international affairs), and

used these positions to further increase their wealth. The centrality that Sorel grants to military affairs in maintaining equality thus unravels. While Sorel would later refer to "classical antiquity before Socrates" as an "organic" epoch, he argues that "nothing appears less constructive" than emphasizing ancient times, "which we are really only beginning to know." Giorgio Sorel, *Saggi di critica del Marxismo* (Milan: Sandron, 1903), 74; *FGS*, 118–19.

24. Sorel, *Saggi*, 13.

25. Jack J. Roth, *The Cult of Violence: Sorel and the Sorelians* (Berkeley: University of California Press, 1980), ix.

26. Karl Marx and Friedrich Engels, *The Communist Manifesto* (New York: Penguin, 2002), 220.

27. This was not an easy task. Not only were the early manuscripts unavailable, but the limited selection of texts that Sorel could access in French meant that—like Lukács a generation later—he "virtually had to unearth and reconstruct" Marxian dialectics on the basis of a few "suggestions" in later texts (Portis, *Georges Sorel*, 12).

28. Perry Anderson excavates the prehistory of the term *hegemony* in socialist circles, albeit not always in reference to ideological struggle, in "The Antinomies of Antonio Gramsci," *New Left Review* 100 (1976–77): 5–78.

29. Eduard Bernstein's own contributions to the debate within the German Sozialdemokratische Partei Deutschlands (SPD) were later published as *Evolutionary Socialism*, trans. E. C. Harvey (New York: Schocken, 1961 [1899]). Bernstein interrogated the validity of several of Marx's "objective" claims, such as the labor theory of value and the assertion that class cleavages would automatically deepen as capitalism developed. The resulting gradualist reformism was countered by Karl Kautsky's reaffirmation of "orthodox" claims, and the nominal opposition within Marxism between "reformist revisionism" and "revolutionary orthodoxy" proliferated antagonistic pairs across the continent, with Jules Guesde and Jean Jaurès standing in as the French representatives of orthodoxy and revisionism, respectively.

30. Foucault, *"Society Must Be Defended,"* 61–62.

31. Sorel, *Saggi*, 12.

32. Sorel, *Saggi*, 175.

33. Sorel, *Saggi*, 92–93; *FGS*, 128–29.

34. J. R. Jennings, "Sorel's Early Marxism and Science," *Political Studies* 31, no. 2 (June 1983): 232.

35. Sorel, *Saggi*, 79; *FGS*, 121.

36. Sorel, *Saggi*, 11, 82.

37. Sorel, *Saggi*, 234. Sorel cites Marx's description of dialectics as a "guiding thread." Despite Sorel's critique of Hegelian dialectics, one could draw out affinities between this narrow historical materialism and Pippin's interpretation of Hegel in *Hegel's Practical Philosophy*.

38. Sorel, *Saggi*, 68, 65; *FGS*, 116, 114.

39. Sorel, *Saggi*, 89, 152, translation modified; *FGS*, 126, 139.
40. Sorel only says "historical dependence," but I follow the English translator in adding the clarifying qualifier "reciprocal" (*Saggi*, 72; *FGS*, 117).
41. Sorel, *Saggi*, 143, 81–82; *FGS*, 135, 122.
42. Sorel, *Saggi*, 87; *FGS*, 125. Sorel's phrasing here notably prefigures Louis Althusser's later turn toward the contingency of what he called "aleatory materialism," although Althusser would be unlikely to admit any direct influence. In the original manuscript of *Marx in His Limits*, Althusser had mentioned Sorel's influence on Antonio Gramsci before scratching out his name, although he retains a similar reference in his later correspondence. In Louis Althusser, *Philosophy of the Encounter: Later Writings, 1978–87* (London: Verso, 2006), 161n148, 239.
43. *FGS*, 127–28. This brief discussion is not included in the edition of *Saggi* published in 1903, but appears in the original Italian version: "La necessità e il fatalismo nel marxismo," *La Riforma Sociale* V 8 (1898): 729–30.
44. Sorel, *Saggi*, 86; *FGS*, 124.
45. Sorel, *Reflections*, 55, 56; *Réflexions*, 74, 76.
46. Sorel, *Reflections*, 43, translation modified; *Réflexions*, 56.
47. Sorel, *Reflections*, 56; *Réflexions*, 76.
48. Sorel, *Reflections*, 66, 68; *Réflexions*, 93, 95.
49. On the role of the ideology of progress, see Georges Sorel, *The Illusions of Progress*, trans. J. Stanley (Berkeley: University of California Press, 1969).
50. Those same socialists who once encouraged agitation against the legal order "combated those in control of public force, [but] they did not at all desire to suppress that force, for they wished to utilize it someday for their own profit," and "they are therefore prepared to commit all the misdeeds of the *ancien régime*." Sorel, *Reflections*, 17, translation modified, 103; *Réflexions*, 23, 145.
51. Sorel, *Reflections*, 101; *Réflexions*, 142.
52. Not only was Sorel an early critic of ideology and what Gramsci would call hegemony, but he could even be understood as an early forerunner of those for whom the twentieth century would come to mark the "real subsumption"—in Marx's terms—of the working class into the capitalist state, via mediating mechanisms such as labor unions and political parties. See Michael Hardt and Antonio Negri, *Labor of Dionysus: A Critique of the State-Form* (Minneapolis: University of Minnesota Press, 1994), 257–62. See also Antonio Negri, "Twenty Theses on Marx," in *Marxism Beyond Marxism*, ed. S. Makdisi, C. Casarino, and R. Karl (London: Routledge, 1996); Endnotes Collective, "The History of Subsumption," *Endnotes* 2 (April 2010), https://endnotes.org.uk/en/endnotes-the-history-of-subsumption.
53. Marx himself did not reduce the class-in-itself purely to objective conditions, but understood it instead as a "class against capital but not yet for itself," with the class-for-itself subsequently emerging "in the struggle . . . [in which] the class becomes united." Marx, *The Poverty of Philosophy* (Peking: Foreign Languages Press, 1977), 168.

54. Ernesto Laclau and Chantal Mouffe, *Hegemony and Socialist Strategy* (London: Verso, 2001 [1985]), 38–40. However, as their title suggests, they view Sorel merely as a stepping-stone to Gramsci and immediately subsume his dialectics into those of his most preeminent disciple. In *Prison Notebooks*, Gramsci is above all critical of Sorel's unwillingness to move from the unifying function of the myth to that of the party. Antonio Gramsci, *Selections From the Prison Notebooks of Antonio Gramsci*, ed. Q. Hoare and G. N. Smith (New York: International Publishers, 1971), 127, 395. Gramsci's translators rightly note that "'Cleavage,' for Sorel, is the equivalent of class consciousness, of the class-for-itself" (126n4).

55. Portis, *Georges Sorel*, 44. Italian Marxist Mario Tronti makes this reversal explicitly. Mario Tronti, *Operai e Capitale*, 2nd ed. (Turin: Einaudi, 1971), 235. I draw out the continuities between Sorel and Tronti in George Ciccariello-Maher, "'Detached Irony Toward the Rest': Working-Class One-Sidedness From Sorel to Tronti," *Commoner* 11 (spring/summer 2006): 54–73.

56. Sorel, *Reflections*, 55, translation modified; *Réflexions*, 75.

57. Sorel, *Reflections*, 58; *Réflexions*, 80.

58. Axel Honneth, *The Struggle for Recognition: The Moral Grammar of Social Conflicts*, trans. J. Anderson (Cambridge, MA: MIT Press, 1995), 151, 153. Honneth continues, however, by predictably attributing the social myth to Bergson's influence and providing a strangely legalistic reading of Sorel's thought. Regardless, his is one of the few studies of Sorel to emphasize important intersections with Hegel's master-slave dialectic, which will prove relevant when we turn to Fanon.

59. Foucault, *"Society Must Be Defended,"* 52. Sorel, *Reflections*, 58; *Réflexions*, 80. Both Sorel and Foucault document the displacement of war to the bounds of the state, doing so in strikingly similar terms: for Sorel, this was when "anarchical elements" like bandits were "confined to *the limits of society*" (*Reflections*, 256; *Réflexions*, 372), for Foucault, when "war was expelled to the limits of the State" (*"Society Must Be Defended,"* 49).

60. Sorel, *Reflections*, 165–66, my emphasis; *Réflexions*, 240. This distinction is lost on most who discuss Sorel, notably Hannah Arendt, *On Violence* (New York: Harcourt, 1970). Even Marx neglected this distinction, in Sorel's view, providing "no other theory than that of bourgeois force," his one-sided account due to the fact that he "did not move in circles which had acquired a satisfactory notion of the general strike." Sorel, *Reflections*, 171–72 and n42; *Réflexions*, 249–50n1.

61. Sorel, *Reflections*, 108; *Réflexions*, 152. This gesture will become crucial when we turn to Fanon, whose apparent support for a national state might make him appear incompatible with Sorel. For a discussion of Sorel's anti-Jacobin antistatism, see Preston King, *Fear of Power: An Analysis of Anti-Statism in Three French Writers* (London: Frank Cass, 1967), 68–91.

62. Sorel, *Reflections*, 165; *Réflexions*, 240.

63. Georg Lukács, "Tactics and Ethics" (1919), in *Tactics and Ethics: Political Writings 1919–1929* (London: NLB, 1972). Jay, *Marxism and Totality*, 122, 98.

64. Sorel, *Reflections*, 68; *Réflexions*, 96. Walter Benjamin, "Critique of Violence," in *Reflections: Essays, Aphorisms, Autobiographical Writings*, ed. P. Demetz (New York: Schocken, 1978), 277–300. Rather than embrace Sorel's force/violence distinction, Benjamin installs a distinction at the heart of violence itself, further confounding Sorelian categories by opposing divine violence to mythical (law-making) violence.

65. Sorel, *Reflections*, 105–6; *Réflexions*, 149. Foucault, *"Society Must Be Defended,"* 58.

66. Sorel, *Reflections*, 251, 78; *Réflexions*, 365, 109–10.

67. Sorel, *Reflections*, 28; *Réflexions*, 38–39.

68. Sorel, *Saggi*, 61–63; FGS, 112–13.

69. Sorel, *Saggi*, 15. In a speech given in 1902, Sorel goes so far as to quote Engels's suggestion that the masses must "have their own interests presented to them in a religious guise in order to create a great turbulence" and popular upheaval. Friedrich Engels, *Ludwig Feuerbach and the Outcome of Classical German Philosophy* in MECW, vol. 26 (London: Lawrence and Wishart, 2010), 395. This is not an admission that myth was religion, however, as Sorel insists that nothing is so religious as the "superstitious belief" that presents Marxism as a "false science" and is upheld by a dogmatic *"socialist clericalism."* *Saggi*, 15–17. His point is instead that religion has no monopoly on nonrational motivation and that both myth and religion occupy "the profounder region of our mental life" (*Reflections*, 30; *Réflexions*, 42).

70. Sorel, *Saggi*, 390.

71. Sorel, *Reflections*, 118, translation modified; *Réflexions*, 169. While Gramsci would rely on the party and other institutions to perform this unifying function, like Sorel he was critical of those like Rosa Luxemburg who deterministically viewed economic crisis as the "field artillery" that not only "opens a breach in the enemy's defenses," but moreover organizes the ranks of the revolution and provides them the necessary "ideological concentration" (*Prison Notebooks*, 233).

72. Sorel, *Reflections*, 29; *Réflexions*, 40.

73. Sorel, *Reflections*, 115; *Réflexions*, 164. Working-class identity as an *absolute* assertion thus enjoys an "infinite quality" like the violence comprising it, and it is this "torment of the infinite" that is capable of producing greatness (24; 33). While still critical of Rousseau's "absolute man," Sorel now believes that through the revolutionary myth, the masses too can and must be "thrust on the road of the absolute [*la voie de l'absolu*]" (263; 383). Joining the two resignified terms together, the general strike points toward an "absolute revolution"—a phrase the early Sorel would never have uttered except in disgust (24; 33).

74. Sorel, *Reflections*, 251; *Réflexions*, 365.

75. Sorel, *Reflections*, 43, translation modified; *Réflexions*, 57.

76. Sorel, *Reflections*, 74, translation modified; *Réflexions*, 105.

77. Sorel, *Reflections*, 75–76, translation heavily modified; *Réflexions*, 106.

78. Sorel, *Reflections*, 76, translation modified; *Réflexions*, 106.

79. Sorel, *Reflections*, 77, translation modified; *Réflexions*, 108.

80. Sorel, *Reflections*, 78, 74–75, translations modified; *Réflexions*, 108–9, 105.

81. Sorel, *Reflections*, 78–79, translation modified; *Réflexions*, 110–11.

82. Sorel, *Reflections*, 85, translation modified; *Réflexions*, 120.

83. Sorel, *Reflections*, 14n13; *Réflexions*, 18n1.

84. Sorel would later compare Greek contempt for barbarians with the xeno-phobia of "the Yankee for the foreign worker" (*Reflections*, 232; *Réflexions*, 337).

85. Contemporary debates surrounding civility in academia and beyond should recognize that even etymologically, civility is a concept that only applies to those within a shared civilizational project—for whom politeness can replace the martial conduct of soldiers. But where exclusions are systematic and the relation is one of war, civility is meaningless.

86. Sorel, *Reflections*, 17, my emphasis; *Réflexions*, 23.

87. Sorel, *Reflections*, 263; *Réflexions*, 384. *Diremption*, one of several terms used by Hegel and Marx to denote a dialectical rupture that precedes reconcilia-tion, evokes a religious fall. See the discussion of the concept, its origins, and its development in Enrique Dussel, *El último Marx (1863–1882) y la liberación latinoamericana* (Mexico City: Siglo XXI, 1990), 346, 356n61; *Método para una filosofía de la liberación: Superación analéctica de la dialéctica hegeliana* (Sala-manca: Sígueme, 1974), 18 and appendix.

88. Foucault's concern thus refers, in Jay's lexicon, to both natural and longitu-dinal totalities. Jay, *Marxism and Totality*, 27–28. Foucault, *"Society Must Be Defended,"* 11.

89. Smith, *Hegel's Critique of Liberalism*, 17.

90. Jay overlooks this, misrepresenting Sorel as a representative of theoretical holism through a faulty interpretation of the role of myth (*Marxism and Totality*, 71n159).

91. Zeev Sternhell, *Neither Right nor Left: Fascist Ideology in France*, trans. D. Maisel (Berkeley: University of California Press, 1986 [1983]), 268–70.

92. Portis, *Georges Sorel*, 16. To which Stanley adds a "curious lack of logical rigor" (*FGS*, 3). For a critique of Sternhell's treatment of Sorel, see Jacques Julliard, "Sur un fascisme imaginaire: A props d'un livre de Zeev Sternhell," *Annales E.S.C.* (July–August 1984), 8496–1; Robert Wohl, "French Fascism, Both Right and Left: Reflections on the Sternhell Controversy," *Journal of Modern History* 63, no. 1 (March 1991): 91–98.

93. Berth, quoted in Stanley, *FGS*, 4.

94. Carl Schmitt, *The Crisis of Parliamentary Democracy*, trans. E. Kennedy (Cam-bridge, MA: MIT Press, 1985 [1923]), 75. This historical observation conceals a normative orientation, in which the friend-enemy conflict, for Schmitt,

must map cleanly onto the a priori boundaries of the nation. Indeed, Schmitt must have shuddered to see Sorel inscribing the anarchy of the international arena at the very heart of the social body itself. While Schmitt's later work embraces aspects of partisan warfare, he nevertheless resists the temptation to extend this sympathy to Lenin's global civil war, and in reserving the position of the ultimate partisan not for the Algerian rebels, but instead for the fascistic settler-terrorist Raoul Salan, Schmitt makes perfectly clear that his approach remains resolutely opposed to decolonization. Carl Schmitt, *The Theory of the Partisan: A Commentary/Remark on the Concept of the Political*, trans. A. C. Goodson (East Lansing: Michigan State University Press, 2004 [1963]).

95. Stanley, *Sociology of Virtue*, 320–26. Stanley's discussion has the virtue of being nuanced, but flies far wide of the mark when he turns his attention to Fanon, toward whom he ironically re-creates errors similar to those frequently leveled at Sorel.

96. David Caute is at pains to rescue Fanon from the Sorelian taint, lest he be deemed a "black neo-Fascist." *Frantz Fanon* (London: Fontana, 1970), 86. At their worst, claims as to the existence of "Black fascism" and "Black racism" fall into the purest of formalism: emphasizing shared rhetorical styles, "military discipline, uniforms, and the readiness to sacrifice," marching bands, and feathered hats. See A. James Gregor, *The Search for Neofascism: The Use and Abuse of Social Science* (Cambridge: Cambridge University Press, 2006), 115–16.

Even more sympathetic arguments, like that of Paul Gilroy, suggest a "common political style" shared by Marcus Garvey and Italian fascism. "Black Fascism," *Transition* 81/82 (2000): 70. Gilroy points toward the "martial technologies of racial becoming" of Garvey's Universal Negro Improvement Association (UNIA) without noting the asymmetry between racial becoming and racial superiority, and defines a "generic fascism" in the least useful way possible, as "brutality and masculinity" (73).

Even C. L. R. James once dismissed Garveyism as "pitiable rubbish" and Garveyites as the "first Fascists," without bothering to wonder what crucial temporal disjuncture was introduced by the suggestion that they were *first*. C. L. R. James, *A History of Negro Revolt* (New York: Haskell House, 1938), 69. However, James would effectively recant this position in a 1961 appendix added to *The Black Jacobins*, praising Garvey for having grasped the role of Black identity in the revolutionary dialectic: "In little more than half of ten years he had made [Blackness] a part of the political consciousness of the world. He did not know the word Negritude but he knew the thing" (397).

97. Malcolm X, a militantly combative and dialectical thinker, would be driven away from the Nation of Islam for breaking the bounds of separatism to antagonize the U.S. political establishment and would eventually abandon

notions of racial supremacy. However, Manning Marable overstates this transformation as though it were a simple pendulum swing toward multicultural universalism, rather than a turn to a more dialectical—indeed Fanonian—concept of race. *Malcolm X: A Life of Reinvention* (New York: Penguin, 2011).

98. Even one of Sorel's sharpest critics argues that "Sorel could be for Libya or against it, for intervention or against it." Jack Roth, "The Roots of Italian Fascism," *Journal of Modern History* 39, no. 1 (March 1967): 30. Quotes in text from Roth, *The Cult of Violence*, 133, 130.

99. José Carlos Mariátegui, *Seven Interpretive Essays on Peruvian Reality*, trans. M. Urquidi (Austin: University of Texas Press, 1971); Robinson, *Black Marxism*, 184.

100. Sorel, *FGS*, 128.

101. Paradigmatic examples of this contingency and reversal include both the tragic view of history in James's *The Black Jacobins* and W. E. B. Du Bois's suggestion in the U.S. context that "the slave went free; stood a brief moment in the sun; then moved back again toward slavery." *Black Reconstruction in America*, 30.

102. Césaire, *Discourse on Colonialism*, 36.

103. Césaire, *Discourse on Colonialism*, 32, 40. For a recent analysis of the "image of the barbaric Left" that brings communism and decolonization together as an object of anxiety, see Brennan, *Borrowed Light*, 178.

104. Walter Mignolo, "The Geopolitics of Knowledge and the Colonial Difference," *South Atlantic Quarterly* 101, no. 1 (2002): 57–96.

105. While Sorel's influence on Fanon is often discussed despite the absence of direct confirmation, Mariátegui was open about his enthusiasm for Sorel, especially in his *Defensa del marxismo, Obras completas*, vol. 5 (Lima: 1974 [1934]). Again, Sorel's maligned status leads many to either distinguish Mariátegui's thought from Sorel's or to note their continuities in order to reject both (as, e.g., insufficiently Marxist). For an example of the first, see Ofelia Schutte's suggestion that Sorel's myth is "masculinist" and "authoritarian and conducive to right-wing ideologies." *Cultural Identity and Social Liberation in Latin American Thought* (Albany: SUNY Press, 1993), 45. For the second, see Hugo García Salvatecci, *Sorel y Mariátegui: Ubicación ideológica del Amauta* (Lima: Delgado Valenzuela, 1979).

106. Sorel, *Reflections*, 287n10.

Chapter 2: Toward a New Dialectics of Race

1. I use the concept of disavowal here in a roughly psychoanalytic sense, following Sibylle Fischer's insightful analysis of the disavowal of the Haitian Revolution. Freud's understanding of the concept is marked by psychic continuity with rather than clean rupture from the object of disavowal, in

which "disavowal is always supplemented by acknowledgement." Sigmund Freud, *An Outline of Psycho-Analysis*, in J. Strachey, et al., eds., *The Standard Edition of the Complete Works of Sigmund Freud*, vol. 23 (London: Hogarth Press, 1974), 204; cited in Fischer, *Modernity Disavowed*, 38.

2. Sartre, "Preface," in Fanon, *Wretched*, xlix, translation modified; Fanon, *Œuvres*, 436.

3. The phrase is borrowed from *Capital* for *Anti-Dühring*, where what Sartre calls violence is generally translated as "force." Where Sorel categorically distinguished violence from force, Étienne Balibar—arguably like Walter Benjamin—locates an "intrinsic ambiguity" within *Gewalt* itself. Étienne Balibar, "Reflections on *Gewalt*," *Historical Materialism* 17 (2009): 101.

4. Fanon, *Wretched*, 63; *Œuvres*, 145. That this comment is too often overlooked owes in part to the fact that it appears at the beginning of the second chapter, far less read than the first.

5. While it is possible to find analyses that do the opposite, the overwhelming weight of the literature seeks to recuperate Fanon by distinguishing him from Sorel. See Alice Cherki, *Frantz Fanon: A Portrait*, trans. N. Benabid (Ithaca, NY: Cornell University Press, 2006 [2000]), 222; Irene L. Gendzier, *Frantz Fanon: A Critical Study* (New York: Grove Press, 1973), 203–4; Hussein A. Buhlan, *Frantz Fanon and the Psychology of Oppression* (New York: Plenum Press, 1985), 145–48; Caute, *Frantz Fanon*, 93; Renate Zahar, *Frantz Fanon: Colonialism and Alienation*, trans. W. Feuser (London: Monthly Review, 1974), 86. More balanced views can be found in L. Adele Jinadu, *Fanon: In Search of the African Revolution* (London: Routledge, 1986), 91–94; Stanley, *Sociology of Virtue*, 328–32; and David Macey, who insists on distinguishing the two, but without taking sides: *Frantz Fanon* (New York: Picador, 2000), 465.

6. Arendt, *On Violence*.

7. Arendt, *On Revolution*, 19.

8. Frantz Fanon, *Black Skin, White Masks*, trans. R. Philcox (New York: Grove Press, 2008 [1952]), 89; *Œuvres*, 153.

9. This metaphorical "crossing" is similar to that experienced by W. E. B. Du Bois, which I discuss in George Ciccariello-Maher, "A Critique of Du Boisian Reason: Kanye West and the Fruitfulness of Double-Consciousness," *Journal of Black Studies* 39, no. 3 (January 2009): 371–401.

10. Fanon, *Black Skin*, 128n10; *Œuvres*, 186n10. Jean-Paul Sartre, *Anti-Semite and Jew: An Exploration of the Etiology of Hate*, trans. G. Becker (New York: Schocken Books, 1995 [1948]), 75.

11. Fanon, *Black Skin*, xvii–xviii; *Œuvres*, 68. The original translation of this chapter's title—"The Fact of Blackness"—was positively misleading, since Blackness was not for Fanon an objective fact. In this passage, the new translation exaggerates the Du Boisian resonances by choosing such words as *striving* and *folk* to complement Fanon's reference to the "black soul."

12. Fanon, *Black Skin*, 90; *Œuvres*, 153.

13. For Jay, this is longitudinal totality as "a belief that history could be understood as a progressively meaningful whole." Jay, *Marxism and Totality*, 26.

14. Fanon, *Black Skin*, xi, translation modified; *Œuvres*, 63.

15. Fanon, *Black Skin*, 206, translation modified; *Œuvres*, 251. Or, alternatively, "I wanted quite simply to be a man among men. I would have liked to enter our world young and sleek, a world we could build together." Fanon, *Black Skin*, 92; *Œuvres*, 91.

16. Fanon, *Black Skin*, xii–xiii, 73; *Œuvres*, 64, 137.

17. Fanon, *Black Skin*, 89, translation modified; *Œuvres*, 153.

18. Fanon, *Black Skin*, 92; *Œuvres*, 155. In fact, Fanon's entire phenomenological treatment of this moment must be read as a critical analog to Sartre's analysis of "The Look," in *Being and Nothingness: A Phenomenological Essay on Ontology*, trans. H. Barnes (New York: Washington Square Press, 1956 [1943]), esp. 340–45.

19. Fanon, *Black Skin*, 94, translation modified; *Œuvres*, 157.

20. Fanon, *Black Skin*, 98–99; *Œuvres*, 160–61.

21. In what follows, I build on ideas present in George Ciccariello-Maher, "Decolonizing Fanaticism," *Theory and Event* 17 (2014): n2.

22. Fanon, *Black Skin*, 22, my emphasis; *Œuvres*, 87.

23. Fanon, *Black Skin*, 98, translation modified; *Œuvres*, 160. For Fanon, following Sartre, anti-Semitism and racism are more than simply irrational; they are forms of existential "bad faith" that are self-referential, circular, and beyond recourse to reason itself. See Lewis Gordon, *Bad Faith and Anti-Black Racism* (New York: Humanity Books, 1995).

24. Fanon, *Black Skin*, 111, translation modified, my emphasis; *Œuvres*, 170.

25. Fanon, *Black Skin*, 106; *Œuvres*, 166.

26. Fanon, *Black Skin*, 100; *Œuvres*, 161. For previous works in this vein, see Lou Turner, "On the Difference between the Hegelian and Fanonian Dialectic of Lordship and Bondage," in *Fanon: A Critical Reader*, ed. L. Gordon, T. Sharpley-Whiting, and R. White (Oxford: Blackwell, 1996); and Ato Sekyi-Otu, *Fanon's Dialectic of Experience* (Cambridge, MA: Harvard University Press, 1997). Arguably the best existing treatment of these questions is that of Nigel Gibson, "Dialectical Impasses: Turning the Table on Hegel and the Black," *parallax* 8, no. 2 (2002): 30–45.

27. Mignolo, "The Geopolitics of Knowledge and the Colonial Difference."

28. G. W. F. Hegel, *Phenomenology of Spirit/Phänomenologie des Geistes*, trans. T. Pinkhard (2010 [1807]), §179–180. The following paragraphs draw upon George Ciccariello-Maher, "The Dialectics of Standing One's Ground," *Theory and Event* 15, no. 3 (2012), where I use Hegel's description of self-consciousness as *Selbstständigkeit*, or "self-standing-ness," to theorize the murder of Trayvon Martin and the debate surrounding "stand your ground" laws.

29. Hegel, *Phenomenology*, §187.

30. Hegel, *Phenomenology*, §182.

31. Hegel, *Phenomenology*, §187.

32. Put briefly, *Grund*—which Hegel discusses extensively in the *Science of Logic*—is the broadest and most basic category of the totality. For an analysis of Hegelian Ground that is more rooted in Hegel's *Logic*, see C. L. R. James, *Notes on Dialectics: Hegel, Marx, Lenin* (Westport, CT: Lawrence Hill, 1980), 95–98.

33. Hegel, *Phenomenology*, §193.

34. Fanon, *Black Skin*, 89–90; *Œuvres*, 153. Like many of his contemporaries, Fanon derives his reading of Hegel, and the importance of the master-slave dialectic, largely from Alexandre Kojève's widely influential lectures given in the 1930s, and through Jean Hyppolite's translation of the *Phenomenology*. Dissecting Fanon through Kojève, Ethan Kleinberg is not convinced by Fanon's claims to have decolonized the Hegelian dialectic, but his attempt to discover in Hegel all aspects of Fanon's reformulation—and to confine Fanon's contributions to the merely phenomenological—are unconvincing in turn. "Kojève and Fanon: The Desire for Recognition and the Fact of Blackness," in T. Stovall and G. Van Den Abbeele, eds., *French Civilization and Its Discontents: Nationalism, Colonialism, Race* (Lanham, MD: Lexington Books, 2003), 115–28. See also Alfred J. López, "Occupying Reality: Fanon Reading Hegel," *South Atlantic Quarterly* 112, no. 1 (winter 2013): 71–78; Gayatri Chakravorty Spivak, "Fanon Reading Hegel," in *Readings* (Calcutta: Seagull Books, 2014). While Macey suggests that this approach to Hegel so prevalent in France was "ill-suited to Fanon's purposes," in some ways it was quite well suited (*Frantz Fanon*, 163).

35. Fanon, *Black Skin*, 95, 91; *Œuvres*, 158, 154–55.

36. Fanon, *Black Skin*, 89; *Œuvres*, 153.

37. Fanon, *Black Skin*, 193; *Œuvres*, 239.

38. Fanon, *Black Skin*, 191; *Œuvres*, 238.

39. Fanon, *Black Skin*, 117n24, translation modified; *Œuvres*, 175n23.

40. Fanon, *Black Skin*, 195n10; *Œuvres*, 241n9.

41. Orlando Patterson points out that the master acquires recognition from other masters, negating the existential need for recognition by the slave. *Slavery and Social Death*, 98–100.

42. Fanon, *Black Skin*, 195n10; *Œuvres*, 241n9.

43. Fanon, *Black Skin*, 90, translation modified; *Œuvres*, 153. If Hegel can be credited with formulating an intersubjective and dialectical ontology, this intersubjectivity incorporates only intraontological difference (differences *within* being) while effectively excluding *subontological* difference (differences *between* being and sub/nonbeing). Nelson Maldonado-Torres uses this term in contrast to Emmanuel Levinas's formulation of *transontological difference*, which marks "the distance between Being and what is beyond Being; or Being and exteriority." Nelson Maldonado-Torres, "On the Coloniality of Being: Contributions to the Development of a Concept," *Cultural Studies* 21,

no. 2 (March 2007): 253–54. See also Nelson Maldonado-Torres, *Against War: Views From the Underside of Modernity* (Durham, NC: Duke University Press, 2008), 106–15.

44. Fanon, *Black Skin*, xii, translation modified; *Œuvres*, 64.

45. Lewis Gordon, "Through the Hellish Zone of Nonbeing: Thinking Through Fanon, Disaster, and the Damned of the Earth," *Human Architecture: Journal of the Sociology of Self-Knowledge* V (summer 2007): 11–12. On politics as publicity, see Hannah Arendt, *The Human Condition* (New York: Doubleday, 1958), 45–53.

46. W. E. B. Du Bois, *The Souls of Black Folk* (New York: Penguin, 1996 [1903]), 8.

47. Fanon, *Black Skin*, 95, translation modified; *Œuvres*, 157.

48. Fanon, *Black Skin*, 94, translation modified; *Œuvres*, 156–57.

49. Fanon, *Black Skin*, 94, translation modified; *Œuvres*, 157.

50. Fanon, *Black Skin*, 103–4; *Œuvres*, 164.

51. Fanon, *Black Skin*, 107–8, translation modified; *Œuvres*, 167–68. Here, borrowing from Sartre's diagnosis of the charitable gaze, Fanon would say that for the colonized to *force* any emotion onto the colonizer is already a step toward ethical reciprocity. See Sartre, *Anti-Semite and Jew*, 77.

52. Fanon, *Black Skin*, xiii; *Œuvres*, 64. I expand upon the question of enthusiasm, fanaticism, and zealotry in Ciccariello-Maher, "Decolonizing Fanaticism."

53. Fanon, *Black Skin*, 95; *Œuvres*, 157.

54. Fanon, *Black Skin*, 102, translation modified; *Œuvres*, 163.

55. Fanon, *Black Skin*, xviii; *Œuvres*, 68. It is revealing that Fanon turns here not to Léopold Senghor—of the more essentialist wing of the Negritude movement—who insisted that "emotion is Negro as reason is Greek" (106; 166), but instead to Césaire whom he immediately cites: "My negritude is not a stone, its deafness hurled against the clamor of day . . . My negritude is neither a tower nor a cathedral" (103; 164). Césaire senses a complicity between a certain form of essentialist negritude and what Sartre would describe as the anti-Semite's desire to possess "the durability of a stone." Sartre, *Anti-Semite and Jew*, 18. On Fanon's relationship to Senghor and Césaire, see Robert Bernasconi, "The Assumption of Negritude: Aimé Césaire, Frantz Fanon, and the Vicious Circle of Racial Politics," *parallax* 8, no. 2 (2002): 69–83.

56. Fanon, *Black Skin*, 102, xviii; *Œuvres*, 163, 68.

57. I have argued elsewhere that, even in *Wretched*, it is "symbolic violence," the two-sided transformation set into motion by this subjective explosion, that matters most. George Ciccariello-Maher, "Jumpstarting the Decolonial Engine: Symbolic Violence From Fanon to Chávez," *Theory and Event* 13, no. 1 (March 2010).

58. Gordon, "Through the Hellish Zone," 12.

59. Lewis Gordon, "Of Illicit Appearance: The L.A. Riots/Rebellion as a Portent of Things to Come," *Truthout.org*, May 12, 2012. http://truth-out.org/news

/item/9008-of-illicit-appearance-the-la-riots-rebellion-as-a-portent-of
-things-to-come. Gordon cites as evidence the perception that professedly
nonviolent civil rights leaders were in fact violent, but almost any example
would suffice. A recent Associated Press poll, carried out in conjunction
with Stanford University, found that a full 20 percent of respondents *openly*
admit to considering blacks "violent" (and data on implicit bias shows that
subtle associations can be much higher). In a broader sense, Enrique Dussel
has charted the *incomprehensibility* of this sort of appearance, in which "the
messianic proposal . . . is *madness* for the old system." Dussel, "The Liberatory Event in Paul of Tarsus," trans. G. Ciccariello-Maher, *Qui Parle* 18, no.
1 (fall/winter 2009): 130. For Gordon, Gandhi's resort to nonviolence had
everything to do with the fact that he was not racialized as already and
necessarily violent in the same way that Fanon was. Lewis Gordon, "Fanon,"
Histories of Violence, http://historiesofviolence.com/thinkers/fanon/.

60. RWW News, "Ben Stein: Michael Brown Was 'Armed With His Incredibly
Strong, Scary Self,'" August 27, 2014. https://www.youtube.com/watch?v
=RtBQUAyLWUI.

61. "Our Nation's Unarmed Teens: Are They Armed?," *The Onion*, August 17 2014.
http://www.theonion.com/graphic/our-nations-unarmed-teens-are-they
-armed-36705.

62. However, it is perhaps more accurate to say, following Spillers, that the
transcendent nature of Black violence is grounded in the inaccessibility of
gender to begin with ("Mama's Baby, Papa's Maybe").

63. Fanon, *Black Skin*, 118–19, translation modified; *Œuvres*, 176. See Richard
Wright, *Native Son* (New York: Harper and Row, 1989 [1940]).

64. Furthermore, to "state" something is to "place" it or to *class-ify* it in the
terms of Aníbal Quijano, "The Coloniality of Power and Social Classification."

65. See Nelson Maldonado-Torres, "On the Coloniality of Being."

66. Fanon, *Black Skin*, 195, translation modified, my emphasis; *Œuvres*, 241.

67. Fanon, *Black Skin*, 194–95, translation modified; *Œuvres*, 240–41.

68. Fanon, *Black Skin*, 195–97, translation modified; *Œuvres*, 241–42. Fanon
sees this situation as specific to France (or perhaps Europe): "In the United
States the black man fights and is fought," and in Africa, many seek to "keep
their alterity—alterity of rupture, of struggle, of combat" (196–97; 242),
although this understates struggle in the French colonies and overstates
struggle—versus ideology—in the United States. Jean Améry confirms
this yearning for struggle, on the basis of his own experiences as a concentration camp inmate, noting his own deep frustrations at having never
"fought the oppressor *weapon in hand*"; Jean Améry, "The Birth of Man From
the Spirit of Violence: Frantz Fanon the Revolutionary," *Wasafiri* 44 (spring
2005): 16.

69. Cited in Fanon, *Black Skin*, 111; *Œuvres*, 170.

70. Cited in Fanon, *Black Skin*, 112, translation modified; *Œuvres*, 171.

71. These passages appear in a 1967 interview, reprinted in Césaire, *Discourse on Colonialism*, 85–86. Césaire had written in 1956: "Provincialism? I am not burying myself in a narrow particularism. But neither do I want to lose myself in a disembodied universalism . . . My conception of the universal is that of a universal enriched by all that is particular, a universal enriched by every particular: the deepening and coexistence of all particulars." Aimé Césaire, "Letter to Maurice Thorez," *Social Text* 103, vol. 28, no. 2 (summer 2010): 152, translation modified. Sartre's insistence that "the most ardent of apostles of Negritude are at the same time militant Marxists" set him up for a serious historical correction less than a decade later: while remaining Marxists, Césaire and many others—including George Padmore, Richard Wright, and C. L. R. James—would soon break with official communism over precisely the sort of myopia that Sartre here embodies (Césaire in the "Letter" itself). See Cedric Robinson, *Black Marxism*, 184.
72. Fanon, *Black Skin*, 112–13, translation modified; *Œuvres*, 171.
73. Fanon, *Black Skin*, 113–14, translation modified; *Œuvres*, 172.
74. Fanon, *Black Skin*, 114, first emphasis mine, translation modified; *Œuvres*, 172.
75. Bernasconi reduces Fanon's critique to the idea that "Sartre's race is the issue for Fanon," rather than his wrongly weighted dialectic. Robert Bernasconi, "The European Knows and Does Not Know," in *Frantz Fanon's* Black Skin, White Masks: *New Interdisciplinary Essays*, ed. M. Silverman (Manchester: Manchester University Press, 2005), 107.
76. Fanon, *Black Skin*, xvi–xvii; *Œuvres*, 67.
77. Fanon, *Black Skin*, 116–17, translation modified; *Œuvres*, 174–75.
78. Fanon's critique of Sartre is too often overlooked and misunderstood. Zamir, for example, misses the dialectical point when he suggests that "Fanon goes on to adopt exactly Sartre's position" regarding the "transitoriness of negritude." Fanon, for Zamir—and in contrast to Du Bois—falls into a "false polarization" between essentialism and transformation; *Dark Voices: W. E. B. Du Bois and American Thought, 1888–1903* (Chicago: University of Chicago Press, 1995), 209. More recently, Glen Coulthard provides a close reading of Fanon to argue in part that he shares Sartre's position: *Red Skin, White Masks*. For our conversation on this and other questions, see the special symposium in *Historical Materialism* 24, no. 3 (2016).

    As I have argued elsewhere, by the time he wrote his preface to *Wretched*, where he insisted that it is decolonization and not the class struggle that constitutes "the last stage of the dialectic," Sartre had accepted the validity of Fanon's critique (lxii; *Œuvres*, 448). See George Ciccariello-Maher, "The Internal Limits of the European Gaze: Intellectuals and the Colonial Difference," *Radical Philosophy Review* 9, no. 2 (fall 2006): 139–65.
79. Fanon, *Black Skin*, 83, 118–19, translation modified; *Œuvres*, 145, 175–76. The position between Nothingness (itself a Sartrean concept) and Infinity

(a concept we would identify more directly with Emmanuel Levinas), opens toward Enrique Dussel. For a work that discusses Fanon, Dussel, and Levinas, see Nelson Maldonado-Torres, *Against War*.

80. Fanon, *Black Skin*, 117, translation modified; *Œuvres*, 175.
81. Fanon, *Black Skin*, 89; *Œuvres*, 153.
82. Fanon, *Black Skin*, 204; *Œuvres*, 249–50. Like Césaire, Fanon can only envision ever arriving at the universal through a struggle with particulars: "Through the particular, he is actually dealing with a more radicalized, universalizing practice, and Fanon himself was a universalist, but again he didn't mean it as a static term, but as a commitment one has to keep struggling for." Gordon, "Fanon."
83. Nigel Gibson, "Radical Mutations: Fanon's Untidy Dialectic of History," in *Rethinking Fanon: The Continuing Dialogue*, ed. N. Gibson (New York: Humanity Books, 1999), 408–46.
84. Fanon, *Black Skin*, 192; *Œuvres*, 239.
85. Fanon, *Black Skin*, 198–99, translation modified; *Œuvres*, 245.
86. Frantz Fanon, "Letter to the Resident Minister (1956)," in *Toward the African Revolution*, trans. H. Chevalier (New York: Grove Press, 1988 [1964]), 53, translation modified; *Œuvres*, 734–35.

Chapter 3: The Decolonial Nation in Motion

1. Du Bois, *The Souls of Black Folk*, chap. 13, "Of the Coming of John." Recall that dialectical rupture as "diremption" refers to just such a religious fall.
2. Jacques Roumain, "Nouveau sermon nègre," in *Anthologie de la nouvelle poésie nègre et malgache de langue française*, ed. L. S. Senghor (Paris: P.U.F., 1969) 119–20. The only English translation, by S. Shapiro, *Ebony Wood* (New York: Interworld Press, 1972), is difficult to acquire. Notably, many English and otherwise translated versions of "L'Internationale" either exclude reference to the damnés, translate it as "oppressed" (thereby shifting a more external relation to an internal one), or even inexplicably invert the condemnation of the damnés into the condemnation of the system.
3. James, *The Black Jacobins*, 317. This is not all: across the Caribbean and Latin America, the example of Haiti—and its concretization of the Rights of Man—fueled revolutionary upheaval. In Venezuela, for example, the free *zambo* José Leonardo Chirino—his mother a free indigenous woman but his father a slave—returned from Haiti imbued with this spirit of transatlantic revolution, and proceeded to lead one of the most important Afro-Indigenous rebellions in Venezuelan history. George Ciccariello-Maher: *We Created Chávez: A People's History of the Venezuelan Revolution* (Durham, NC: Duke University Press, 2013), 148–50.
4. Slavoj Žižek, *First as Tragedy, Then as Farce* (London: Verso, 2009), 111–12. Aimé Césaire, "Décolonisation pour les Antilles," in *Caribbean Critique:*

Antillean Critical Theory From Toussaint to Glissant, ed. Nick Nesbitt (Liverpool: Liverpool University Press, 2013), 86; thanks to Richard Pithouse for drawing my attention to this passage. See also Miguel Mellino, "The *Langue* of the Damned: Fanon and the Remnants of Europe," *South Atlantic Quarterly* 112, no. 1 (2013): 79–89.

5. Fanon, *Wretched*, 6, translation modified, my emphasis; *Œuvres*, 455.

6. Fanon, "Letter to the Resident Minister," in *Toward the African Revolution*, 52; *Œuvres*, 734.

7. Fanon, *Wretched*, 63; *Œuvres*, 509. Macey admits that Fanon had read Sorel's *Réflexions*, but adds that "there is little evidence that he was influenced by it" (*Frantz Fanon*, 465). Here, as with Macey's similar denial that Sartre was influenced by Fanon, an absence of citation conceals a deep and evident theoretical influence (452).

8. In an interesting double gesture, the Fanon of *Wretched* cites his own account of racism as Manichaean in *Black Skin* (6n1; *Œuvres*, 456n1), while the Fanon of *Black Skin* cites (160; 210) Sartre's account of anti-Semitism as Manichaeism (*Anti-Semite and Jew*, 40). On the question of Manichaeism, Sartre's text shares an immobility akin to *Black Skin*: whereas Fanon had denied being a zealot, Sartre similarly insisted that "we are not Manichaeans" (*Anti-Semite and Jew*, 59). But in both his call for Jewish authenticity and his critique of the democrat as a "feeble protector" of the Jews, Sartre nevertheless gestures toward Fanon's eventual inversion and harnessing of Manichaean identity: "If the democrat were to put some warmth into pleading the cause of the Jew, he would have to be a Manichaean too, and equate the Jew with the principle of the Good" (73).

9. Fanon, *Wretched*, 14–15, translation modified; *Œuvres*, 463.

10. Fanon, *Wretched*, 2; *Œuvres*, 452.

11. Fanon, *Wretched*, 3–4, translation modified; *Œuvres*, 453–54.

12. Fanon, *Wretched*, 4–5; *Œuvres*, 454.

13. Fanon, *Wretched*, 4, translation modified; *Œuvres*, 454.

14. Fanon, *Wretched*, 5; *Œuvres*, 455. Whereas Fanon had previously concretized the abstract hostility of the Sartrean Other, in the colonial context this Other gains an additional layer of geopolitical materiality.

15. Fanon, *Wretched*, 23; *Œuvres*, 470.

16. Fanon, *Wretched*, 6; *Œuvres*, 456.

17. Fanon, *Wretched*, 43; *Œuvres*, 488.

18. Fanon, *Wretched*, 14; *Œuvres*, 462.

19. Fanon, *Wretched*, 6, translation modified; *Œuvres*, 455.

20. Fanon, *Wretched*, 1, translation modified; *Œuvres*, 451.

21. We may rightly wonder, however, whether Fanon's formulation might have the opposite effect: weakening the national stage (as Sartre had weakened the Black stage) by pointing toward its overcoming. But here we must remember that Fanon could already see on the horizon the mortal danger posed by *not* transcending the national stage.

22. Jameson, *Valences of the Dialectic*, 19.

23. Fanon, *Wretched*, 43n5, quoting from Sartre's *Critique of Dialectical Reason*; *Œuvres*, 488n5.

24. Fanon, *Wretched*, 3, translation modified; *Œuvres*, 453.

25. Fanon, *Wretched*, 5–6, my emphasis; *Œuvres*, 455. The translation here is slightly misleading, but captures the essence of what Fanon is trying to say. As he adds elsewhere: "The very same people who had it constantly drummed into them that the only language they understood was that of force, now decide to express themselves with force. In fact the colonist has always shown them the path they should follow to liberation. The argument chosen by the colonized was conveyed to them by the colonist, and by an ironic twist of fate it is now the colonized who state that it is the colonizer who only understands the language of force" (Fanon, *Wretched*, 42; *Œuvres*, 488).

26. Fanon, *Wretched*, 46, my emphasis; *Œuvres*, 491–92.

27. While Fanon does not discriminate as clearly in his usage of the terms *force* and *violence* as Sorel, he uses force most often to refer to the ontological lines dividing the colonial world (i.e., "forces of order," the "force of the bayonet") (Fanon, *Wretched*, 4, translation modified, 43; *Œuvres*, 454, 488). But even then the homology persists: when the colonized takes up Manichaeism, she enters into a "struggle of forces" [*rapport de forces*] but also notably "discovers that only violence pays" (23, translation modified; 470). Further Fanon occasionally characterizes the colonizer-colonized relationship ambiguously as one of "mass" [*rapports de masse*], but this ambiguity is intentional, since he adds: "Against the greater number the colonist pits his force" (17; 84). Mass then appears as an intermediary category, one that simultaneously recognizes the "mass" of weaponry ("force") maintaining colonialism while avoiding technological reductionism and insisting on the potential of the "masses" who engage in "violence" to undermine it.

28. Fanon, *Wretched*, 23; *Œuvres*, 470.

29. Fanon, *Wretched*, 65; *Œuvres*, 510.

30. Fanon, *Wretched*, 4, translation modified, 8; *Œuvres*, 454, 457.

31. Fanon, *Wretched*, 30–32, translation modified; *Œuvres*, 477–78.

32. Fanon, *Wretched*, 25, translation modified; *Œuvres*, 472.

33. Friedrich Engels, *Anti-Dühring*, trans. E. Burns (New York: International Publishers, 1976 [1877]), 184. On Engels's arguably more complex position, see Yves Winter, "Debating Violence on the Desert Island: Engels, Dühring and Robinson Crusoe," *Contemporary Political Theory* 13 (November 2014): 318–38.

34. Fanon, *Wretched*, 33; *Œuvres*, 480.

35. Here, it would be difficult to overlook parallels to Lenin's formulation of the dictatorship of the proletariat in the pages of *State and Revolution*, where "force" is similarly taken up by the proletariat as a strategic necessity only to set into motion an immediate process of transformation ("withering away"). V. I. Lenin, *State and Revolution* (Chicago: Haymarket, 2014 [1918]), 51–58.

36. Fanon, *Wretched*, 45–46, my emphasis; *Œuvres*, 489–91. Macey claims that the citation was inserted at the last minute, suggesting that, as Édouard Glissant had reported—with the Algerian Revolution nearing its conclusion—Fanon's sights were beginning to turn back to his native Antilles (*Frantz Fanon*, 425–26, 462). But the organic suitability of the passage remains, as does the fact that he had quoted the same piece in *Black Skin*—albeit in a slightly different sense and toward a different end—yet another indication of the striking continuity of the two works.

37. Sartre, "Preface," in Fanon, *Wretched*, lv; *Œuvres*, 442.

38. Fanon, *Wretched*, 50–51; *Œuvres*, 495–96. Crucially, these subjective effects of violence can be present "even if the armed struggle has been symbolic."

39. Fanon, *Wretched*, 10; *Œuvres*, 459.

40. Fanon, *Wretched*, 5; *Œuvres*, 455.

41. This mutual determination both echoes Sorel and prefigures Dussel's insistence on the same, as when he suggests that it is not only the case that "the lonely hour of the final instance never comes," but that there is no such thing to begin with. See Enrique Dussel, *Twenty Theses on Politics*, trans. G. Ciccariello-Maher (Durham, NC: Duke University Press, 2008 [2006]), 8, 59 fig. 7.

42. Fanon, *Wretched*, 66, translation modified; *Œuvres*, 512.

43. Fanon, *Wretched*, 67, translation modified; *Œuvres*, 512–13.

44. Fanon, *Wretched*, 71; *Œuvres*, 516.

45. Fanon, *Wretched*, 68; *Œuvres*, 514.

46. Fanon, *Wretched*, 78–79; *Œuvres*, 522–23.

47. Fanon, *Wretched*, 80–81; *Œuvres*, 524–25.

48. Fanon, *Wretched*, 82–83, translation modified; *Œuvres*, 527.

49. Fanon, *Wretched*, 84, translation modified; *Œuvres*, 528.

50. Fanon, *Wretched*, 85, translation modified; *Œuvres*, 529.

51. Fanon, *Wretched*, 86, translation modified; *Œuvres*, 530.

52. Fanon, *Wretched*, 88, translation modified; *Œuvres*, 532.

53. Fanon, *Wretched*, 64; *Œuvres*, 510. The English translation misleadingly gives the appearance that Fanon later repeats this claim (75; 520).

54. Fanon, *Wretched*, 100; *Œuvres*, 546.

55. For a discussion of Amilcar Cabral's development of the concept of class suicide, see Tom Meisenhelder, "Amilcar Cabral's Theory of Class Suicide and Revolutionary Socialism," *Monthly Review* 45 (November 1993): 40–49.

56. Fanon, *Wretched*, 99, translation modified, my emphasis; *Œuvres*, 544–45.

57. Fanon, *Wretched*, 145; *Œuvres*, 589.

58. Fanon, *Wretched*, 101, translation modified; *Œuvres*, 546–47.

59. Fanon, *Wretched*, 119; *Œuvres*, 563.

60. Fanon, *Wretched*, 120–21; *Œuvres*, 563–64.

61. Fanon, *Wretched*, 89, translation modified; *Œuvres*, 532.

62. Fanon, *Wretched*, 94, translation modified, my emphasis; *Œuvres*, 537.

63. Fanon, *Wretched*, 95, translation modified; *Œuvres*, 537–38.

64. Fanon, *Wretched*, 93, translation modified; *Œuvres*, 536.

65. Fanon, *Wretched*, 51.

66. Fanon, *Wretched*, 144, translation modified; *Œuvres*, 585.

67. Fanon, *Wretched*, 96, translation modified; *Œuvres*, 539.

68. Fanon, *Wretched*, 140–41, translation modified, my emphasis; *Œuvres*, 582.

69. Fanon, *Wretched*, 51–52, translation modified; *Œuvres*, 495–96.

70. Fanon, *Wretched*, 144; *Œuvres*, 585.

71. As Immanuel Wallerstein puts it in his classic essay on Fanon: "He simply said, let us look again to see who has how many chains, and which are the groups who, having the fewest privileges, may be the most ready to become a 'revolutionary class.'" Immanuel Wallerstein, "Fanon and the Revolutionary Class," in *The Essential Wallerstein* (New York: New Press, 2000), 26.

72. Ernesto Laclau, *On Populist Reason* (London: Verso, 2005), 152.

73. Specifically, the later chapters are fundamentally dedicated to both diagnosing in an utterly prescient way the looming dangers of (post)colonial rule and to demonstrating the powerfully *negative*, if equally generative, implications of violence on the colonial subject. As Lewis Gordon puts it, violence is in this sense tragic: "He brings out the monstrosity of what happens to people engaged in those struggles. . . . The tragedy of it is that these are battles that needed to be waged" ("Fanon").

74. Fanon, *Wretched*, 179; *Œuvres*, 621.

75. While this is no place to fully enter into the errors of Laclau's analysis, several merit brief mention. First, Laclau exaggerates the importance of the lumpenproletariat in Fanon's analysis to the detriment of the peasantry. The effect of this is, second, to neglect the particular claims the peasantry puts forward (which Laclau insists do not exist). Third, then, against Laclau there indeed exists something to be articulated in the struggle, through what I have called above a "dialectic-within-a-dialectic."

76. In some senses, then, it may be true—as Edward Said suggested—that Fanon was an heir to the radical combativeness of which Lukács's concept of reification was ultimately sapped (his suggestion that Fanon derived his concept of Manichaeism from Lukács seems both unnecessary and unlikely). However, Fanon effectively shunned Lukács most central and overbearing category: that of the totality. Edward Said, "Traveling Theory Reconsidered," in *Reflections on Exile* (London: Granta, 2001), 445–46. I am grateful to an anonymous reviewer for drawing my attention to this claim.

77. Fanon, *Wretched*, 3–4, translation modified; *Œuvres*, 454. Compare to Sorel's attacks on the "preachers of ethics [*prédicateurs de morale*]," so patently similar as to suggest direct influence (*Reflections*, 76; *Réflexions*, 106).

78. Fanon, *Wretched*, 4, translation modified; *Œuvres*, 453–54.

79. Gramsci, *Selections from the Prison Notebooks*, 207.

80. Fanon, *Wretched*, 182, translation modified, my emphasis; *Œuvres*, 626. On the importance of the colonized as naturalized backdrop, see Gil Anidjar's analysis of the Palestinian in Zionist literature: *The Jew, the Arab: A History of the Enemy* (Stanford, CA: Stanford University Press, 2003).

81. Slavoj Žižek seems to begin to grasp this in his endorsement of Simone de Beauvoir's insistence that, by virtue of the ontological function of racism, U.S. blacks *actually were inferior* (as opposed to being merely *seen as inferior by racists*). However, he missteps in rejecting the term *inferiorization*, since in negating racialization as a *process* and granting whites a too complete symbolic power, he effectively places any symbolic-ontological resistance beyond the grasp of the racialized. Slavoj Žižek, *Violence* (New York: Picador, 2008), 71–73.

82. Césaire, *Discourse on Colonialism*, 36. Césaire prevaricates slightly: in some moments grouping Jews and Blacks together and in others suggesting that Nazism was only scandalous for having applied colonial procedures to white Europeans.

83. As a pioneer of "world-systems theory," Wallerstein was among the first to insist on this shift in unit of analysis, and it is no surprise that Wallerstein was heavily influenced by Fanon. The addendum of the qualifier *colonial* to Wallerstein's "modern world-system" resulted from critical dialogue with the decolonial thinker Aníbal Quijano.

84. Michael Hardt and Antonio Negri, *Empire* (Cambridge, MA: Harvard University Press, 2000), 65.

85. Hardt and Negri, *Empire*, xiv.

86. Hardt and Negri, *Empire*, xv.

87. Fanon, *Wretched*, 238; *Œuvres*, 676.

88. According to Gordon, "Fanon is subverting some of the themes of the Internationale" by connecting them to a "different universalizing praxis connected to the question of the anti-colonial struggle" ("Fanon"), and he further draws out a comparison with Dante's *Inferno*.

89. Fanon, *Wretched*, 236, translation modified; *Œuvres*, 674.

90. Fanon, *Wretched*, 237, translation modified; *Œuvres*, 675.

91. If Foucault's error is to neglect alternative sources for a radicalized dialectics beyond Europe, something similar could be said of his rejection of humanism and failure to seek alternatives. While Foucault insisted on the particularity of his conclusions, he did not hedge when it came to rejecting humanism or dialectics out of hand. As one notable Foucauldian puts it: "ignoring the imperial context of his own theories, Foucault seems actually to represent an irresistible colonizing movement"; Edward Said, *Culture and Imperialism* (London: Vintage, 1994), 336.

92. Fanon, *Black Skin*, xii; *Œuvres*, 64.

93. Fanon, *Wretched*, 238; *Œuvres*, 676.

94. Fanon, *Wretched*, 235; *Œuvres*, 673. For Gordon, truly turning away requires abandoning revenge and "letting go of those attachments that link them to their colonization" ("Fanon"). These attachments, to use Wendy Brown's concept, are nothing if not fundamentally "wounded"; "Wounded Attachments," *Political Theory* 21, no. 3 (August 1993): 390–410.

95. Fanon, *Wretched*, 239, translation modified; *Œuvres*, 676.

96. Fanon, *Wretched*, 238, translation modified; *Œuvres*, 676.

97. On the notion of a "decolonial turn," see *El giro decolonial: Reflexiones para una diversidad epistémica más allá del capitalismo global*, ed. S. Castro-Gómez and R. Grosfoguel (Bogotá: Siglo de Hombres Editores, 2007).

98. According to Chateaubriand, "The patricians started the revolution: the plebeians finished it," whereas for James, in successive chapter titles in *The Black Jacobins*, "The San Domingo Masses Begin" and "And the Paris Masses Complete," the origin is as important as the conclusions. For Fredric Jameson, Fanon's refiguring of the master-slave dialectic in terms of anticolonial struggle sets him apart from recognition-based identity politics while making him "easily assimilable" to questions of class struggle. *The Hegel Variations*, 90.

Chapter 4: Latin American Dialectics and the Other

1. See in particular the reception of Fanon's *Wretched* from Mexico to Bolivia and beyond, in Magalí Rabasa, "Re-reading The Wretched of the Earth in Spanish: Tracing Fanon's Movement Through Radical Politics (Past and Present) in Latin America" (unpublished).

2. Salvatecci, *Sorel y Mariátegui*. Having limited access to Marx's own texts, Mariátegui in fact derived his heterodox Marxism directly from Sorel (who, along with Gramsci, Benedetto Croce, and Gabriele D'Annunzio, Mariátegui met at the crucial 1921 Congress of Italian Socialists in Livorno). Sorel's influence is particularly pronounced in Mariátegui's 1928 *Defense of Marxism*, which Salvatecci scornfully dismisses as a "defense of Sorel." Elizabeth Garrels, editorial notes of José Carlos Mariátegui, 7 *Ensayos Sobre la Realidad Peruana* (Caracas: Biblioteca Ayacucho, 2007), 326. In the same volume Aníbal Quijano disagrees with some accounts of how little Marx Mariátegui actually read ("José Carlos Mariátegui: Reencuentro y Debate," ix–cxii).

3. José Carlos Mariátegui, *An Anthology*, ed. H. Vanden and M. Becker (New York: Monthly Review Press, 2011), 125, 128, translation modified.

4. Fanon, *Wretched*, 101; *Œuvres*, 547.

5. It is by now recognized that Marx later came around to something like this position, especially in his now-famous 1881 letter to Vera Zasulich, in which the Russian communes, or *obshchina*, figure as the basis for potentially skipping stages or indeed their disintegration. Marx's method in this letter is

to look precisely at the "reality" in question, to analyze the communes and their bifurcated historical content in context. For a fuller discussion of the question, see Anderson, *Marx at the Margins*.

6. See especially Gunder Frank's *Latin America: Underdevelopment or Revolution* (New York: Monthly Review, 1970).

7. Ramón Grosfoguel, "Developmentalism, Modernity, and Dependency Theory in Latin America," *Nepantla: Views From South* 1, no. 2 (2000): 360. But, Grosfoguel adds, some dependentistas did not manage in the end to overcome the developmentalist tendencies they themselves had critiqued.

8. Enrique Dussel, *Philosophy of Liberation*, trans. A. Martinez and C. Morkovsky (Eugene, OR: Wipf and Stock, 1985), viii; *Filosofía de la Liberación* (Bogotá: Nueva América 1996 [1977]), 10. When pressed, however, Dussel will admit that his engagement with Fanon was incomplete. Nelson Maldonado-Torres has sought to fill in the gaps in the conversation in *Against War*.

9. Dussel, *Philosophy of Liberation*, 13; *Filosofía de la Liberación*, 25.

10. Dussel, *Philosophy of Liberation*, 51; *Filosofía de la Liberación*, 68.

11. Michael Barber, *Ethical Hermeneutics: Rationality in Enrique Dussel's Philosophy of Liberation* (New York: Fordham University Press, 1998), 26.

12. Linda Martín Alcoff and Eduardo Mendieta show that much of Dussel's work from 1969 was more clearly Heideggerian and that his *Para una ética de liberación*, from 1973, contains a "very noticeable and disconcerting shift" between Heideggerian and Levinasian registers. "Introduction," in *Thinking from the Underside of History: Enrique Dussel's Philosophy of Liberation*, ed. L. M. Alcoff and E. Mendieta (Lanham, MD: Rowman and Littlefield, 2000), 20–21. Dussel himself explains the transition as follows: "I had discovered the subject of totality long before reading Levinas (in Paris as early as 1962, with [Jean-]Yves Jolif). The idea of overcoming totality was clarified by Levinas, although Sartre had suggested it. We read Levinas as a group (with [Juan Carlos] Scannone) by the end of 1969, in the context of my classes on Hegel . . . in which Levinas did not appear, but we had begun to read him. The concept of exteriority and the overcoming of the totality is Levinasian" (personal communication, October 11, 2009).

13. Alcoff and Mendieta, "Introduction," 21.

14. Dussel, "From Critical Theory to the Philosophy of Liberation," 34n4.

15. Dussel, *Philosophy of Liberation*, 49, translation modified; *Filosofía de la liberación*, 66–67.

16. Dussel, *Philosophy of Liberation*, 6, translation modified; *Filosofía de la liberación*, 17.

17. Dussel, *Philosophy of Liberation*, 5–6; *Filosofía de la liberación*, 17. This translation is not precise for the edition cited here, but the meaning is accurate.

18. Dussel, *Philosophy of Liberation*, 51, translation modified; *Filosofía de la liberación*, 68.

19. Dussel, *Philosophy of Liberation*, 52–53, translation modified; *Filosofía de la liberación*, 69–70.

20. Dussel, *Philosophy of Liberation*, 157, translation modified; *Filosofía de la liberación*, 184–85.

21. Dussel, *Philosophy of Liberation*, 158–59, translation modified; *Filosofía de la liberación*, 186.

22. Some see Levinas as fundamentally Hegelian, but the tension between this assertion and Levinas's own critique of Hegel can be seen as a doubling of the difficulty we have faced from the outset: the distance that separates dialectics conservatively understood as totalizing, perfect division of the totality, and the unity of opposites, versus dialectics as a generative and open-ended motion whose effects are largely unpredictable. Robert Bernasconi insists that "Levinas is not simply opposed to Hegel" and to insist so is "wrong and self-defeating," in "Hegel and Levinas: The Possibility of Reconciliation and Forgiveness," *Archivio di Filosofia* 54 (1986): 325; see also "Levinas Face to Face—with Hegel," *Journal of the British Society for Phenomenology*, 13/3 (October 1982): 267–76; Peter C. Hodgson, *Hegel and Christian Theology: A Reading of the Lectures on the Philosophy of Religion* (Oxford: Oxford University Press, 2005), 265.

23. Emmanuel Levinas, *Totality and Infinity: An Essay on Exteriority* (The Hague: Kluwer, 1991 [1961]), 35, 290. The following paragraphs draw upon and reformulate arguments from George Ciccariello-Maher, "Decolonial Realism: Ethics, Politics, and Dialectics in Fanon and Dussel," *Contemporary Political Theory* 13, no. 1 (February 2014): 2–22.

24. Dussel, *Philosophy of Liberation*, 39, 48; *Filosofía de la liberación*, 56, 65.

25. Dussel, *Philosophy of Liberation*, 42; *Filosofía de la liberación*, 58.

26. Dussel, *Philosophy of Liberation*, 44; *Filosofía de la liberación*, 60.

27. Dussel, *Philosophy of Liberation*, 6; *Filosofía de la liberación*, 17.

28. Dussel, *Philosophy of Liberation*, 71; *Filosofía de la liberación*, 92. While he speaks frequently in terms of "absolute" or "total" exteriority, Dussel admits that this "spatial metaphor . . . can lead to more than one equivocation," and is better understood as a "beyond," adding that "Exteriority and interior transcendentality have the same signification in this philosophical discourse" (40; 56).

29. Enrique Dussel, *Para una fundamentación filosófica de la liberación Latinoamericana* (Buenos Aires: Editorial Bonum, 1974), 8. For a similar critique, see Robert Bernasconi, "African Philosophy's Challenge to Continental Philosophy," in *Postcolonial African Philosophy*, ed. E. Eze, 183–96 (Oxford: Blackwell, 1997). Barber frames this as "overcoming Levinas," but is at pains to emphasize that this overcoming involves the dialectical preservation of much of Levinas's contribution (*Ethical Hermeneutics*, 50–51). Shannon Bell has argued that whereas "Levinas does not politicize his concept of the other," Dussel does. "Levinas and Alterity Politics," in A. Horowitz and G. Horowitz, eds., *Difficult Justice* (Toronto: University of Toronto Press, 2006), 112. Santiago Slabodsky has sought to use Dussel toward reconsidering this critique of Levinas's Eurocentrism. "Emmanuel Levinas's Geopolitics:

Overlooked Conversations between Rabbinical and Third World Decolonialisms," *Journal of Jewish Thought and Philosophy* 18, no. 2 (2011): 147–65.

30. Dussel, *Método para una filosofía de la liberación*, 181. While his own decision to cut the Gordian knot of metaphysics by mapping alterity onto global geopolitics can be critiqued, it is not for these same reasons. Kohn and McBride, for example, diagnose Dussel's slippage between abstract metaphysics and concrete particularity and between a multiplicity of overlapping systems and subject positions and singular references to a single system. *Political Theories of Decolonization* (New York: Oxford University Press, 2011), 133.

31. Barber, *Ethical Hermeneutics*, 57.

32. Dussel, *Philosophy of Liberation*, 173, translation modified, my emphasis; *Filosofía de la liberación*, 200.

33. Like Sorel, Dussel grants some importance to the concept of diremption to describe such rupture. See Dussel, *El último Marx*, 346, 356n61; *Método para una filosofía de la liberación*, 18 and appendix.

34. Dussel, *Philosophy of Liberation*, 159; *Filosofía de la liberación*, 187.

35. Dussel, *Philosophy of Liberation*, 62, translation modified; *Filosofía de la Liberación*, 81.

36. Dussel, *Philosophy of Liberation*, 159, 48, translation modified; *Filosofía de la Liberación*, 187, 65.

37. Dussel, *Philosophy of Liberation*, 159, translation modified; *Filosofía de la liberación*, 187.

38. Dussel, *Philosophy of Liberation*, 158, translation modified; *Filosofía de la liberación*, 187.

39. Dussel, *Philosophy of Liberation*, 160, translation modified; *Filosofía de la liberación*, 188.

40. Dussel, *Philosophy of Liberation*, 158, translation modified; *Filosofía de la liberación*, 186.

41. Dussel, *Philosophy of Liberation*, 159–60, translation modified; *Filosofía de la liberación*, 187–88.

42. Dussel, *Philosophy of Liberation*, 136–37, translation modified; *Filosofía de la liberación*, 162.

43. Dussel, *Philosophy of Liberation*, 166, translation modified; *Filosofía de la liberación*, 194.

44. Dussel, *Philosophy of Liberation*, 96, translation modified, my emphasis; *Filosofía de la liberación*, 118–19.

45. Dussel, *Philosophy of Liberation*, 4, translation modified; *Filosofía de la liberación*, 16. That peripheral thought enjoys "second sight" is no guarantee that it will embrace that outlook. In fact, the constant temptation for peripheral thought—one verified in the content of university curricula—is to look toward the core, toward Europe, in a sort of repetition of what Fanon found so perverse in the deactivated colonial master-slave dialectic. For Dussel, this turn toward the master constitutes "its death as philosophy; it is its birth as completed ontology and as ideology. Thought that takes refuge

in the core ends up thinking it to be the only reality." Dussel, *Philosophy of Liberation*, 4, translation modified; *Filosofía de la Liberación*, 16.

46. Dussel, *Philosophy of Liberation*, 14, translation modified; *Filosofía de la liberación*, 26.

47. Dussel, *Philosophy of Liberation*, 61–62, translation modified; *Filosofía de la liberación*, 80.

48. Here echoing Fanon and Lewis Gordon, this ontological breach of the system will always be perceived as violent, even if it entails little or no concrete violence, and as such is inevitably "illegal." Dussel, *Philosophy of Liberation*, 66, translation modified; *Filosofía de la liberación*, 85.

49. Dussel, *Philosophy of Liberation*, 179, translation modified; *Filosofía de la liberación*, 208.

50. On the fear of penetration as a central aspect of racism, see George Ciccariello-Maher, "Toward a Racial Geography of Caracas: Neoliberal Urbanism and the Fear of Penetration," *Qui Parle* 16, no. 2 (spring/summer 2007): 39–72.

51. Maldonado-Torres, *Against War*, 182.

52. Maldonado-Torres, *Against War*, 183.

53. Maldonado-Torres, *Against War*, 183.

54. It is here that Dussel also avoids some of the sharpest critiques of the Levinasian approach by, for example, Alain Badiou, who critiques Levinas precisely for the decontextualized, nonsituatedness of his transcendent other. See *Ethics*, xxii–xxiii.

55. In terms of this precolonial exteriority and its legacies in the present, Dussel draws frequently upon Mariátegui. See, for example, *Política de la liberación*, vol. 1: *Historia mundial y crítica* (Madrid: Trotta, 2007), 34.

56. Dussel, *Philosophy of Liberation*, 145; *Filosofía de la liberación*, 172.

57. Dussel, *Philosophy of Liberation*, 70, translation modified; *Filosofía de la liberación*, 91.

58. Dussel, *Philosophy of Liberation*, 70, translation modified; *Filosofía de la liberación*, 91.

Chapter 5: Venezuela's Combative Dialectics

1. See Paolo Virno, *Grammar of the Multitude: For an Analysis of Contemporary Forms of Life*, trans. I. Bertoletti, J. Cascaito, and A. Casson (New York: Semiotext(e), 2004 [2001]); the trilogy by Hardt and Negri: *Empire*; *Multitude: War and Democracy in the Age of Empire* (New York: Penguin, 2004); and *Commonwealth* (Cambridge, MA: Harvard University Press, 2009)

2. The distinction between people and multitude first appears in developed form in Paolo Virno, "Virtuosity and Revolution: The Political Theory of Exodus," in P. Virno and M. Hardt, eds., *Radical Thought in Italy: A Potential Politics* (Minneapolis: University of Minnesota Press, 1996), esp. 200–202. Negri's contribution to this volume, by contrast, is notably pre-*Empire* in its formulations, even suggesting

we redefine "the people" in a way suited to our post-Fordist era. Antonio Negri, "Constituent Republic," in *Radical Thought in Italy*, 215.

3. Hardt and Negri, *Multitude*, xiv.

4. Hardt and Negri, *Multitude*, 99.

5. Hardt and Negri, *Empire*, 103. Previously, Virno and Hardt had defined constituent power in radically dialectical terms: "a form of power that continually creates and animates a set of juridical and political frameworks. Its perpetually open processes should be contrasted with the static and closed character of constituted power." *Radical Thought in Italy*, 261. See also Antonio Negri, *Insurgencies: Constituent Power and the Modern State*, trans. M. Boscagli (Minneapolis: University of Minnesota Press, 1999 [1992]).

6. Virno, *Grammar of the Multitude*, 21. For Hardt and Negri, the people "tends toward identity and homogeneity internally while posing its difference from and excluding what remains outside of it" (*Empire*, 103).

7. Hardt and Negri, *Empire*, 103; Virno, *Grammar of the Multitude*, 22–23.

8. Thomas Hobbes, *Elementa philosophica de cive* (Lausanne: Grasset, 1782 [1642]), XII.viii, 209: "*multitudinem* contra *populum*."

9. Virno, *Grammar of the Multitude*, 22.

10. Hardt and Negri, *Empire*, 103–4.

11. Hardt and Negri, *Empire*, 101.

12. Hardt and Negri, *Multitude*, 328–29. In an effort to head off such concerns, they clumsily add that unitary sovereignty is "not limited to the European tradition. The history of Chinese philosophy too, for example, is dominated by notions of immutable unity and a dictating center."

13. Even Thermidor itself could stand to be decolonized, as C. L. R. James does in *The Black Jacobins*, by providing a more sophisticated understanding of the real struggles that occurred between constituted and constituent power, all the while placing this French struggle in the context of a global colonial system.

14. Hardt and Negri, *Empire*, 106, emphasis in original.

15. Hardt and Negri, *Empire*, 107.

16. Hardt and Negri, *Empire*, 109, my emphasis.

17. Hardt and Negri, *Empire*, 109.

18. Hardt and Negri, *Empire*, 128–29, emphasis in original.

19. Hardt and Negri, *Empire*, 132.

20. Quijano, "The Coloniality of Power and Social Classification."

21. Enrique Dussel, *Twenty Theses on Politics*; *Política de la Liberación*, vol. 1: *Historia mundial y crítica*; *Política de la Liberación*, vol. 2: *Arquitectónica* (Madrid: Trotta, 2009); *Política de la Liberación*, vol. 3: *Crítica* (Madrid: Trotta, forthcoming).

22. Dussel's intervention, while specific to Latin America, nevertheless appears in the context of a resurgent debate on the concept of the people (provoked in part by political developments in Venezuela) in which a number of thinkers have underlined the rupture marked by the people. Jodi Dean, for

example, insists on the people not as unity but instead as the rest, and in so doing is sharply critical of the Multitude. *The Communist Horizon*, 78. The people in this sense, like the radicalized dialectics I have put forth here, points toward *"the impossibility of totalizing or enclosing the political"* (101). Against Dussel's emphasis on exclusion however, Dean argues—erroneously, in my view—that the language of exclusion necessarily implies inclusion as its solution. For Dussel, it instead entails the opposite: the radical breaching and outward expansion of that totality. Dean builds on similar suggestions by Giorgio Agamben, who describes the people as "not a unitary subject but a dialectical oscillation" between the whole and the excluded, and on Susan Buck-Morss, for whom "democratic sovereignty" attempts to "monopolize" the people, thereby "attesting to its *non*-identity with the people." Giorgio Agamben, *Homo Sacer: Sovereign Power and Bare Life* (Stanford, CA: Stanford University Press, 1998), 177; Susan Buck-Morss, *Dreamworld and Catastrophe: The Passing of Mass Utopia in East and West* (Cambridge, MA: MIT Press, 2002), 7.

To these thinkers, we could add two more directly relevant to Dussel's formulation: the consistent contributions of Ernesto Laclau—especially *On Populist Reason*—and Jacques Rancière's suggestion that "The people (*demos*) exists only as a rupture of the logic of *arche*," and therefore designates "the supplement that inscribes 'the count of the unaccounted-for' or 'the part of those who have no part.'" "Ten Theses on Politics," *Theory and Event* 5, no. 3 (2001). For a recent analysis of the people that sets out from a Latin American context, see Paulina Ochoa Espejo, *The Time of Popular Sovereignty: Process and the Democratic State* (University Park: Penn State University Press, 2011).

23. We can find a similar ambiguity in the English derivation: whereas the idea of a people as a unity appears in the thirteenth century, an alternate meaning emerges only a few short years later to refer exclusively to the common people against the nobility.

24. Dussel, *Twenty Theses*, 74.

25. Dussel, *Twenty Theses*, 75.

26. Dussel, *Twenty Theses*, 73.

27. Dussel, *Twenty Theses*, 74. Fidel Castro Ruz, *History Will Absolve Me*, trans. C. González Díaz (Havana: Editorial José Martí, 1998 [1953]), 56. Many translations butcher the meaning of this admittedly cryptic sentence. Here we can note some resonances with Jason Frank's analysis of the people in the context of the U.S. founding as the effect of its own emergence in political action, whose unity can only be confirmed retroactively. *Constituent Moments: Enacting the People in Postrevolutionary America* (Durham, NC: Duke University Press, 2010).

28. Dussel, *Twenty Theses*, 74–75.

29. Dussel, *Twenty Theses*, 78.

30. Here, Dussel's people also constitutes a notable advance over Latin American liberation theology, a field to which he himself contributed significantly.

According to Nelson Maldonado-Torres, liberation theology (like the dependency theory with which it was allied) focused exclusively on a sociological conception of "the poor," and as a result "failed to realize the complexity of the coloniality of power, in particular, the situation of *colonial heterogeneity* . . . The struggles and demands of certain groups of women and black and indigenous peoples remained in the periphery of their concerns [i.e., peripheralized even by theorists of the core-periphery relation]. In this way liberation theology became complicit with an elite mestizo Latin American consciousness that gave only partial expression to the needs for liberation in the region." Nelson Maldonado-Torres, "Liberation Theology and the Search for the Lost Paradigm: From Radical Orthodoxy to Radical Diversality," in *Latin American Liberation Theology: The Next Generation*, ed. I. Petrella (Maryknoll, NY: Orbis, 2005), 55.

31. Dussel, *Twenty Theses*, 72–73.
32. Laclau, *On Populist Reason*, 7.
33. This privileging of form over content leads many to conclusions as non-sensical as those who would speak of a "Black fascism." See, for example, the counterposition of Hugo Chávez with Ross Perot—which only makes sense if grounded in the assumption that the two are talking about the *same thing*—in Francisco Panizza, "Introduction: Populism and the Mirror of Democracy," in *Populism and the Mirror of Democracy*, ed. F. Panizza (London: Verso, 2005), 4. What I would do through Fanon and Dussel, Benjamin McKean has recently done through W. E. B. Du Bois, providing a nuanced critique of Laclau that, rather than simply pointing toward the potential inclusiveness of populism, identifies those exclusionary barriers that remain present in Laclau's account. Benjamin L. McKean, "Toward an Inclusive Populism? On the Role of Race and Difference in Laclau's Politics," *Political Theory* (advance online publication, May 4, 2016).
34. Here, I consciously use the language of, among others, Gloria Anzaldúa, *Borderlands/La Frontera: The New Mestiza* (San Francisco: Aunt Lute, 1987).
35. Michael Hardt denies the absoluteness of such oppositions in his translator's foreword to Negri's *Savage Anomaly*, xiii, but even then falls short of the dialectical interplay of Dussel's approach.
36. Dussel, *Twenty Theses*, 18.
37. Dussel, *Twenty Theses*, 20.
38. Dussel, *Twenty Theses*, 82.
39. Dussel, *Twenty Theses*, 79; see also fig. 9.
40. Rómulo Betancourt, *Tres años de gobierno democrático*, vol. 2 (Caracas: Imprenta Nacional, 1962), 245.
41. Betancourt, *Tres años de gobierno democrático*, 245.
42. Fernando Coronil and Julie Skurski, "Dismembering and Remembering the Nation: The Semantics of Political Violence in Venezuela," in *Politics in the Andes: Identity, Conflict, and Reform*, ed. J.-M. Burt and P. Mauceri

(Pittsburgh: University of Pittsburgh Press, 2004), 96. In fact, shortly after Betancourt came to power, the journalist and popular hero of the resistance to the dictatorship, Fabricio Ojeda, invoked those same phrases in a speech resigning his congressional seat to join the guerrilla struggle against the Venezuelan government. Ciccariello-Maher, *We Created Chávez*, 23. The mobility with which the anthem was interpreted in Venezuela is also reflected in the politics of its translation, with more conservative translations replacing *death to* with *down with*, prioritizing the obligation to respect the law over the obligations of lawmakers to obey the people, and even substituting *nation* for *people*.

43. Alí Primera, "Yo no sé filosofar," *Volumen 2*. I cite from his collected lyrics: Alí Primera, *Que mi canto no se pierda* (Caracas: Fundarte, 2006). Song titles are followed by album titles.

44. "Gloria al Bravo Pueblo," *Alí ¡En Vivo!*

45. "Me lo contó Canelón," *Adios en dolor mayor*.

46. "Piraña con diente de oro," *Con el sol a medio cielo*.

47. "El que cantó con Zamora," *Abrebrecha*.

48. "Tin Marín," *Abrebrecha*. For an analysis of the mythical elements of popular identity in Latin America that similarly foregrounds the importance of popular culture, see William Rowe and Vivian Schelling, *Memory and Modernity: Popular Culture in Latin America* (London: Verso, 1991).

49. "Yo vengo de donde usted no ha ido," *Lo Primero de Alí Primera*.

50. Dussel, *Philosophy of Liberation*, 62; *Filosofía de la liberación*, 80.

51. Ramón Piñango, "Muerte de la armonía," in *En esta Venezuela: Realidades y nuevos caminos*, ed. Patricia Márquez y Ramón Piñango (Caracas: Instituto de Estudios Superiores de la Administración, 2003), 22.

52. See for example Deborah L. Norden, "Sowing Conflict in Venezuela: Political Violence and Economic Policy," in *Economic Development Strategies and the Evolution of Violence in Latin America*, ed. W. Ascher and N. Mirovitskaya (New York: Palgrave MacMillan, 2012), 168; Medófilo Medina and Margarita López Maya, *Venezuela: Confrontación social y polarización política* (Bogotá: Ediciones Aurora, 2003).

53. Here I build upon ideas first formulated in Ciccariello-Maher, "Jumpstarting the Decolonial Engine."

54. Íñigo Errejón, "We Are (Almost) All Chávez: Challenges in the Deployment of Chavista Political Identity," trans. G. Ciccariello-Maher, *Venezuela Analysis* (September 15, 2013), http://venezuelanalysis.com/analysis/10024.

55. Patricia Márquez, "Vacas flacas y odios gordos: la polarización en Venezuela," in *En esta Venezuela*, ed. Márquez and Piñango, 31, my emphasis.

56. Fernando Saldivia Najul, "Chávez dividió al país," *Aporrea.org* (May 28, 2014), http://www.aporrea.org/actualidad/a188867.html.

57. Miguel Angel Landa, "Venezuela Desapareció," *Noticia Al Día* (August 1, 2013), http://noticiaaldia.com/2013/08/el-desgarrador-articulo-del-actor

-miguel-angel-landa-venezuela-desaparecio/. Revealingly, Landa continues, "The country disappeared from the memory of universal things," but he reveals much about his own conception of the universal by mourning the fact that Venezuela is no Titanic, no Pompeii, no Troy, no Homer telling the glory of Achilles: "We will not be wool for weaving legends. Our end will leave us only shame."

58. Fanon, *Wretched*, 182, translation modified, my emphasis; *Œuvres*, 626.

59. *Ciudad de despedidas* (May 3, 2012), https://www.youtube.com/watch?v =GfxToCNh6rQ.

60. José Roberto Duque, "Miguel Ángel Landa llora por el país que se le desapareció, y tiene razón," *Misión Verdad* (25 August 2013), http://misionverdad .com/la-guerra-en-venezuela/miguel-angel-landa-llora-por-el-pais-que-se-le -desaparecio-y-tiene-razon.

61. Márquez, "Vacas flacas," in *En esta Venezuela*, ed. Márquez and Piñango, 31.

62. Márquez, "Vacas flacas," in *En esta Venezuela*, ed. Márquez and Piñango, 32. For an alternative decolonial view of the virtues of so-called resentment, see Glen Sean Coulthard, *Red Skin, White Masks*.

63. On race in the media, see Jun Ishibashi, "Hacia una apertura del debate sobre el racismo en Venezuela: Exclusión y inclusion estereotipada de personas 'negras' en los medios de comunicación," in *Políticas de identidades y diferencias sociales*, ed. D. Mato (Caracas: Facultad de Ciencias Económicas y Sociales, 2003), 33–63. Electoral registry data is from the Consejo Nacional Electoral; population is from the Instituto Nacional de Estadística.

64. Jon Beasley-Murray, for example, establishes too firm a distinction between the Caracazo as an expression of the Multitude and the dynamics that it set into motion. *Posthegemony: Political Theory and Latin America* (Minneapolis: University of Minnesota Press, 2011), 232. For Michael Bray, this has everything to do with Beasley-Murray's worry that Laclau's logic of representation tacitly comes down on the side of the state—and seeing Chávez as having confirmed that—whereas I would argue that the reality was far more complex. Michael Bray, "*El Estado Somos Todos, El Pueblo Soy Yo?* On *Chavismo* and the Necessity of the Leader," *Theory and Event* 17, no. 1 (2014).

65. Chávez and other midlevel officers had formed a radical "Bolivarian Pact" alongside revolutionary guerrillas years before, but it was only after the repression of the Caracazo that, according to Chávez, they "realized we had passed the point of no return and we had to take up arms." Hugo Chávez and Marta Harnecker, *Understanding the Bolivarian Revolution*, trans. C. Boudin (New York: Monthly Review Press, 2005), 32.

66. See George Ciccariello-Maher, *Building the Commune: Radical Democracy in Venezuela* (London: Jacobin-Verso, 2016).

67. Elías Jaua, "Chavismo," trans. R. Boothroyd, *Venezuela Analysis* (January 4, 2013), available online at http://venezuelanalysis.com/analysis/7586, translation modified. This genealogy is confirmed by LexisNexis searches that reveal almost no references to *Chavism* or *Chavismo* prior to 2001.

68. Ivan Briscoe, "Un caudillo inclasificable," *El País*, May 20, 2006. http://elpais .com/diario/2006/05/20/babelia/1148080638_850215.html.

69. Reinaldo Iturriza López, "The Vitality of the Revolution," trans. C. Fischer-Hoffman. *Venezuela Analysis*, September 3, 2014, translation modified. http://venezuelanalysis.com/analysis/10878.

70. Íñigo Errejón, "We Are (Almost) All Chávez."

71. Caldera quoted in Angela Zago, *La Rebelión de los ángeles* (Caracas: Fuentes, 1992), 30.

72. Errejón, "We Are (Almost) All Chávez."

73. Ociel Alí López, *¡Dale Más Gasolina! Chavismo, Sifrinismo y Burocracia* (Caracas: Fundación Casa Nacional de las Letras Andrés Bello, 2015), 27.

74. López, *¡Dale Más Gasolina!*, 28, 32.

75. López, *¡Dale Más Gasolina!*, 106.

76. López, *¡Dale Más Gasolina!*, 27, 33.

77. López, *¡Dale Más Gasolina!*, 28, 32.

78. See Jesús María Herrera Salas, "Ethnicity and Revolution: The Political Economy of Racism in Venezuela," *Latin American Perspectives* 32, no. 2 (March 2005): 72–91; Ciccariello-Maher, "Toward a Racial Geography of Caracas."

79. Herrera Salas, "Ethnicity and Revolution," 84.

80. Ciccariello-Maher, *We Created Chávez*, 154.

81. This concept emerges early on in Quijano's "Notas sobre el concepto de 'marginalidad social'" (Santiago: División de Asuntos Sociales, CEPAL, 1966) and more recently in Quijano, "Coloniality of Power and Social Classification."

82. Jameson, *Valences of the Dialectic*, 10.

83. Simón Rodríguez, *Inventamos o erramos* (Caracas: Monte Avila, 2004), 138.

84. Errejón, "We Are (Almost) All Chávez."

85. Errejón, "We Are (Almost) All Chávez."

86. Iturriza, "The Vitality of the Revolution." Iturriza does better than most to incorporate the spontaneity of power from below into the institutionalization of power from above, even better than Dussel himself, who in *Twenty Theses* presents an overly sanguine picture of the Venezuelan Constitution of 1999 as having smoothly incorporated participation into the structures of power. However, the institutionalization of spontaneity—the shift from the *barrio* assemblies of the 1990s to the communal councils of today—carries real risks. Dussel remains correct, however, that the riskiness of the shift from potentia to potestas is no grounds for rejecting its necessity.

87. Hugo Chávez Frías, *Golpe de Timón* (Caracas: Correo del Orinoco, 2012), 25–26.

Spirals

1. Brennan, *Borrowed Light*, 99.

2. Frederick Douglass, *My Bondage and My Freedom* (New York: Miller, Orton and Mulligan, 1855), 212.

3. Douglass, *My Bondage*, 230. Fanon, *Black Skin*, 83; *Œuvres*, 145.

4. Douglass, *My Bondage*, 234, 241. Recall that diremption originally referred to a religious fall.

5. Douglass, *My Bondage*, 239. It is no coincidence that this lesson was provided by Sandy, a sinful autodidact, whose magic root—Douglass's only protection—proved the "limits of enlightenment rationalism." Margaret Kohn, "Frederick Douglass's Master-Slave Dialectic," *Journal of Politics* 67, no. 2 (May 2005): 511.

6. Frederick Douglass, "The Meaning of July Fourth for the Negro" (1852), in *Frederick Douglass: Selected Speeches and Writing*, ed. P. Foner (Chicago: Chicago Review Press, 2000), 196. Kohn reads Hegel's progression from the master-slave dialectic through stoicism as erroneously suggesting that Christian universalism undermined slavery, whereas in reality the institution was constantly expanding. Whether we opt to read Hegel this way, or in the less literal and more Kojèvean sense, Kohn is correct to insist that "Douglass's story is the story of the enlightenment, but not one based on reason, consensus, and moral suasion. It is a story that foregrounds brutality and conflict in the struggle for freedom. The slave, who learned the meaning of liberty in face of death and the darkness of bondage, was to be the bearer of progress" (Kohn, "Frederick Douglass's Master-Slave Dialectic," 505). See also Leonard Cassuto, "Frederick Douglass and the Work of Freedom: Hegel's Master-Slave Dialectic in the Fugitive Slave Narrative," *Prospects* 21 (October 1996): 229–59.

7. Fanon, *Black Skin*, 117n24; *Œuvres*, 175n23.

8. Douglass, *My Bondage*, 242–43.

9. Douglass, *My Bondage*, 245.

10. Douglass, *My Bondage*, 246–47.

11. Willett rightly breaks out of the strict two-ness of the dialectic toward exteriority, insisting that "the slave is not *in fact* the mirror reversal of the master" and that "the experience of the African-American slave demands a second dialectic, one that is irreducible to the Hegelian model of selfhood and freedom." Cynthia Willett, "The Master-Slave Dialectic: Hegel vs. Douglass," in *Subjugation and Bondage: Critical Essays on Slavery and Social Philosophy*, ed. T. Lott (Lanham, MD: Rowman and Littlefield, 1998), 151–52. This second dialectic, rather than stoically negating nature, involves a positive "social eroticism of the self" that undermines western notions of rationality.

12. According to Zamir (*Dark Voices*, 1995), some American Hegelians used submission to slavery in the face of death to justify the peculiar institution as voluntary or deserved, and for Paul Gilroy, "Douglass's preference for death" over servitude distinguishes his dialectic from Hegel's. *The Black Atlantic: Modernity and Double Consciousness* (London: Verso, 1993), 63. Hegel does seemingly suggest that the slave is responsible for slavery, when he writes that "if someone is a slave, his own will is responsible, just as the responsibility lies with the will of a people if that people is subjugated. Thus

the wrong of slavery is the fault not only of those who enslave or subjugate people, but of the slaves and the subjugated themselves." This is not the Hegel of the *Phenomenology*, however, a text in which Hegel's firm indication is that one *ought* choose life (even in slavery) over death, but of the *Philosophy of Right*, 88 (§57).

13. For a less common take on the relationship between death and the "return to the collective consciousness of the present-day masses in the future," see Arash Davari, "A Return to Which Self? 'Ali Shari'ati and Frantz Fanon on the Political Ethics of Insurrectionary Violence." *Comparative Studies of South Asia, Africa and the Middle East* 34, no. 1 (2014): 104.

14. Arendt seems utterly incapable of grasping this qualitative distinction when she critiques the phrase "hunger with dignity is preferable to bread eaten in slavery" as an example of "Fanon's worst rhetorical excesses," adding that "no history and no theory are needed to refute this statement; the most superficial observer of the processes in the human body knows its untruth." Arendt, *On Violence*, 19.

15. According to Cook, Douglass cited this passage frequently to justify the violent resistance of the enslaved. James H. Cook, "Fighting With Breath, Not Blows: Frederick Douglass and Antislavery Violence," in *Antislavery Violence: Sectional, Racial, and Cultural Conflict in Antebellum America*, ed. J. McKivigan and S. Harrold (Knoxville: University of Tennessee Press, 1999), 156. Byron himself doesn't say "first," but this misquote is common in the Black radical tradition, for reasons that may be obvious.

16. W. E. B. Du Bois, *Souls* Byron himself doesn't say "first," but this misquote is common in the Black radical tradition, for reasons that may be obvious. 36, 50.

17. Du Bois, *Souls*, 8. Indeed, nothing drives home the weight of white supremacy and the insufficiency of education and reason so painfully as "Of the Coming of John." Elsewhere, I have argued that we can read in the progression of *Souls*, whose chapters were written over a period of years, an inflection in Du Bois's radical trajectory. George Ciccariello-Maher, "A Critique of Du Boisian Reason." On Du Bois's ambivalent appropriation of Hegelian teleology—which entailed a critique of the universal similar to Fanon's—see Winfried Siemerling, "W. E. B. Du Bois, Hegel, and the Staging of Alterity," *Callaloo* 24, no. 1 (2001): 325–33.

18. Du Bois, *Black Reconstruction*, 30.

19. Fischer, *Modernity Disavowed*.

20. Buck-Morss, *Hegel, Haiti, and Universal History*.

21. Malcolm X, *Malcolm X Speaks* (New York: Grove Press, 1965), 34. The dialectical nature of Malcolm X's mature thought is lost on both Black essentialists and those who, for example, Manning Marable, bend the stick too far in the opposite direction, making of Malcolm a veritable multicultural universalist. Manning Marable, *Malcolm X: A Life of Reinvention* (New York: Penguin, 2011).

22. Roberto Bolaño, *2666*, trans. N. Wimmer (New York: Farrar, Straus, and Giroux, 2008 [2004]), 266–67.

23. Theodor Adorno, *Negative Dialectics* (New York: Continuum, 1973), xix; Herbert Marcuse, *One-Dimensional Man* (Boston: Beacon Press, 1991 [1964]), 253.

24. Dussel, *Philosophy of Liberation*, 159–60, translation modified; *Filosofía de la liberación*, 187.

25. Fanon, *Black Skin*, xii, 197; *Œuvres*, 64 (the reference to "cosmic harmonies" is absent), 242–43. Fanon counterposes this actional stance to Nietzschean *ressentiment*, whereas Dussel would set out from a "will to live" that he distinguished sharply from Nietzsche's will to power (Dussel, *Twenty Theses*, 13). Sorel was not, as is often suggested, Nietzschean, and his only discussion of Nietzsche's distinction between master and slave morality occurs at a crucial moment of the *Reflections*, with the American conqueror of the U.S. West ambiguously standing in for the "blonde beast" (231–32).

26. Fanon, *Black Skin*, 206; *Œuvres*, 251. In *Against War*, Nelson Maldonado-Torres speaks of decolonial love, a phrase he takes from Chela Sandoval.

27. Sorel, *Reflections*, 227–28.

28. Sorel, *Reflections*, 244. This reading of quasi-exteriority and positivity into the European working class does not straightforwardly contradict the decolonial turn of Fanon and Dussel. Where Fanon was less optimistic about the European working class, the multifaceted character of Dussel's concept of exteriority grants a degree of exteriority to the worker, which is confirmed in Dussel's own systematic rereading of the role of living labor as a category of exteriority in Marx's thought. See *El último Marx*.

29. Adorno diagnoses the ontological incompleteness of the world, and Dussel would agree, but he attempts to move forward both by centering that ontological divide and thinking through the subjects that lie beyond it. Even for Hegel, we should remember, there is a difference between absolute and determinate negativity, the latter of which bears within it the historicity so crucial to grasping dialectical progress.

30. Frank B. Wilderson, III, "The Prison Slave as Hegemony's (Silent) Scandal," *Social Justice* 30, no. 2 (2003): 25–26.

31. Robinson, *Black Marxism*, 73.

32. I thank Robert Nichols for pressing me on this point, although I don't claim to have resolved it sufficiently. Glen Coulthard comes closer to the question in his critique of Fanon in *Red Skin, White Masks*.

33. The colonizer, according to Fanon, "reactivates the tribes" (*Wretched*, 67, translation modified; *Œuvres*, 513).

34. Fanon, *Wretched*, 70; *Œuvres*, 515. On self-criticism and its reinforcement as a tradition, see *Wretched*, 12, 92–93; *Œuvres*, 460–61, 535.

35. See Fanon, *Wretched*, 12; Mariátegui, *Seven Interpretive Essays*, 42, 56–58; Dussel, *Twenty Theses*, 74.

36. Fanon, *Wretched*, 67; *Œuvres*, 512.

37. Fanon, *Wretched*, 160. This is in fact the underlying theme of *A Dying Colonialism* as a whole, where Fanon demonstrates how ostensibly antimodern sentiments among the rural masses were in fact anticolonial and moreover mutable

in the heat of revolutionary struggle (especially radio and medicine) while the inverse was true of so-called traditions (familial structures and the veil).

38. Fanon, *Wretched*, 65; *Œuvres*, 510.

39. Frantz Fanon, "Letter to the Resident Minister (1956)," in *Toward the African Revolution*, 53, translation modified; *Œuvres*, 735.

40. Grégoire Chamayou, *Manhunts: A Philosophical History*, trans. S. Rendall (Princeton, NJ: Princeton University Press, 2012 [2010]), 2.

41. Chamayou, *Manhunts*, 56.

42. Chamayou, *Manhunts*, 58.

43. Chamayou, *Manhunts*, 67.

44. Chamayou, *Manhunts*, 6–7, 3.

45. Maldonado-Torres, *Against War*, chap. 6. See also the "readily killable" subject tracked by Abdul R. JanMohamed, *The Death-Bound-Subject: Richard Wright's Archaeology of Death* (Durham NC: Duke University Press, 2005), 10. See also Gastón Gordillo's reflections on the mobility of "The Killable Horde" (September 3, 2014), http://spaceandpolitics.blogspot.com/2014/09/the-killable-horde.html.

46. Chamayou, *Manhunts*, 3.

47. Chamayou, *Manhunts*, 75–76. This error of this apparent impasse is shared by Buck-Morss, in her turn to so-called cycles of violence and the "dilemmas of the insurgent" in *Hegel, Haiti, and Universal History*.

48. Angela Davis, "Reflections on the Black Woman's Role in the Community of Slaves," *Massachusetts Review* 13, nos. 1/2 (winter–spring 1972): 86.

49. James Scott provides a similar account for the origins of what he calls the "hidden transcript" in the "systematic *frustration of reciprocal action*" in the Hegelian dialectic. *Domination and the Arts of Resistance* (New Haven, CT: Yale University Press, 1990), 37. Scott, however, emphasizes not the master-slave dialectic of the *Phenomenology*, but instead the analysis of the duel—which Hegel considered particular to civil society and feudalism more specifically—in the later *Philosophy of Subjective Spirit*. Even there, Hegel insists that the duel "is in no way to be confused with" the struggle for recognition itself. *The Philosophy of Subjective Spirit*, vol. 3, trans. M. Petry (Boston: Reidel, 1978 [1930]), 61. As a result, the emphasis falls more on honor and standing than on self-consciousness proper, and Scott's ostensibly optimistic account falls back into pessimism by rendering almost all resistance mere fantasy: thus he recounts Richard Wright's reference to rumors about a Black man who "hit a white man, knocked him cold, and nobody did a damned thing," as an exemplification of the psychological release of the hidden transcript (39). But Douglass did the same in reality, not in fantasy.

However, an interesting decolonial and feminist reading emerges once we recognize that *duelo* in Spanish means both duel and grief or mourning, a fact that Yomaira Figueroa recently pointed out to me. The result is a dialectic doubly transformed: filled with the positivity of loss in decolonial suffering and reinforced by the often feminized impact of the grieving process.

50. Davis, "Reflections on the Black Woman's Role," 87, my emphasis.

51. Davis, "Reflections on the Black Woman's Role," 89.
52. Davis, "Reflections on the Black Woman's Role," 97.
53. See Kramer, *Excluded Within*; "Derrida's 'Antigonanette.'" I have hardly touched upon the relationship between this decolonized dialectic and its feminist or queered variants and aspects. When revolutionary Italian feminists considered the master-slave dialectic in 1970, they noted its insufficiency in terms that parallel—albeit without recognizing it—the decolonial critique of the same, therefore insisting that "We spit on Hegel." Rivolta Femminile, "Let's Spit on Hegel," trans. V. Newman (Secunda, 2010), http://zinelibrary.info/lets-spit-hegel-carla-lonzi-rivolta-femminile-0.
54. On the escape from slavery as the epitome of freedom, see Neil Roberts, *Freedom as Marronage* (Chicago: University of Chicago Press, 2015).
55. Fanon, *Wretched*, 4; *Œuvres*, 454. Jean Améry, "The Birth of Man From the Spirit of Violence," 16.
56. Sorel, *Reflections on Violence*, 34–35.
57. Fanon, *Wretched*, 77; *Œuvres*, 522.
58. Dussel, *Twenty Theses*, 67, 131–32.
59. Francois Bondy, "The Black Rousseau," *New York Review of Books*, March 31, 1966.
60. James, *Black Jacobins*, 177, 286.
61. James, *Black Jacobins*, 276n6.
62. On the importance of this distinction between authoritarian and radically democratic brutality in contemporary Venezuela, see my article, "Venezuelan Jacobins," *Jacobin Magazine* (March 13, 2014), https://www.jacobinmag.com/2014/03/venezuelan-jacobins/.
63. Césaire, "Décolonisation pour les Antilles," in Nesbitt, *Caribbean Critique*.
64. Occasionally, this Eurocentrism is worn quite openly, as in Lucien van der Walt and Michael Schmidt, *Black Flame: The Revolutionary Class Politics of Anarchism and Syndicalism* (Oakland, CA: AK Press, 2009), in which the authors declare that anarchism is anticolonial while simultaneously embracing its hyperrationalism and Enlightenment legacy. See my critique, Ciccariello-Maher, "An Anarchism That Is Not Anarchism." It should be noted that Schmidt has since been outed as a white supremacist, and it appears that his class-centrism is complicit in his racism. See Alexander Reid Ross and Joshua Stephens, "About Schmidt: How a White Nationalist Seduced Anarchists Around the World," *Medium* (October 12, 2015), https://medium.com/@rossstephens/about-schmidt-how-a-white-nationalist-seduced-anarchists-around-the-world-chapter-1–1a6fa255b528#.quk7jx2cd. While the related volume by Steven Hirsch and Lucien van der Walt is more promising in this respect for its intention "to recover the history of anarchist and syndicalist anti-imperialism," this is done with an uneven degree of nuance. *Anarchism and Syndicalism in the Colonial and Postcolonial World, 1870–1940* (Leiden: Brill, 2010), xxxii. See also Benedict Anderson, *Under Three Flags: Anarchism and the Anticolonial Imagination* (London: Verso, 2007). On the "race problem"

in anarchism and the tendency to subsume white supremacy into a resistance against all oppressions, see the wonderful work of the late Joel Olson, "The Problem With Infoshops and Insurrection," in *Contemporary Anarchist Studies*, ed. R. Amster, et al. (London: Routledge, 2009), 35–45.

65. Maldonado-Torres, "On the Coloniality of Being," 263.

66. Maia Ramnath, *Decolonizing Anarchism: An Antiauthoritarian History of India's Liberation Struggle* (Oakland, CA: AK Press, 2011), 15.

67. Fanon, *Black Skin*, 191; *Œuvres*, 237.

68. Cited in Fanon, *Black Skin*, 76; *Œuvres*, 139.

.

BIBLIOGRAPHY

Adorno, Theodor. *Negative Dialectics*. New York: Continuum, 1973 [1966].

Agamben, Giorgio. *Homo Sacer: Sovereign Power and Bare Life*. Stanford, CA: Stanford University Press, 1998.

Alcoff, Linda Martín, and Eduardo Mendieta, eds. *Thinking from the Underside of History: Enrique Dussel's Philosophy of Liberation*. Lanham, MD: Rowman and Littlefield, 2000.

Althusser, Louis. *Philosophy of the Encounter: Later Writings, 1978–87*. London: Verso, 2006.

Améry, Jean. "The Birth of Man from the Spirit of Violence: Frantz Fanon the Revolutionary." *Wasafiri* 44 (spring 2005): 13–18.

Anderson, Benedict. *Imagined Communities*. London: Verso, 1982.

———. *Under Three Flags: Anarchism and the Anticolonial Imagination*. London: Verso, 2007.

Anderson, Kevin. *Marx at the Margins: On Nationalism, Ethnicity, and Non-Western Societies*. Chicago: University of Chicago Press, 2010.

Anidjar, Gil. *The Jew, the Arab: A History of the Enemy*. Stanford, CA: Stanford University Press, 2003.

Anzaldúa, Gloria. *Borderlands/La Frontera: The New Mestiza*. San Francisco: Aunt Lute, 1987.

Arendt, Hannah. *The Human Condition*. New York: Doubleday, 1958.

———. *On Revolution*. New York: Penguin, 1990 [1963].

———. *On Violence*. New York: Harcourt, 1970.

Badiou, Alain. *The Communist Hypothesis*. London: Verso, 2010.

———. *Ethics: An Essay on the Understanding of Evil*. Trans. P. Hallward. London: Verso, 2001.

———. *Metapolitics*. Trans. J. Barker. London: Verso, 2005.

————. *The Rebirth of History*. London: Verso, 2012.

Balibar, Étienne. "Reflections on *Gewalt*." *Historical Materialism* 17 (2009): 99–125.

Barber, Michael. *Ethical Hermeneutics: Rationality in Enrique Dussel's Philosophy of Liberation*. New York: Fordham University Press, 1998.

Barreto, José-Manuel, ed. *Human Rights from a Third World Perspective: Critique, History, and International Law*. Newcastle, UK: Cambridge Scholars, 2013.

Baum, Bruce. "Decolonizing Critical Theory." *Constellations* 22, no. 3 (2015): 420–34.

Beasley-Murray, Jon. *Posthegemony: Political Theory and Latin America*. Minneapolis: University of Minnesota Press, 2011.

Bell, Shannon. "Levinas and Alterity Politics." In *Difficult Justice: Commentaries on Levinas and Politics*, ed. A. Horowitz and G. Horowitz. Toronto: University of Toronto Press, 2006.

Beltrán, Cristina. *The Trouble with Unity: Latino Politics and the Creation of Identity*. New York: Oxford University Press, 2010.

Benjamin, Walter. *Illuminations: Essays and Reflections*. New York: Schocken, 1968.

————. *Reflections: Essays, Aphorisms, Autobiographical Writings*. New York: Schocken, 1978.

Bernasconi, Robert. "African Philosophy's Challenge to Continental Philosophy." In *Postcolonial African Philosophy*, ed. E. Eze, 183–96. Oxford: Blackwell, 1997.

————. "The Assumption of Negritude: Aimé Césaire, Frantz Fanon, and the Vicious Circle of Racial Politics." *parallax* 8, no. 2 (2002): 69–83.

————. "The European Knows and Does Not Know." In *Frantz Fanon's* Black Skin, White Masks: *New Interdisciplinary Essays*, ed. M. Silverman. Manchester, UK: Manchester University Press, 2005.

————. "Hegel and Levinas: The Possibility of Reconciliation and Forgiveness." *Archivio di Filosofia* 54 (1986): 325–46.

————. "Levinas Face to Face—with Hegel." *Journal of the British Society for Phenomenology* 13, no. 3 (October 1982): 267–76.

Bernstein, Eduard. *Evolutionary Socialism*. Trans. E. C. Harvey. New York: Schocken, 1961 [1899].

Betancourt, Rómulo. *Tres años de gobierno democrático*. Vol. 2. Caracas: Imprenta Nacional, 1962.

Bolaño, Roberto. *2666*. Trans. N. Wimmer. New York: Farrar, Straus, and Giroux, 2008 [2004].

Bondy, Francois. "The Black Rousseau." *New York Review of Books*, March 31, 1966.

Bosteels, Bruno. *The Actuality of Communism*. London: Verso, 2011.

Bray, Michael. "*El Estado Somos Todos, El Pueblo Soy Yo?* On *Chavismo* and the Necessity of the Leader." *Theory and Event* 17, no. 1 (2014).

Brennan, Timothy. *Borrowed Light: Vico, Hegel, and the Colonies*. Stanford, CA: Stanford University Press, 2014.

Brown, Wendy. "'The Most We Can Hope For . . .': Human Rights and the Politics of Fatalism." *South Atlantic Quarterly* 103, nos. 2/3 (2004): 451–63.

————. "Wounded Attachments." *Political Theory* 21, no. 3 (August 1993): 390–410.

Buck-Morss, Susan. *Dreamworld and Catastrophe: The Passing of Mass Utopia in East and West*. Cambridge, MA: MIT Press, 2002.

———. *Hegel, Haiti, and Universal History*. Pittsburgh: University of Pittsburgh Press, 2009.

Buhlan, Hussein A. *Frantz Fanon and the Psychology of Oppression*. New York: Plenum Press, 1985.

Cassuto, Leonard. "Frederick Douglass and the Work of Freedom: Hegel's Master-Slave Dialectic in the Fugitive Slave Narrative." *Prospects* 21 (October 1996): 229–59.

Castro-Gómez, Santiago, and Ramón Grosfoguel, eds. *El giro decolonial: Reflexiones para una diversidad epistémica más allá del capitalismo global*. Bogotá: Siglo de Hombres Editores, 2007.

Castro Ruz, Fidel. *History Will Absolve Me*. Trans. C. González Díaz. Havana: Editorial José Martí, 1998 [1953].

Caute, David. *Frantz Fanon*. London: Fontana, 1970.

Césaire, Aimé. *Discourse on Colonialism*. Trans. J. Pinkham. New York: Monthly Review, 2000 [1956].

———. "Letter to Maurice Thorez." *Social Text* 103 28, no. 2 (summer 2010 [1956]): 145–52.

Chamayou, Grégoire. *Manhunts: A Philosophical History*. Trans. S. Rendall. Princeton, NJ: Princeton University Press, 2012 [2010].

Chávez, Hugo, and Marta Harnecker. *Understanding the Bolivarian Revolution*. Trans. C. Boudin. New York: Monthly Review Press, 2005.

Chávez Frías, Hugo. *Golpe de Timón*. Caracas: Correo del Orinoco, 2012.

Cherki, Alice. *Frantz Fanon: A Portrait*. Trans. N. Benabid. Ithaca, NY: Cornell University Press, 2006 [2000].

Ciccariello-Maher, George. "An Anarchism That Is Not Anarchism: Notes toward a Critique of Anarchist Imperialism." In *How Not to Be Governed: Readings and Interpretations from a Critical Anarchist Left*, ed. J. Klausen and J. Martel. Lanham, MD: Lexington Books, 2011.

———. *Building the Commune: Radical Democracy in Venezuela*. London: Jacobin-Verso, 2016.

———. "A Critique of Du Boisian Reason: Kanye West and the Fruitfulness of Double-Consciousness." *Journal of Black Studies* 39, no. 3 (January 2009): 371–401.

———. "Decolonial Realism: Ethics, Politics, and Dialectics in Fanon and Dussel." *Contemporary Political Theory* 13, no. 1 (February 2014): 2–22.

———. "Decolonizing Fanaticism." *Theory and Event* 17, no. 2 (2014).

———. "'Detached Irony toward the Rest': Working-Class One-Sidedness from Sorel to Tronti." *Commoner* 11 (spring-summer 2006): 54–73.

———. "The Dialectics of Standing One's Ground." *Theory and Event* 15, no. 3 (2012).

———. "The Internal Limits of the European Gaze: Intellectuals and the Colonial Difference." *Radical Philosophy Review* 9, no. 2 (fall 2006): 139–65.

———. "Jumpstarting the Decolonial Engine: Symbolic Violence from Fanon to Chávez." *Theory and Event* 13, no. 1 (March 2010).

———. " 'So Much the Worse for the Whites': Dialectics of the Haitian Revolution." *Journal of French and Francophone Philosophy* 22, no. 1 (2014): 19–39.

———. "Toward a Racial Geography of Caracas: Neoliberal Urbanism and the Fear of Penetration." *Qui Parle* 16, no. 2 (spring-summer 2007): 39–72.

———. "Venezuelan Jacobins." *Jacobin Magazine*, March 13, 2014. https://www.jacobinmag.com/2014/03/venezuelan-jacobins/.

———. *We Created Chávez: A People's History of the Venezuelan Revolution*. Durham, NC: Duke University Press, 2013.

Ciudad de despedidas, May 3, 2012. https://www.youtube.com/watch?v=GfxToCNh6rQ.

"Communiqué from Decolonize Oakland," March 18, 2012. http://unsettlingamerica.wordpress.com/2012/03/18/communique-from-decolonize-oakland/.

Cook, James H. "Fighting with Breath, Not Blows: Frederick Douglass and Antislavery Violence." In *Antislavery Violence: Sectional, Racial, and Cultural Conflict in Antebellum America*, ed. J. McKivigan and S. Harrold. Knoxville: University of Tennessee Press, 1999.

Coronil, Fernando, and Julie Skurski. "Dismembering and Remembering the Nation: The Semantics of Political Violence in Venezuela." In *Politics in the Andes: Identity, Conflict, and Reform*, ed. J.-M. Burt and P. Mauceri. Pittsburgh: University of Pittsburgh Press, 2004.

Coulthard, Glen. *Red Skin, White Masks: Rejecting the Colonial Politics of Recognition*. Minneapolis: University of Minnesota Press, 2014.

Davari, Arash. "A Return to Which Self? 'Ali Shari'ati and Frantz Fanon on the Political Ethics of Insurrectionary Violence. *Comparative Studies of South Asia, Africa and the Middle East* 34, no. 1 (2014): 86–105.

Davis, Angela. "Reflections on the Black Woman's Role in the Community of Slaves."*Massachusetts Review* 13, nos. 1/2 (winter–spring 1972): 81–100.

Dean, Jodi. *The Communist Horizon*. London: Verso, 2012.

Douglas, Andrew. *In the Spirit of Critique: Thinking Politically in the Dialectical Tradition*. Albany: SUNY Press, 2013.

Douglass, Frederick. "The Meaning of July Fourth for the Negro" (1852). In *Frederick Douglass: Selected Speeches and Writing*, ed. P. Foner. Chicago: Chicago Review Press, 2000.

———. *My Bondage and My Freedom*. New York: Miller, Orton and Mulligan, 1855.

Du Bois, W. E. B. *Black Reconstruction in America, 1860–1880*. New York: Free Press, 1998 [1935].

———. *The Souls of Black Folk*. New York: Penguin, 1996 [1903].

Dunayevskaya, Raya. "On C. L. R. James' Notes on Dialectics," *News and Letters* (1997 [1972]): 4. http://www.marxists.org/archive/dunayevskaya/works/1972/misc/james.htm.

Duque, José Roberto. "Miguel Ángel Landa llora por el país que se le desapareció, y tiene razón." *Misión Verdad*, August 25, 2013. http://misionverdad .com/la-guerra-en-venezuela/miguel-angel-landa-llora-por-el-pais-que-se-le -desaparecio-y-tiene-razon.

Dussel, Enrique. *El último Marx (1863–1882) y la liberación latinoamericana*. Mexico City: Siglo XXI, 1990.

———. "From Critical Theory to the Philosophy of Liberation: Some Themes for Dialogue." Trans. G. Ciccariello-Maher. *Transmodernity* 1, no. 2 (2011): 16–43.

———. "The Liberatory Event in Paul of Tarsus." Trans. G. Ciccariello-Maher. *Qui Parle* 18, no. 1 (fall-winter 2009): 111–80.

———. *Método para una filosofía de la liberación: Superación analéctica de la dialéctica hegeliana*, 2nd ed. Salamanca: Sígueme, 1974.

———. *Para una fundamentación filosófica de la liberación Latinoamericana*. Buenos Aires: Editorial Bonum, 1974.

———. *Philosophy of Liberation*. Trans. A. Martinez and C. Morkovsky. Eugene, OR: Wipf and Stock, 1985. In Spanish: *Filosofía de la liberación*. Bogotá: Nueva América, 1996 [1977].

———. *Política de la Liberación*. Vol. 1: *Historia mundial y crítica*. Madrid: Trotta, 2007.

———. *Política de la Liberación*. Vol. 2: *Arquitectónica*. Madrid: Trotta, 2009.

———. *Política de la liberación*. Vol. 3: *Crítica*. Madrid: Trotta, forthcoming.

———. *Twenty Theses on Politics*. Trans. G. Ciccariello-Maher. Durham, NC: Duke University Press, 2008 [2006].

Endnotes Collective. "The History of Subsumption." *Endnotes* 2 (April 2010). https://endnotes.org.uk/en/endnotes-the-history-of-subsumption.

Engels, Friedrich. *Anti-Dühring*. Trans. E. Burns. New York: International Publishers, 1976 [1877].

———. *Ludwig Feuerbach and the Outcome of Classical German Philosophy*. In *MECW*. Vol. 26. London: Lawrence and Wishart, 2010 [1886].

Errejón, Íñigo. "We Are (Almost) All Chávez: Challenges in the Deployment of Chavista Political Identity." Trans. G. Ciccariello-Maher. *Venezuela Analysis*, September 15, 2013. http://venezuelanalysis.com/analysis/10024.

Fanon, Frantz. *Black Skin, White Masks*. Trans. R. Philcox. New York: Grove Press, 2008 [1952].

———. *A Dying Colonialism*. Trans. H. Chevalier. New York: Grove Press, 1965 [1959].

———. *Œuvres*. Paris: La Découverte, 2011.

———. *Toward the African Revolution*. Trans. H. Chevalier. New York: Grove Press, 1988 [1964].

———. *The Wretched of the Earth*. Trans. R. Philcox. New York: Grove Press, 2004 [1961].

Fischer, Sibylle. *Modernity Disavowed: Haiti and the Cultures of Slavery in the Age of Revolution*. Durham, NC: Duke University Press, 2004.

Ford, Glen. "Obama's Siren Song." *Counterpunch*, June 14, 2007. http://www .counterpunch.org/2007/06/14/obama-s-siren-song/.

Foucault, Michel. *Discipline and Punish: The Birth of the Prison*. Trans. A. Sheridan. New York: Vintage, 1979 [1975].

———. *History of Madness*. Trans. J. Murphy and J. Khalfa. London: Routledge, 2006 [1961].

———. *History of Sexuality*, vol. 1: *An Introduction*. New York: Pantheon, 1978 [1976].

———. "Intellectuals and Power: A Conversation Between Michel Foucault and Gilles Deleuze" (1972). In *Language, Counter-Memory, Practice: Selected Essays and Interviews*. Ithaca, NY: Cornell University Press, 1977.

———. *Remarks on Marx*. Trans. R. J. Goldstein and J. Cascaito. New York: Semiotext(e), 1991 [1978/1981].

———. *"Society Must Be Defended": Lectures at the Collège de France, 1975–1976*. Trans. D. Macey. New York: Picador, 2003 [1997].

———. "What Is Critique?." Trans. L. Hochroth. In *The Politics of Truth*, ed. S. Lotringer. New York: Semiotext(e), 1997.

Foucault, Michel, Colin Gordon, and Paul Patton. "Interview: Considerations on Marxism, Phenomenology and Power. Interview with Michel Foucault; Recorded on April 3rd, 1978." *Foucault Studies* 14 (September 2012): 98–114.

Frank, André Gunder. *Latin America: Underdevelopment or Revolution*. New York: Monthly Review, 1970.

Frank, Jason. *Constituent Moments: Enacting the People in Postrevolutionary America*. Durham, NC: Duke University Press, 2010.

Freud, Sigmund. *An Outline of Psycho-Analysis*. In *The Standard Edition of the Complete Works of Sigmund Freud*, vol. 23, ed. J. Strachey, et al. London: Hogarth Press, 1974.

Fukuyama, Francis. *The End of History and the Last Man*. New York: Simon and Schuster, 2006 [1992].

García Salvatecci, Hugo. *Sorel y Mariátegui: Ubicación ideológica del Amauta*. Lima: Delgado Valenzuela, 1979.

Gendzier, Irene L. *Frantz Fanon: A Critical Study*. New York: Grove Press, 1973.

Gibson, Nigel. "Dialectical Impasses: Turning the Table on Hegel and the Black." *parallax* 8, no. 2 (2002): 30–45.

———. "Radical Mutations: Fanon's Untidy Dialectic of History." In *Rethinking Fanon: The Continuing Dialogue*, ed. N. Gibson. New York: Humanity Books, 1999.

Gilroy, Paul. *The Black Atlantic: Modernity and Double Consciousness*. London: Verso, 1993.

———. "Black Fascism." *Transition* 81/82 (2000): 70–91.

Gooding-Williams, Robert. "Race, Multiculturalism and Democracy." *Constellations* 5, no. 1 (1998): 18–41.

Gordillo, Gaston. "The Killable Horde," September 3, 2014. http://spaceand politics.blogspot.com/2014/09/the-killable-horde.html.

Gordon, Lewis. *Bad Faith and Anti-Black Racism*. New York: Humanity Books, 1995.

———. "Fanon." *Histories of Violence*, May 29, 2012. https://vimeo.com/43036768.

———. "Fanon's Tragic Revolutionary Violence." In *Fanon: A Critical Reader*, ed. L. Gordon, T. Sharpley-Whiting, and R. White. Oxford: Blackwell, 1996.

———. "Of Illicit Appearance: The L.A. Riots/Rebellion as a Portent of Things to Come." *Truthout.org*, May 12, 2012. http://truth-out.org/news/item/9008-of -illicit-appearance-the-la-riots-rebellion-as-a-portent-of-things-to-come.

———. "Through the Hellish Zone of Nonbeing: Thinking through Fanon, Disaster, and the Damned of the Earth." *Human Architecture: Journal of the Sociology of Self-Knowledge* V (summer 2007): 5–12.

Gramsci, Antonio. *Selections from the Prison Notebooks of Antonio Gramsci*, ed. Q. Hoare and G. N. Smith. New York: International Publishers, 1971.

Grant, John. *Dialectics and Contemporary Politics: Critique and Transformation from Hegel through Post-Marxism*. London: Routledge, 2013.

Greenwald, Glenn. "Two Short Paragraphs That Summarize the U.S. Approach to Human Rights Advocacy." *Intercept*, September 13, 2015. https://theintercept .com/2015/09/13/two-short-paragraphs-summarize-us-approach-human -rights-advocacy/.

Gregor, A. James. *The Search for Neofascism: The Use and Abuse of Social Science*. Cambridge: Cambridge University Press, 2006.

Grosfoguel, Ramón. "Developmentalism, Modernity, and Dependency Theory in Latin America." *Nepantla: Views from South* 1, no. 2 (2000): 347–74.

Hardt, Michael, and Antonio Negri. *Commonwealth*. Cambridge, MA: Harvard University Press, 2009.

———. *Empire*. Cambridge, MA: Harvard University Press, 2000.

———. *Labor of Dionysus: A Critique of the State-Form*. Minneapolis: University of Minnesota Press, 1994.

———. *Multitude: War and Democracy in the Age of Empire*. New York: Penguin, 2004.

Hegel, G. W. F. *Elements of the Philosophy of Right*. Trans. H. B. Nisbet. Cambridge: Cambridge University Press, 1991 [1820].

———. *The Encyclopaedia Logic*. Trans. T. F. Geraets, W. A. Suchting, and H. S. Harris. Cambridge, MA: Hackett, 1991 [1817].

———. *Phenomenology of Spirit/Phänomenologie des Geistes*. Trans. T. Pinkhard. Cambridge: Cambridge University Press, 2010 [1807].

———. *The Philosophy of Subjective Spirit*. Vol. 3. Trans. M Petry. Boston: Reidel, 1978 [1830].

———. *The Science of Logic*. Trans. G. di Giovanno. Cambridge: Cambridge University Press, 2010 [1812–16].

Herrera Salas, Jesús María. "Ethnicity and Revolution: The Political Economy of Racism in Venezuela." *Latin American Perspectives* 32, no. 2 (March 2005): 72–91.

Hirsch, Steven, and Lucien van der Walt. *Anarchism and Syndicalism in the Colonial and Postcolonial World, 1870–1940*. Leiden: Brill, 2010.

Hobbes, Thomas. *Elementa philosophica de cive*. Lausanne: Grasset, 1782 [1642].

Hodgson, Peter C. *Hegel and Christian Theology: A Reading of the Lectures on the Philosophy of Religion*. Oxford: Oxford University Press, 2005.

Honneth, Axel. *The Struggle for Recognition: The Moral Grammar of Social Conflicts.* Trans. J. Anderson. Cambridge, MA: MIT Press, 1995.

Ishibashi, Jun. "Hacia una apertura del debate sobre el racismo en Venezuela: Exclusión y inclusión estereotipada de personas 'negras' en los medios de comunicación." In *Políticas de identidades y diferencias sociales*, ed. D. Mato. Caracas: Facultad de Ciencias Económicas y Sociales, 2003.

Iturriza López, Reinaldo. "The Vitality of the Revolution." Trans. C. Fischer-Hoffman. *Venezuela Analysis*, September 3, 2014. http://venezuelanalysis.com /analysis/10878.

James, C. L. R. *The Black Jacobins: Toussaint L'Overture and the San Domingo Revolution.* New York: Vintage, 1989 [1938].

———. *A History of Negro Revolt.* New York: Haskell House, 1938.

———. *Notes on Dialectics: Hegel, Marx, Lenin.* Westport, CT: Lawrence Hill, 1980 [1948].

Jameson, Fredric. *The Hegel Variations: On the* Phenomenology of Spirit. London: Verso, 2010.

———. *Valences of the Dialectic.* London: Verso, 2009.

JanMohamed, Abdul R. *The Death-Bound-Subject: Richard Wright's Archaeology of Death.* Durham NC: Duke University Press, 2005.

Jaua, Elías. "Chavismo." Trans. R. Boothroyd. *Venezuela Analysis*, January 4, 2013. http://venezuelanalysis.com/analysis/7586.

Jay, Martin. *Marxism and Totality: The Adventures of Concept from Lukács to Habermas.* Berkeley: University of California Press, 1984.

———. "The Concept of Totality in Lukács and Adorno." In *Varieties of Marxism*, ed. S. Avineri. The Hague: Martinus Nijhoff, 1977.

Jennings, J. R. "Sorel's Early Marxism and Science." *Political Studies* 31, no. 2 (June 1983): 224–38.

Jinadu, L. Adele. *Fanon: In Search of the African Revolution.* London: Routledge, 1986.

Julliard, Jacques. "Sur un fascisme imaginaire: A props d'un livre de Zeev Sternhell." *Annales E.S.C.* (July–August 1984): 849–61.

King, Preston. *Fear of Power: An Analysis of Anti-Statism in Three French Writers.* London: Frank Cass, 1967.

Kleinberg, Ethan. "Kojève and Fanon: The Desire for Recognition and the Fact of Blackness." In *French Civilization and Its Discontents: Nationalism, Colonialism, Race*, ed. T. Stovall and G. Van Den Abbeele. Lanham, MD: Lexington Books, 2003.

Kohn, Margaret. "Frederick Douglass's Master-Slave Dialectic." *Journal of Politics* 67, no. 2 (May 2005): 497–514.

Kohn, Margaret, and Keally McBride. *Political Theories of Decolonization.* New York: Oxford University Press, 2011.

Koopman, Colin. *Genealogy as Critique: Foucault and the Problems of Modernity.* Bloomington: Indiana University Press, 2013.

Kramer, Sina. *Excluded Within: The (Un)Intelligibility of Radical Political Actors.* Oxford: Oxford University Press, forthcoming.

———. "Derrida's 'Antigonanette': On the Quasi-Transcendental." *Southern Journal of Philosophy* 52, no. 4 (December 2014): 521–51.

Laclau, Ernesto. *On Populist Reason.* London: Verso, 2005.

Laclau, Ernesto, and Chantal Mouffe. *Hegemony and Socialist Strategy.* London: Verso, 2001 [1985].

Lendon, J. E. *Soldiers and Ghosts: A History of Battle in Classical Antiquity.* New Haven, CT: Yale University Press, 2006.

Lenin, V. I. *State and Revolution.* Chicago: Haymarket, 2014 [1918].

Levinas, Emmanuel. *Totality and Infinity: An Essay on Exteriority.* The Hague: Kluwer, 1991 [1961].

López, Alfred J. "Occupying Reality: Fanon Reading Hegel." *South Atlantic Quarterly* 112, no. 1 (winter 2013): 71–78.

López, Ociel Alí. *¡Dale Más Gasolina! Chavismo, sifrinismo y burocracia.* Caracas: Fundación Casa Nacional de las Letras Andrés Bello, 2015.

Lovato, Brian. *Democracy, Dialectics, and Difference: Hegel, Marx, and 21st Century Social Movements.* London: Routledge, 2015.

Lukács, Georg. "Tactics and Ethics." In *Tactics and Ethics: Political Writings 1919–1929.* London: NLB, 1972.

Luxemburg, Rosa. *Reform or Revolution and Other Writings.* Mineola, NY: Dover, 2006.

Macey, David. *Frantz Fanon.* New York: Picador, 2000.

Maldonado-Torres, Nelson. *Against War: Views from the Underside of Modernity.* Durham, NC: Duke University Press, 2008.

———. "Decolonization and the New Identitarian Logics after September 11." *Radical Philosophy Review* 8, no. 1 (2005): 35–67.

———. "Liberation Theology and the Search for the Lost Paradigm: From Radical Orthodoxy to Radical Diversality." In *Latin American Liberation Theology: The Next Generation,* ed. I. Petrella. Maryknoll, NY: Orbis, 2005.

———. "On the Coloniality of Being: Contributions to the Development of a Concept." *Cultural Studies* 21, no. 2 (March 2007): 240–70.

Marable, Manning. *Malcolm X: A Life of Reinvention.* New York: Penguin, 2011.

Marasco, Robyn. *The Highway of Despair: Critical Theory after Hegel.* New York: Columbia University Press, 2015.

Marcuse, Herbert. *One-Dimensional Man.* Boston: Beacon Press, 1991 [1964].

Mariátegui, José Carlos. *An Anthology.* Edited by H. Vanden and M. Becker. New York: Monthly Review Press, 2011.

———. *Defensa del marxismo. Obras completas.* Vol. 5. Lima: Biblioteca Amauta, 1974 [1934].

———. *7 Ensayos sobre la realidad peruana.* Caracas: Biblioteca Ayacucho, 2007 [1928]. In English: *Seven Interpretive Essays on Peruvian Reality.* Trans. M. Urquidi. Austin: University of Texas Press, 1971.

Markell, Patchen. *Bound by Recognition*. Princeton, NJ: Princeton University Press, 2003.

Márquez, Patricia, and Ramón Piñango, eds. *En esta Venezuela: Realidades y nuevos caminos*. Caracas: Instituto de Estudios Superiores de la Administración, 2003.

Marx, Karl. *The Poverty of Philosophy*. Peking: Foreign Languages Press, 1977.

Marx, Karl, and Friedrich Engels. *The Communist Manifesto*. New York: Penguin, 2002 [1848].

McInnes, Neil. "Georges Sorel on the Trial of Socrates." *Politics: Australian Journal of Political Science* 10, no. 1 (May 1975): 37–43.

McKean, Benjamin L. "Toward an Inclusive Populism? On the Role of Race and Difference in Laclau's Politics." *Political Theory* (advance online publication, May 4, 2016).

McWhorter, Ladelle. *Racism and Sexual Oppression in Anglo-America: A Genealogy*. Bloomington: Indiana University Press, 2009.

Medina, Medófilo, and Margarita López Maya. *Venezuela: Confrontación social y polarización política*. Bogotá: Ediciones Aurora, 2003.

Meisenhelder, Tom. "Amilcar Cabral's Theory of Class Suicide and Revolutionary Socialism." *Monthly Review* 45, no. 6 (November 1993): 40–49.

Mellino, Miguel. "The *Langue* of the Damned: Fanon and the Remnants of Europe." *South Atlantic Quarterly* 112, no. 1 (2013): 79–89.

Mendieta, Eduardo. "'To Make Live and Let Die': Foucault on Racism," published in Spanish in *Tabula Rasa* 6 (2007): 138–52. Available in English (April 25, 2002), http://www.stonybrook.edu/commcms/philosophy/people/faculty_pages/docs/foucault.pdf.

Mignolo, Walter. "The Geopolitics of Knowledge and the Colonial Difference." *South Atlantic Quarterly* 101, no. 1 (2002): 57–96.

Miller, James. *The Passion of Michel Foucault*. New York: Simon and Schuster, 1993.

Moussa, Mario, and Ron Scapp. "The Practical Theorizing of Michel Foucault: Politics and Counterdiscourse." *Cultural Critique* 33 (spring 1996): 87–112.

Murray, Stuart J. "Myth as Critique?" *Philosophy and Social Criticism* 30, no. 2 (2004): 247–62.

Negri, Antonio. *Insurgencies: Constituent Power and the Modern State*. Trans. M. Boscagli. Minneapolis: University of Minnesota Press, 1999 [1992]. http://antonionegriinenglish.wordpress.com/2010/11/25/some-thoughts-on-the-use-of-dialectics/.

———. *Savage Anomaly: The Power of Spinoza's Metaphysics and Politics*. Trans. M. Hardt. Minneapolis: University of Minnesota Press, 1991 [1981].

———. "Some Thoughts on the Use of Dialectics." Trans. Ariana Bove. Contribution to Critical Thought in the 21st Century conference, Moscow, June 2009.

———. "Twenty Theses on Marx." In S. Makdisi, C. Casarino, and R. Karl, eds., *Marxism beyond Marxism*. London: Routledge, 1996.

Nesbitt, Nick. *Caribbean Critique: Antillean Critical Theory from Toussaint to Glissant*. Liverpool: Liverpool University Press, 2013.

Norden, Deborah L. "Sowing Conflict in Venezuela: Political Violence and Economic Policy." In *Economic Development Strategies and the Evolution of Violence in Latin America*, ed. W. Ascher and N. Mirovitskaya. New York: Palgrave MacMillan, 2012.

Ochoa Espejo, Paulina. *The Time of Popular Sovereignty: Process and the Democratic State*. University Park: Penn State University Press, 2011.

Ollman, Bertell. *Dance of the Dialectic: Steps in Marx's Method*. Champaign: University of Illinois, 2003.

Olson, Joel. "The Problem with Infoshops and Insurrection." In *Contemporary Anarchist Studies*, ed. R. Amster, et al. London: Routledge, 2009.

———. "Whiteness and the 99%." In *We Are Many: Reflections on Movement Strategy from Occupation to Liberation*, ed. K. Khatib, M. Killjoy, and M. McGuire. Oakland, CA: AK Press, 2012.

Panizza, Francisco. "Introduction: Populism and the Mirror of Democracy." In *Populism and the Mirror of Democracy*, ed. F. Panizza. London: Verso, 2005.

Patterson, Orlando. *Slavery and Social Death: A Comparative Study*. Cambridge, MA: Harvard University Press, 1982.

Pippin, Robert. *Hegel's Practical Philosophy: Rational Agency as Ethical Life*. Cambridge: Cambridge University Press, 2008.

Portis, Larry. *Georges Sorel*. London: Pluto Press, 1981.

Primera, Alí. *Que mi canto no se pierda*. Caracas: Fundarte, 2006.

Quijano, Aníbal. "The Coloniality of Power and Social Classification." Trans. G. Ciccariello-Maher. Published in Spanish in *Journal of World-Systems Research* 6, no. 2 (2000): 342–86.

———. "Notas sobre el concepto de 'marginalidad social.'" Santiago: División de Asuntos Sociales, CEPAL, 1966.

Rabasa, Magalí. "Re-reading *The Wretched of the Earth* in Spanish: Tracing Fanon's Movement through Radical Politics (Past and Present) in Latin America" (unpublished).

Ramnath, Maia. *Decolonizing Anarchism: An Antiauthoritarian History of India's Liberation Struggle*. Oakland, CA: AK Press, 2011.

Rancière, Jacques. "Ten Theses on Politics." *Theory and Event* 5, no. 3 (2001).

Reid Ross, Alexander, and Joshua Stephens. "About Schmidt: How a White Nationalist Seduced Anarchists around the World." *Medium*, October 12, 2015. https://medium.com/@rossstephens/about-schmidt-how-a-white-nationalist-seduced-anarchists-around-the-world-chapter-1–1a6fa255b528#.quk7jx2cd.

Rivolta Femminile. "Let's Spit on Hegel." Trans. V. Newman. Secunda, 2010. http://blogue.nt2.uqam.ca/hit/files/2012/12/Lets-Spit-on-Hegel-Carla-Lonzi.pdf.

Roberts, Neil. *Freedom as Marronage*. Chicago: University of Chicago Press, 2015.

Robinson, Cedric. *Black Marxism: The Making of the Black Radical Tradition*. Chapel Hill: University of North Carolina Press, 2000 [1983].

Rodríguez, Simón. *Inventamos o erramos*. Caracas: Monte Avila, 2004.

Roth, Jack J. *The Cult of Violence: Sorel and the Sorelians*. Berkeley: University of California Press, 1980.

———. "The Roots of Italian Fascism: Sorel and Sorelismo." *Journal of Modern History* 39, no. 1 (March 1967): 30–45.

Roumain, Jacques. "Nouveau sermon nègre." In *Anthologie de la nouvelle poésie nègre et malgache de langue française*, ed. L. S. Senghor. Paris: P.U.F., 1969. In English: "New Black Sermon." In *Ebony Wood*, ed. S. Shapiro. New York: Interworld Press, 1972.

Rowe, William, and Vivian Schelling. *Memory and Modernity: Popular Culture in Latin America*. London: Verso, 1991.

RWW News. "Ben Stein: Michael Brown Was 'Armed with His Incredibly Strong, Scary Self,'" August 27, 2014. https://www.youtube.com/watch?v=RtBQUAyLWUI.

Said, Edward. *Culture and Imperialism*. London: Vintage, 1994.

———. "Traveling Theory Reconsidered." In *Reflections on Exile*. London: Granta, 2001.

Saldivia Najul, Fernando. "Chávez dividió al país." *Aporrea.org*, May 28, 2014. http://www.aporrea.org/actualidad/a188867.html.

Sartre, Jean-Paul. *Anti-Semite and Jew: An Exploration of the Etiology of Hate*. Trans. G. Becker. New York: Schocken Books, 1995 [1948].

———. *Being and Nothingness: A Phenomenological Essay on Ontology*. Trans. H. Barnes. New York: Washington Square Press, 1956 [1943].

———. "Preface." In Frantz Fanon, *The Wretched of the Earth*. In French: Fanon, *Œuvres*.

Schmitt, Carl. *The Crisis of Parliamentary Democracy*. Trans. E. Kennedy. Cambridge, MA: MIT Press, 1985 [1923].

———. *The Theory of the Partisan: A Commentary/Remark on the Concept of the Political*. Trans. A. C. Goodson. East Lansing: Michigan State University Press, 2004 [1963].

Schutte, Ofelia. *Cultural Identity and Social Liberation in Latin American Thought*. Albany: SUNY Press, 1993.

Scott, David. *Conscripts of Modernity: The Tragedy of Colonial Enlightenment*. Durham, NC: Duke University Press, 2004.

Scott, James. *Domination and the Arts of Resistance*. New Haven, CT: Yale University Press, 1990.

Sekyi-Otu, Ato. *Fanon's Dialectic of Experience*. Cambridge, MA: Harvard University Press, 1997.

Sheth, Falguni. *Toward a Political Philosophy of Race*. Albany: SUNY Press, 2009.

Siemerling, Winfried. "W. E. B. Du Bois, Hegel, and the Staging of Alterity." *Callaloo* 24, no. 1 (2001): 325–33.

Slabodsky, Santiago. "Emmanuel Levinas's Geopolitics: Overlooked Conversations between Rabbinical and Third World Decolonialisms." *Journal of Jewish Thought and Philosophy* 18, no. 2 (2011): 147–65.

Smith, Stephen B. *Hegel's Critique of Liberalism: Rights in Context*. Chicago: University of Chicago Press, 1989.

Sorel, Georges. *From Georges Sorel*. Edited by J. L. Stanley. New Brunswick, NJ: Transaction, 1987.

———. *The Illusions of Progress*. Trans. J. Stanley. Berkeley: University of California Press, 1969 [1908].

———. "La necessità e il fatalismo nel marxismo." *La Riforma Sociale* V, vol. 8 (1898): 729–30.

———. *Le Procès de Socrate: Examen critique des thèses socratiques*. Paris: Alcan, 1889.

———. *Reflections on Violence*. Cambridge: Cambridge University Press, 2004. In French: *Réflexions sur la violence*. Paris: Marcel Rivière, 1910 [1908].

———. *Saggi di critica del Marxismo*. Milan: Sandron, 1903.

Spillers, Hortense. "Mama's Baby, Papa's Maybe: An American Grammar Book." *Diacritics* 17, no. 2 (summer 1987): 65–81.

Spivak, Gayatri Chakravorty. "Fanon Reading Hegel." In *Readings*. Calcutta: Seagull Books, 2014.

Stanley, John L. *The Sociology of Virtue: The Political and Social Theories of George Sorel*. Berkeley: University of California Press, 1981.

Sternhell, Zeev. *Neither Right nor Left: Fascist Ideology in France*. Trans. D. Maisel. Berkeley: University of California Press, 1986 [1983].

Stewart, Jon, ed. *Hegel Myths and Legends*. Evanston, IL: Northwestern University Press, 1996.

Stoler, Anna Laura. *Race and the Education of Desire: Foucault's* History of Sexuality *and the Colonial Order of Things*. Durham, NC: Duke University Press, 1995.

Stone, I. F. *The Trial of Socrates*. New York: Anchor, 1989.

Terdiman, Richard. *Discourse/Counterdiscourse*. Ithaca, NY: Cornell University Press, 1985.

Toscano, Alberto. "Communism without Guarantees: On Franco Fortini." *Salvage*, September 18, 2015. http://salvage.zone/in-print/communism-without-guarantees-on-franco-fortini/.

———. *Fanaticism: On the Uses of an Idea*. London: Verso, 2010.

———. "Politics in a Tragic Key." *Radical Philosophy* 180 (July–August 2013): 25–34.

Tronti, Mario. *Operai e Capitale*. 2nd ed. Turin: Einaudi, 1971.

Turner, Lou. "On the Difference between the Hegelian and Fanonian Dialectic of Lordship and Bondage." In *Fanon: A Critical Reader*, ed. L. Gordon, T. Sharpley-Whiting, and R. White. Oxford: Blackwell, 1996.

van der Walt, Lucien, and Michael Schmidt. *Black Flame: The Revolutionary Class Politics of Anarchism and Syndicalism*. Oakland, CA: AK Press, 2009.

Vázquez-Arroyo, Antonio. "Universal History Disavowed: On Critical Theory and Postcolonialism," *Postcolonial Studies* 11, no. 4 (2008): 451–73.

Virno, Paolo. *Grammar of the Multitude: For an Analysis of Contemporary Forms of Life*, trans. I. Bertoletti, J. Cascaito, and A. Casson. New York: Semiotext(e), 2004 [2001].

Virno, Paolo, and Michael Hardt, eds. *Radical Thought in Italy: A Potential Politics.* Minneapolis: University of Minnesota Press, 1996.

Wallerstein, Immanuel. "Fanon and the Revolutionary Class." In *The Essential Wallerstein.* New York: New Press, 2000.

Wilderson, Frank B., III. "The Prison Slave as Hegemony's (Silent) Scandal." *Social Justice* 30, no. 2 (2003): 18–27.

Willett, Cynthia. "The Master-Slave Dialectic: Hegel vs. Douglass." In *Subjugation and Bondage: Critical Essays on Slavery and Social Philosophy*, ed. T. Lott. Lanham, MD: Rowman and Littlefield, 1998.

Winter, Yves. "Debating Violence on the Desert Island: Engels, Dühring and Robinson Crusoe." *Contemporary Political Theory* 13 (November 2014): 318–38.

Wohl, Robert. "French Fascism, Both Right and Left: Reflections on the Sternhell Controversy." *Journal of Modern History* 63, no. 1 (March 1991): 91–98.

Wright, Richard. *Native Son.* New York: Harper and Row, 1989 [1940].

X, Malcolm. *Malcolm X Speaks.* New York: Grove Press, 1965.

Young, Iris Marion. *Justice and the Politics of Difference.* Princeton, NJ: Princeton University Press, 1990.

Zago, Angela. *La Rebelión de los ángeles.* Caracas: Fuentes, 1992.

Zahar, Renate. *Frantz Fanon: Colonialism and Alienation.* Trans. W. Feuser. London: Monthly Review, 1974.

Zamir, Shamoon. *Dark Voices: W. E. B. Du Bois and American Thought, 1888–1903.* Chicago: University of Chicago Press, 1995.

Žižek, Slavoj. "Against Human Rights." *New Left Review* 34 (July–August 2005): 115–31.

———. *First as Tragedy, Then as Farce.* London: Verso, 2009.

———. "In the Wake of Paris Attacks the Left Must Embrace Its Radical Western Roots." *In These Times*, November 16, 2015. http://inthesetimes.com/article /18605/breaking-the-taboos-in-the-wake-of-paris-attacks-the-left-must -embrace-its.

———. "A Leftist Plea for 'Eurocentrism.'" *Critical Inquiry* 24, no. 4 (summer 1998): 988–1009.

———. *Less Than Nothing.* London: Verso, 2012.

———. *Violence.* New York: Picador, 2008.

communism, 29, 45, 170, 175n18, 179n59, 194n71; Césaire on, 67; and decolonization, 12, 188n103; indigenous, 107, 163; Negritude movement and, 75; renewal of, 172n4

constituent power, 132–33, 143, 206n5, 206n13

constituted power, 133, 135, 136, 142, 206n5, 206n13

Cook, James H., 213n15

Coulthard, Glen, 172n7, 194n78, 214n32

counterdiscourse, 6–8, 12, 15–16, 18, 21, 157, 177nn30–31, 177n39, 178n46

Davis, Angela, 166–67

Dean, Jodi, 206–7n2

death, 85, 107, 155–56, 213n13

De Beauvoir, Simone, 200n81

decolonial critique, 15, 112, 216n53

decolonial feminisms, 173n11

decolonial nation, 8, 48, 73, 77–78, 82, 86, 88–89, 101, 103–4, 120, 121, 126–27, 132

decolonial thought, 2, 54, 104, 107, 176n20

decolonial turn, 101, 201n97, 214n28

decolonization, 7, 11, 22, 41, 80, 86–88, 97, 103–4, 113, 115, 153, 167; African, 96; Algerian, 87; anarchism and, 168–70; of being, 63; class struggle and, 43, 45, 101, 153, 194n78; communism and, 12, 188n103; critique of identity politics and, 172n7, 187n94; dialectics and, 2, 19, 21, 49, 57, 66, 70, 78, 97, 93, 103, 117, 159, 164; epistemic/epistemological, 10, 52, 54, 109; Fanon and, 48, 128, 165; Manichaeism and, 82; philosophy of, 107; project of, 6; rural-urban divide in, 87–88, 90, 97; symbolic, 86; theoretical, 158; totality and, 18. *See also* Manichaeism: inversion of

Decolonize Oakland, 5–6, 173n10

deconstruction, 13–14

Deleuze, Gilles, 173n12

dependency theory, 105, 107, 109, 202n7, 208n30

determinism, 7, 9–10, 24, 29–31, 53–54, 68, 148, 158; dialectical, 21, 114; economic, 43, 45; Hegelian, 76; historical, 19; indeterminate, 38; Marxist, 37–38, 45

Dien Bien Phu, 84

difference, 5, 7, 52, 80, 98, 109–10, 114, 116, 131, 144, 150, 176n29; class, 117; colonial (*see* colonial difference); dialectical, 110; diversity and, 9, 11, 80, 108, 110, 116–17, 148; ethics of, 3; indifference of, 174n16; ontological, 66, 158–59, 191n43; racial, 52; sameness and, 20; transontological versus subontological, 118

diremption, 41, 71, 186n87, 195n1, 204n33; ethical, 35, 44, 79; religious origins of, 85, 212n4

disavowal (psychoanalysis), 188–89n1

diversity, 12, 98, 124, 159, 167; difference and, 9, 11, 80, 108, 110, 117, 148; in Hegel's dialectic, 174n16

Douglass, Frederick, 12, 211nn5–6, 211n12, 215n49; citation of Byron, 213n15; master-slave dialectic and, 153; struggle with Edward Covey, 153–55, 166

Du Bois, W. E. B., 52, 58, 76, 116, 176n52, 194n78, 208n33; citation of Byron, 156; crossing, 189n9; dialectic and, 156; Hegelian dialectic and, 213n17; racial trajectory of, 213n17; on slavery, 188n101

duelo (duel/grief), 215n49

Dühring, Eugen K., 84

Dussel A., Enrique, 8, 17, 107–21, 126, 128–35, 137–38, 140, 142, 144–47, 150, 153, 157–61, 193n59, 195n79, 203n29, 205n54, 206–7n22, 207n30, 214n25; anadialectical method of, 113; anarchism and, 116, 168, 170; bombing of, 108; critique of totality, 9; decolonial

Jaurès, Jean, 182n29
Jay, Martin, 9, 32, 36, 174n15, 186n88, 186n90, 190n13
Jews: Fanon on, 49, 98, 176n8; Césaire on, 200n82; Sartre on, 196n8. *See also* anti-Semitism

Kautsky, Karl, 182n29
Kleinberg, Ethan, 191n34
Kohn, Margaret, 204n30, 212n6
Kojève, Alexandre, 171n2, 191n34
Kramer, Sina, 173n11, 174n16

Laclau, Ernesto, 34, 96, 199n75, 210n64; on populism, 131–32, 207n22, 208n33
Landa, Miguel Ángel, 139, 210n57
Lefebvre, Georges, 169
Leibniz, Gottfried W., 12
Lenin, Vladimir, 14, 23, 45, 187n94, 197n35; *Conspectus* on Hegel's *The Science of Logic*, 174n18
Levinas, Emmanuel, 109–13, 118–20, 130, 191n43, 195n79, 202n12, 203n29; critique of Hegel, 203n22; critique of ontology, 108; decolonization of (Dussel), 111; ethics of alterity, 8, 104, 108; exteriority, 104; as Hegelian, 203n22; transontological difference, 191n43
liberation theology, 207–8n30
López, Ociel Alí, 145–46
L'Ouverture, Toussaint, 20, 76, 156, 168–69
Lukács, Georg, 36, 182n27, 199n76
lumpenproletariat, 88, 96, 199n75
Luxemburg, Rosa, 24, 40, 185n71

Macey, David, 189n5, 191n34, 196n7, 198n36
Malcolm X, 42, 127, 157, 187n97, 213n21
Maldonado-Torres, Nelson, 191n43, 202n8, 208n31, 214n26; critique of Dussel, 118–20
mandar obediciendo (commanding by obeying), 133

Manichaeism, 37, 52, 78–82, 84, 87, 95, 118, 123, 127, 159, 196n8; antiessentialist, 93; colonial, 128, 197n27, 199n76; global, 99–100; inversion of, 79, 81, 87, 90, 93, 100
Marable, Manning, 188n97
Marcuse, Herbert, 114, 160, 161
Mariátegui, José Carlos, 43, 44, 45, 105–7, 131, 147, 148, 157; anarchism and, 168; on *ayllu*, 129, 163; on class, 69; Dussel and, 205n55; enthusiasm for Sorel, 188n105, 201n2; prefigures Fanon, 106; *Peruvian Reality*, 105; *Seven Interpretive Essays*, 105
Markell, Patchen, 174n18
Maroon communities, 156, 167
Martin, Trayvon, 4, 61
Marx, Karl, 2, 10–12, 14, 23–24, 28–31, 36, 38, 43, 87, 108, 116, 130, 142, 167, 176n28, 178n46, 183n53, 184n60, 186n87; *Capital*, 178n46, 189n3; letters to Vera Zasulich, 175n18, 201n5; on *Obshchina* (Russian peasant communes), 45, 201n5
Marxism, 15, 17–18, 24, 27, 33, 36, 45, 153, 178n44, 178n46, 181n22, 182n29, 201n2; European, 7; indigenous, 107; Latin American, 105; as myth (Sorel), 28; orthodox, 29, 31, 157; scientific aspirations of, 30; as "social poetry" (Sorel), 27; Tunisian, 18; vulgar, 86; Western, 23, 114, 175n19
Marxist dialectics of history, 7, 37–38, 40, 50, 116, 118, 157
mass, 95, 197n27
master-slave dialectic, 7, 39, 49, 54, 153, 159, 166–67, 184n58, 212n6, 215n49; decolonization of, 8, 50, 118, 128, 165, 201n98, 215n53 (*see also* decolonization: dialectics and); Dussel on, 107; Fanon's critique of, 57, 62, 66, 70, 112, 191n34, 204n45; race and, 59
McBride, Keally, 204n30
McBride, Renisha, 4

McDonald, CeCe, 4

McKean, Benjamin, 208n33

Mendieta, Eduardo, 202n12

mestizaje, 146

Michels, Robert, 42

Mignolo, Walter, 54, 159

mimicry, 44–45, 80, 99–100

Mouffe, Chantal, 34

Muhammad, Elijah, 42

Multitude, 99, 124–25, 127, 133–34, 141, 159, 168; Caracazo and, 210n64; criticism of, 207n2; Latin American struggles and, 128; the people (el pueblo) and, 205n2

Mussolini, Benito, 42

myth, 1, 18, 25, 27–28, 42, 71, 89, 138, 181n22, 184n54, 185n69, 186n90, 188n105; Chávez, 144; Homeric, 25–26; of the nation, 89; revolutionary, 34, 36–37, 144, 185n73

national consciousness, 71, 76–77, 85, 87–88, 90–91, 94, 96–97, 106

national identity, 81, 86, 94, 103; decolonial, 84, 119

nationalism, 42, 48, 83–84, 88, 90–91, 93–94, 96–97, 112, 121, 123, 126, 133, 135; anticolonial, 40; bourgeois, 11; class, 37, 40; decolonial, 82, 126, 170; essentialist, 83, 89; fascism and, 44; Manichaean, 81; of the powerful, 44; proletarian, 42; third-world, 120, 126; vulgar, 89; of the weak, 44

national liberation, 12, 81, 88

Nation of Islam, 42

nation-state, 124; Westphalian, 77

negativity, 67, 114–15, 127, 162, 174n18, 214n29

Negri, Antonio, 175n19. *See also* Hardt, Michael, and Antonio Negri)

Negritude movement, 66–67, 71, 75, 187n96, 192n55, 194n71

neoliberalism, 1–2, 123, 134

Nichols, Robert, 214n32

nonbeing, 11, 44, 58, 61, 63, 70–71, 77–78, 111, 167; concrete existence of, 112; exteriority and, 147, 159–60, 163; zone of (*see* Fanon, Frantz: zone of nonbeing)

nostalgia, 25, 27, 28, 92

Obama, Barack, 3–4

objectivity, 34, 38, 39, 40, 67, 83–84, 117

Occupy movement, 2, 4–6, 173n10

Occupy Oakland, 5–6, 173n10

Ojeda, Fabricio, 209n42

The Onion, 61

ontology, 109, 113, 165, 191n43, 204n45; colonial, 114; Heideggerian, 108

optimism, 3, 158; in Du Bois, 156; in Dussel, 119, 133; in Fanon, 51, 77, 78, 81, 96, 99, 214n28; liberal, 2. *See also* Afro-Pessimism

Other, 51, 56, 69, 109–10, 112–14, 118–19, 130, 140; appeal to, 104; as exteriority, 8, 116; face of, 111; gaze of, 51; white, 55, 154

Padmore, George, 12, 43, 194n71

Palestine, 126, 200n80

Patterson, Orlando, 191n41

the people (el pueblo), 8, 18, 103–4, 120–21, 123–28, 131–34, 144, 147, 150–51, 206–7n22; ambiguity of, 136–37; as category of rupture, 128–31, 206n22; centripetal function of (Virno), 124; Hardt and Negri on, 124–26, 206n2, 206n6; as identity of identities, 147; as pejorative, 143; the state and, 132–33; in the United States, 207n27; in Venezuela, 134–35, 146. *See also* "Gloria al Bravo Pueblo"

"pink tide," 2

Pippin, Robert, 176n28, 182n37

Podemos, 138

popular identity, 8, 103–4, 121, 125–26, 128–30, 134–38, 141–42, 145, 147; in Latin America, 129, 134, 142, 209n48

will, 33, 37, 45, 84, 89, 125, 212n12,
214n25
Willett, Cynthia, 212n11
world-system, 91, 97, 99, 106, 112, 120
world-systems theory, 200n83
Wright, Richard, 12, 43, 61, 194n71,
215n49

Young, Iris Marion, 176n29

Zamir, Shamoon, 194n78, 212n12
Žižek, Slavoj, 3, 173n10, 200n81;
Eurocentrism and, 3; on the Haitian
Revolution, 76; universalism and, 6,
172n3, 172n7